THE PHILOSOPHY OF RACE

The Philosophy of Race

Albert Atkin

Routledge
Taylor & Francis Group

LONDON AND NEW YORK

In memory of Edna Sara Ann Brown (1918–93),
from whom I learned the value of *race*.

First published 2012 by Acumen

Published 2014 by Routledge
2 Park Square, Milton Park, Abingdon, Oxon OX14 4RN
711 Third Avenue, New York, NY 10017, USA

Routledge is an imprint of the Taylor & Francis Group, an informa business

ISBN: 978-1-84465-514-4 (hardcover)
ISBN: 978-1-84465-515-1 (paperback)

British Library Cataloguing-in-Publication Data
A catalogue record for this book is available from the British Library.

Designed and typeset in Warnock Pro by JS Typesetting Ltd,
Porthcawl, Mid Glamorgan

Contents

Acknowledgements

This book has benefited from the input of various people. I'd like to mention and thank Alison Beale, Rachael Briggs, Emma Buxton, Wendy Carlton, David Lah, Mianna Lotz, Peter Menzies, Mari Mikkola, Stephanie Rennick, Cynthia Townley and Jennifer Saul, who have all contributed something different but important. Thanks must also go to Tristan Palmer at Acumen, who has pressed, pursued and guided this project with encouragement and generosity.

On a more personal level, my concern with *race* and *racism* started early, and I am sure I would have remarkably different ideas were it not for my maternal grandparents, Edna and Albert Brown, my mother, Mary, and my brother and sisters, Rudi, Laura and Christine. Although I have discussed little of the material in this book with them, they have contributed to my thinking in immeasurable ways. I also have to give extra special thanks to my wife, Hannah, and my children, Tristan and Iris, who have found the time and patience to allow me to write this book. Hannah also picked up plenty of infelicities in my writing (though I'm sure plenty remain) and Tristan was at all times forthcoming with opinions on potential book covers.

Finally, I would like to mention John Richardson and single him out for special praise and gratitude. John and I have discussed questions of *race*, *racism* and *ethnicity* for as long as I can remember, and I hold a deep admiration for the work he does. Indeed, the idea for this book grew out of our earlier joint projects. Failing to acknowledge him would be to ignore one the most important reasons for my interest in questions of *race*. Thank you John.

Introduction

The majority of us take *race* to be a feature of the world. When we meet new people, or describe old friends, we often pick out their *race* as a characteristic. Moreover, we think we see the effects of *race*-thinking all around us. In Australia, 83.3 per cent of people believe that there is *racism* in Australian society (see Dunn *et al.* 2004). In Europe, 71 per cent of people think those from racial and ethnic minority groups suffer discrimination in the job market (Brika *et al.* 1997). In the USA, 69 per cent of white people and 41 per cent of black people think there is equal treatment of *races* in their local community (see Newport *et al.* 2001). Central to these ideas about the prevalence of *racism* seems to be the idea that there are such things as *races*. But it turns out that *race* and *racism* are not nearly so clear-cut as our views here might suggest.

To begin with, it turns out that from the point of view of science and biology *race* is not a very coherent idea at all. As the great genetic anthropologist Frank Livingstone put it, "there are no races, only clines" (Livingstone 1962: 279).[1] I will explore this idea further in Chapter 1, but here we can note that for the vast majority of people the idea that there are no *races* for the scientist to study makes little sense. As we have already said, *race* seems to be one of the more tangible characteristics of people

---

1. We shall talk more about *Clines* in Chapter 1, but here it is enough to know that this is a simple biological concept that describes a gradual change in some physical or bodily trait relating to some corresponding geographical transition. For example, a tree species grows across a range that moves from sea level to high altitude. Increases in altitude see a gradual reduction in the height of trees that grow there. This gradual change in the tree, tied to a transitional geographical change, is a cline.

– it's just obvious what *race* someone is, isn't it? But what we take to be obvious turns out to be complex, and difficult, and nothing like as simple as it seems.

Similar things hold for our thoughts on *racism* and racial discrimination too. For example, while 83.3 per cent of Australians believe there to be *racism* in society, only 38 per cent believe white Australians experience any racial privilege, and only 12 per cent self-ascribe any racist views (see Dunn *et al.* 2004). Similarly, in Europe, although 77 per cent think there are dimensions of discrimination in society, and 54 per cent would worry about the quality of education in a highly multicultural school, only 33 per cent would self-ascribe any racist views (see Brika *et al.* 1997). And in the USA, even though 69 per cent of white people and 41 per cent of black people assume that there is racial equality in their local areas, some startling findings suggest matters are otherwise: black males with no criminal convictions are less likely to be called for job interviews than their white counterparts who do have criminal convictions (see Pager 2003); black people convicted of murder are much more likely to receive the death penalty than white counterparts (see Eldridge 2002); black students are much more likely to be excluded from honours classes than their white counterparts, even where their grades meet the requirements (see Fischer *et al.* 1996: 163). I could go on. Clearly, something doesn't quite add up here either.

So, we think there are *races*, and quite obviously so, but, in at least one very important respect, there are not, and matters are not nearly as obvious as they seem. And we tend to see the impact of *race* all around us in the form of *racism*, yet we don't seem to notice just how much of it there really is, few us seem to think we are implicated in it, and those who admit to being implicated tend to see this as a source of pride (Dunn *et al.* 2004: 422–3). *Race*, then, is a mysterious and deeply interesting thing – we notice it all around us, but it isn't *really* there; we are aware that the notion of *race* has an impact, but fail to see that the impact is everywhere, and that we play a key part in it. Curious.

With all this said, then, it is unsurprising that *race* and *racism* should be of interest to us. Indeed, we can see the interest that *race* creates for us by the number of disciplines and researchers that see themselves as contributing to the debates that circle the concept. Sociologists find themselves deeply intrigued by the concept of *race*, which seems to be an organizing structure within society on a par with *gender* or *class*. And, indeed, we ask questions about the interaction of *race* and *gender*, about whether or not *race* is really reducible to *class*, and so on. Art historians and museologists ask about the portrayal of *race* and *racism* in art; or whether or not we should have ethnographic collections in a museum setting, and how we ought to handle such collections given certain interacting conceptions like "the other", post-colonialism, and so on. And historians find the history of *race* and related notions to be central concepts worthy of deep interest – the role of slavery in the rise of global capitalism; the rise of anti-Semitism in Germany; the adaptation and manipulation of the caste system in British India; the rise of the civil rights movement – all deeply interesting historical questions for which *race* is a central feature. Even law in the USA has seen the Critical Race Theory movement – which attempts to analyse the social, political and legal history of the USA through its avoidance of its racial and racialized past.

At this point, however, it is worth noting that mainstream philosophy has managed to make itself something of a notable exception in contributing to debates on *race*.[2] Although there are many philosophers who have made important and insightful contributions to discussions of *race* – and we shall acquaint ourselves with these philosophers and their work during the course of this book – as an entire discipline philosophy's contribution has been smaller than we might hope. And in many ways philosophy has simply excused itself from considerations of *race*. It is intriguing to speculate as to just why this should be so, and we shall engage in such intrigue in a moment, but first, it is worth noting that in the last decade or so there has been a growth of interest among the philosophical mainstream in questions about *race*, and the tide of neglect from mainstream philosophy seems to be turning. One hope is that this book captures some of this recent vigour, and draws attention to both the exciting work that is now emerging and to the important foundational work that it draws upon.

So, what of philosophy's engagement with *race*? As we have noted, even allowing for the current growth in interest, there has been less of it than there perhaps should be. But this raises some very important questions about philosophical engagement with *race*, especially for a book such as this: Why hasn't philosophy engaged with *race*? Why should philosophy engage with *race*? And what does the study of *race* have to gain from

---

2. It's worth being clear that there are pockets and areas of philosophy where there has been lots of work on race. However, mainstream analytic philosophy, which represents the largest and most influential body of philosophical endeavour in the discipline, has paid very little attention to race.

philosophical engagement? The main concern of this book, as will become apparent, is the third question – our aim is to see just what a philosophically informed study of *race* looks like. All the same, let's say a little about each of these questions here.

As I pointed out, race *appears* to be real, but in an important respect (which we shall examine in Chapter 1) it isn't; and the degree of *racism* in society appears to be of one magnitude, but is in fact, in reality, many magnitudes greater. This is the clash of appearance and reality, and it is normally the kind of thing that brings philosophers flocking. But in the case of *race*, this has not been so. An intriguing speculation as to why this could be is that the very nature of philosophical theorizing is such that philosophers simply haven't noticed *race* with its potential philosophical interest.[3] To be more specific, the thought is that philosophy, at least since Descartes, sees part of its task as drawing general conclusions and abstracting out extraneous details. In many philosophical concerns, *race* looks as though it is one of these extraneous details, and so is abstracted away.

Consider, for example, the famous philosophical conundrum of 1960s epistemology – is *knowledge* merely *justified true belief*? In that enterprise, we imagine cases where these conditions seem to hold – a proposition is believed, true, and justified – yet knowledge doesn't seem to obtain. And we take ourselves to learn very hard-won lessons from all of this – perhaps what makes something knowledge is all a matter of ensuring we aren't correct by virtue of luck; perhaps knowledge isn't a composite concept at all. In truth, the epistemological lessons don't matter to us here. The real point is that in this entire philosophical endeavour and in all the lessons learned, the concept of *race* is notably absent. The abstractness, the questioning at an intellectual remove that is so characteristic of philosophy, means that these issues, and the upshots of our theorizing about them, have no special conclusions for *race* – if *knowledge* is justified true belief, then it is justified true belief whether you're black, white, red or yellow. Moreover, *race* has no particular input for these questions either – black knowledge is justified true belief, white knowledge is justified true belief, and so on. In making the generalized point, *race*, if it was ever even noticed, simply drops away.

---

3. In many ways this is an observation made by Charles Mills in his book *Blackness Visible* (1998), and anyone interested in the relationship between the discipline of philosophy and race – and in particular the *whiteness* of philosophy – would do well to read (at least) the first two chapters of Mills's book.

As it happens, this assumption has come in for increasing scrutiny,[4] but it is not our concern here to explore this. Rather, we are interested in noting that within a general practice of abstracting away certain kinds of detail, *race* has frequently found itself sidelined. It would be unsurprising, then, if philosophers have either not noticed *race*, or have assumed that it holds no philosophical interest. And put like this, it seems to make sense why philosophical reflection on *race* is so thin and in some areas entirely missing. Indeed, in all but a few very applied areas of the discipline – the very places where the abstractness of philosophy is supposed to relent – questions of *race* in philosophy are absent.

But, of course, these are not good reasons. They are an explanation, not an excuse. Which brings us to our second question: why should philosophy engage with *race*? In many ways, we have already hinted at the philosophical promise *race* might offer – in the gap between the way things are and the way we take them to be there is clear room for philosophers to do their work. What's more, I hope that anyone who reaches the end of this book will be able to see for themselves just how rich a philosophical subject *race* can be. Nonetheless, it's worth pre-empting a little and noting that the questions of *race* and *racism* that philosophy could engage with are plentiful. *Race* may not be as we take it to be, but what exactly do we think "race" means? And if *race* is not as we take to be, what on Earth is it? If it's true that we are failing to see and understand our role in *racism*, perhaps we don't understand what that is either. So what is *racism*? And given that we see the effects of *race* and *racism* everywhere around us, we perhaps need to ask how our understanding of *race* and *racism* affects this – if there is no *race*, can there still be *racism*? If we manage to work out what *racism* is, what should we do about it? We take *racism* to be wrong, but is it? And why?

We'll explore these kinds of questions in detail in the coming chapters, but it should be clear, I hope, that these are questions that can grab the attention of philosophers. As we noted, the normal assumption about philosophical engagement with *race* is that it occurs somewhere at the interface between ethics and real world decisions – concerns in applied ethics about affirmative action, for instance. But the questions we have

---

4. In many ways, feminist philosophers have led the way here in questioning just how gender and epistemology interact – Antony (2002) gives a good overview of feminist epistemology – but there are attempts to rethink the interaction between race and epistemology too. See chapter 3 of Mills (1998) for instance.

just raised have greater philosophical breadth than that. Questions about what we really mean by "race", what *race* really is, what *racism* is – these are questions with a broadly metaphysical flavour. Of course, concerns about how our answers to these questions should be incorporated into applied and social areas mean that our study of *race* will still retain its "value" and "ethics" dimensions. But the point is obvious – *race* is a broad philosophical topic. In terms of our question – why should philosophy engage with *race*? – the answer is that there is plenty here to cause a philosophical itch. And wherever there is such an itch, philosophers are inclined to scratch. But this is not the only reason for philosophy to engage with *race*.

An additional reason, but one I won't really pursue further in this book, is this: just as with *gender* and the call for philosophy to reflect upon its "maleness", it might well do philosophy, as a discipline, some good to reflect upon its "whiteness". We mentioned that philosophy tends to abstract away from matters of *race*, but it is also worth noting that white men have written all the perceived "Great Works" of philosophy. This may mean that philosophy's view of which problems and questions are its concern may be the result of a peculiarly white gaze. Some engagement with *race* might increase our sensitivity to this. It's worth being clear about what this means, though, since it is an easy claim to misconstrue.

To continue with our earlier example of epistemology and the question of how to define *knowledge*, the observation that philosophy might reflect upon its "whiteness" does not mean that looking at *race* and the epistemological make-up of non-white people will somehow change our definitions. To say that black people have different kinds or notions of *knowledge* to white people is as ridiculous as the claim that girls can't do logic. Rather, the point is that ideas about what epistemology is, which questions and problems matter, and how we think it should be conducted might change if we diminish the whiteness of the philosophical gaze. To give a strained analogy, if we say that our particular interest in food is "too white", or "too Western", and that we should reflect upon that, we don't mean to say that non-white people or non-Western people taste food in a different way – that sugar isn't as sweet for them, say. Rather, we mean our menu may be more restricted and limited than it should be – the principles and ideas behind what makes good cuisine might be much more varied, interesting and enlightening than we have so far been assuming.

As we've already said, our concern in this book will be with pointing out why *race* is interesting as a philosophical topic rather than reflecting on the methodological effect of philosophy's white gaze. Which brings us to the last of the three questions we mentioned – what does the study of *race* have to gain from philosophy? As we pointed out above, sociologists, anthropologists, historians, museologists and psychologists all work on *race* and *racism*. Which means there is plenty of work and research around. So what exactly does philosophy bring to the table?

Again, my hope is that this book will demonstrate at least some of the interesting contributions that philosophy and philosophers are bringing to debates about *race* and *racism*, but again it is worth saying a little here. In particular, it seems important to draw attention to the tools and methods of philosophy, especially those geared towards conceptual precision and analysis. These are an incredibly important part of what philosophers do, and arguably an incredibly useful thing for philosophers to bring to debates about *race*. To be precise, there are concepts that underlie any theorizing about *race* across the humanities, social sciences and physical sciences, which are frequently left implicit or unanalysed. These are exactly the kinds of detail that philosophers can address, and invariably delight in addressing. Let me try to furnish this point with an example.

In a comment for the American Sociological Association, the sociologist Troy Duster asks:

> If biological research now questions the utility of the concept for scientific work in this field, how, then, can racial categories be the subject of valid scientific investigation? The answer is that our social and economic lives are integrally organized around race as a social construct. ... [R]ace has been a sorting mechanism for friendship, mating, and marriage; a basis for the distribution of social privileges and resources; and a reason to organize social movements to preserve or challenge the status quo. Sociologists are interested in explaining how and why social definitions of race persist and change.   (Duster 2002)

In a 2003 discussion of Duster's claims, the anthropologist Yehudi Webster laments:

> A lack of attention to reasoning, or a pursuit of "racial justice" without regard for logical consistency, largely explains why social scientists are not able to rid themselves of a clearly absurd tradition of grouping persons according to certain anatomical attributes. Sociologists are often particularly guilty of this. They

have initiated one of the most developed sub-disciplines in the social sciences—the sociology of race relations.

(Webster 2003)

This exchange takes place in the context of the American Sociological Association's support of the collection of *race* data, while the American Anthropology Association had called for the US Census Bureau to phase out the use of racial classification. Here we have sociologists calling for the continued study of *race* and anthropologists calling for the abandonment of *race*. But what is at the core of this disagreement?

Webster continues his complaint, "certain biologists and geneticists do not simply 'question the utility' of the race concept. They demonstrate that it is arbitrary and internally inconsistent ... therefore, [there are] no races". At least part of the worry seems to be that if there are no *races* in scientific terms – a claim we've already mentioned – then how can there be a continued and legitimate study of this concept? Yet the sociologists seem to be right when they observe that *race* moves us in social dimensions with such force that it looks absurd to abandon its study. The concern, then, seems to be that these groups are being pulled in different directions – one is compelled by the lack of scientific reality for *race*, the other is compelled by the power of its social impact. How, if at all, are these kinds of concern to be reconciled?

As we shall see in coming chapters, this kind of worry is front and centre of the philosophers' interest in *race*, and it is precisely where philosophy can begin to make its presence felt. In particular, we, as philosophers, can begin to draw distinctions between different conceptions of *race*. We can begin to see how a lack of reality for a concept in one dimension does not settle any ontological question outright – that is, questions about its existence may well still be up for grabs. None of this is to say that philosophical input is somehow prior to, or foundational for, sociological and anthropological questions about *race*. It isn't. However, the philosophers' concern for making concepts precise, for identifying the various dimensions of their reality and for drawing out hidden implications is exactly what is called for here.[5] *Race* is a strange and elusive notion in its own right, and

---

5. To be clear, the kinds of points I'm making in favour of philosophy are tools that anthropologists and sociologists use too, and have brought to bear in the kinds of disagreement I have mentioned. My point, though, is that these are profoundly philosophical methods and tools, and as philosophers we can help in their employment in such debates.

philosophers can do much in making it clear and precise. That this concept has such an impact in the world around us should give us extra interest in bringing our best philosophical work to questions of *race*.

I hope, at this point, that we are in a position to see that *race* and *racism* are interesting in their own right, that they are interesting for philosophical reasons, and that we can see some grounds for thinking philosophy has interesting contributions to make in discussion of them. The purpose of the remainder of this book, then, is to introduce some of the interesting contributions that philosophers can make. All that remains for me to do here is to give a brief outline of what is to come.

In Chapter 1 we shall turn our attention to the very first claim made in this book – that many of us see *race* as being an obvious feature of the world, yet in at least one very important respect it is not real. In particular, we shall spend some time trying to recover just what our ordinary, everyday notion of *race* is. We shall then spend some time making it philosophically robust – that is, we shall make it as clear and precise as possible. Once we have done this, we shall examine just how little support such a concept receives from the natural sciences, and in particular from biology.

In Chapter 2, we shall turn our attention to the other feature of *race* that we have noted throughout this Introduction – its profound social impact. In particular we will explore the socio-historical facts and background behind our concept of *race*, and look at how different social pressures give rise to different kinds of racial categorization. Having done this we shall look at various philosophical ideas about what we should make of this. In particular, we shall look at views which suggest these socio-historical facts make *race* real, views which take the social impact of *race* seriously but fall shy of claiming that this confers genuine reality on *race*, and the views of those who think we can use the social elements of *race* to change our concept into something different.

In Chapter 3, we shall, in an important sense, bring the lessons and insights of the first two chapters together by asking just what we should do with *race*. As we shall see, combining the view that our ordinary concept of *race* has no scientific reality with various ideas about the social reality of *race* can lead us to very different conclusions about whether we should retain our thought and talk of *race*. In particular we shall see arguments for shedding the concept of *race*, arguments for keeping the concept of *race*, and arguments for changing our concept of *race*.

In Chapter 4, we turn to the question of *racism*. Our primary interest is in defining what *racism* is, but, as we shall see, there is much work on *racism* from disciplines such as sociology and psychology. Consequently, among the requirements we have for a philosophical account of *racism* is to accommodate this work. We will also look for our accounts of *racism* to offer us some explanation of why it is wrong. With these requirements in place, we shall examine three broad theories of what *racism* is: an account that treats *racist belief* as central to *racism*, an account that treats *racist behaviour* as central to *racism*, and an account that treats *racist feelings* or sentiment as central to *racism*.

In our final chapter, Chapter 5, we shall turn to questions of the impact of *race* and *racism* on everyday lives. Our particular concern will be to show just how the kinds of philosophical consideration we have entertained in our first four chapters can have a direct bearing on more applied questions. Specifically, we shall address the question of racial profiling and ask whether such a practice could ever be justifiable. As we shall see, this will require of us that we work out how such a notoriously troubling practice could be made more robust and free of the clear problems that plague its current use. We will then subject that version of racial profiling to scrutiny by examining cases for and against its justifiability.

CHAPTER ONE

Is *race* real?

Is *race* real? At first blush, this may seem like an odd question. After all, *race* seems to be all around us. We have no difficulty ascertaining its presence in our daily interactions with others – if you ask me, I can tell you the *race* of the woman who drove the bus I caught to work this morning, or the *race* of the man who sold me a newspaper on my way home. And of course, *race* looms large in how we consider the world to be – it seems significant that the USA elected its first black president in 2008; it seems right that Australia's "Stolen Generation" should seek compensation for injustices inflicted upon them on account of their *race*; it seems contentious that the commissioner of the Metropolitan Police in London thinks young black men should be the focus of anti-crime initiatives in Britain's capital; it seems to be an advance that in the 2011 UK census, the racial category of "Romany" has been added for the first time. In light of what looks like the ubiquity and mundanity of *race* talk and thought in our daily lives, then, the oddness of the question "Is *race* real?" becomes apparent. Are we really supposed to question the reality of something that is so obviously a part of our everyday lives, and the subject of everyday talk everywhere? If we are, it looks as though it will simply be one of those esoteric philosophical questions that raise unlikely doubts about what is blindingly obvious to anyone who doesn't want to play the philosopher's game. But, as it happens, questions about the reality of *race* are not quite like that. They are the foundation of serious enquiry with significant import and ramifications for our everyday thought and talk.

In asking if *race* is real, we are trying to do some serious philosophical work, and one of the first things we must learn to do in such work is question what seems to be obvious. But questions, philosophical or otherwise, about the reality of *race* arguably have deeper consequences than questions of merely esoteric philosophical concern – those questions we ask simply because we can. After all, the first black American to take office in the USA is an event of no small moment, just as the compensatory entitlements of Australia's indigenous people or the possibility of race-led policing in London are hardly issues without practical friction in the world. And these things are premised on the notion that there really is such a thing as *race*. So, odd as the question may seem, to ask whether *race* is real is to take a serious question about our behaviours, beliefs and ways of thinking and talking, and to look for the assumptions that lie beneath. That's the philosophical project of this chapter.

The first thing to note is that we do seem to assume that *race* is real. After all, that's what our observations about the ubiquity and mundanity of *race* talk are meant to show. In our non-philosophical garb, in our role as ordinary folk with pre-theoretical ideas, we talk, think and behave as though there really is such a thing as *race* in the world. But what are we really assuming here? What are our pre-theoretical, ordinary-folk assumptions about *race*? What do we think that word picks out in the world? And by assuming or even boldly asserting that *race* is real, even if only pre-theoretically, what do we honestly mean? That we *behave* as though there are *races*, or that there *really* are *races*? That it is a fact about our *behaviour*, or that it is a fact about the *world*? In short, what do we ordinary thinkers mean when we talk about *race*, and is that thing, the thing we take ourselves to be talking about, real?

In this chapter we will begin to answer these questions about our pre-theoretical ideas of *race* and its reality. Indeed, we shall deal with these questions in two separate sections, first examining what our ordinary *race* talk purports to be about, and then examining whether that thing really exists. However, for the sake of clarity it is worth saying here and now that among the key themes underlying our ordinary talk and thought about *race* are the following ideas: that the key markers of *race* are bodily or somatic traits; that *race* involves genealogy or inheritance; that *race* is crucially tied to geographical origins; that *race* indicates, generates or constrains certain physical or mental abilities and capacities; that *race* indicates, generates or constrains certain cultural and attitudinal behaviours; that *race* involves notions of purity. As for the question of reality, we seem to assume that *race* is real and that its reality is underpinned by biological and genetic facts made readily available by our best scientific theories. We shall of course examine and elaborate on all of these points in the rest of this chapter.

We'll start by spending some time looking at our ordinary ideas about *race* by introducing and making sense of the common themes, assertions and ideas that seem prevalent in our ordinary notions and talk of *race*. We shall also spend some time trying to make that "ordinary notion" a little more robust – we want to find a concept that can do justice to the ordinary pre-theoretical idea of *race*, while at the same time being coherent and well-formed enough to do some philosophical work. We'll then move on to examine what our ordinary assumptions about the reality of *race* are, and see if there is any clear way in which those assumptions are borne out by scientific fact. In particular, we shall see that our assumptions about the scientific underpinnings of *race* are not supported by science at all and that if our ordinary thinking about the reality of *race* assumes that there are solid scientific facts that bear it out, then we are wrong.

WHAT DO WE MEAN BY "RACE"?

Part of the problem of asking what we mean by "race" is that because our use of the term is often unreflective, we seldom stop to ask exactly what it is we take ourselves to be referring to when we talk about it. However, some time spent reflecting on the ways we talk about and use the concept of *race* in our day-to-day interactions with the world can allow us to recover an awful lot of the features that we seem to assume are bound to *race*. The following is a list of notions that seem to be more or less implicit on our ordinary *race* talk:

1. *Race* and racial difference is marked by certain somatic markers and bodily differences (e.g. skin colour, facial features, hair texture).
2. *Race* is something that we inherit from our parents, grandparents, etc.
3. Racial differences are tied to geographical origins (e.g. black people originate from Africa).
4. Different *races* have different physical and mental capabilities.
5. Different *races* have different cultural and attitudinal behaviours.
6. *Races* are more or less pure.

We will examine the elements on this list in a little more detail very shortly, but it is worth noting a few things before we begin. First of all this is not an exhaustive list of the assumptions that are implicit in our *race* talk. Second,

Does this mean: some individual may be more or less purely of one race?

this is not meant to be a simple list of necessary and sufficient conditions, just a cluster of ideas that seem to circulate around our ordinary uses of the term "race". And third, confronted with this list, it is unlikely that everyone will agree that this captures what *they* mean when they talk and think of *race*. Indeed, they may think all of these ideas should be included in a clarification of the term "race", but they might just as easily think this list too extensive, or even totally inadequate. Nonetheless, I think this list forms a good working core of ordinary pre-theoretical assumptions about *race*,[1] and it certainly includes what are arguably non-negotiable features of our *race* thinking – we shall return to this when we try to make our ordinary concept of *race* more robust. But before we do that, let's examine the elements of the list above more closely and see just what reasons we might have for thinking these are the assumptions that underpin ordinary talk about *race*.

Racial difference as bodily difference

What reason do we have for claiming that in our ordinary thinking *race* and *racial difference* is supposedly marked by bodily difference? In fact, I take this to be a relatively non-contentious claim – it simply attempts to capture the fact that we think people of different *races* look different, and people of the same *races* look similar. And the features we most often tend to think of when talking of *race* are skin colour (black skin, brown skin, white skin, yellow skin, etc.), facial features (thin noses, broad noses, thick lips, round heads, etc.) and hair type and colour (thick and frizzy, thin and straight, etc.). We can support such a claim by pointing to a number of facts.

First, our everyday practices of noting *race* and racial difference tend to rely on physical descriptions, and in particular on skin colour. Had you asked me the *race* of the woman who drove the bus I caught to work, or the *race* of man who sold me a newspaper on the way home, I would probably have answered by making reference to skin colour – "she was *white*" or "he was *black*". Indeed, in a variety of contexts, our names and descriptions (including pejoratives) for the different *races* are meant to reference

---

1. See Glasgow (2009a), Hardimon (2003), Zack (1997a, b), and Smedley and Smedley (2005) for a similar (though not isomorphic) set of "ordinary assumptions" about race.

perceived differences in skin colour: "blacks", "whites", "red-skins", and so on. Physical difference, then, is readily used in ordinary discourse as a marker of *race* and racial difference.

Second, the assumption of racial difference as bodily difference is made explicit in official contexts too. Skin-based racial markers are often included in our census categories, with the USA, UK and Australia frequently including black and white among their classifications, and countries such as Brazil on occasion including as many as twenty-eight colour-related census classifications for *race*.[2] There are even examples of police training manuals that demarcate *races* in wholly physical terms – South Carolina's *Gypsies, Tramps and Thieves* describes "European Gypsies" thus: *"Average height – 5'9" (tend to be stocky); average weight – medium to heavy; hair – dark; eyes – dark; complexion – olive to dark".* Physical difference, then, plays a role in our more official attempts to organize and demarcate members of our broader social groups.

And finally, we often use perceived bodily differences between *races* as the explanatory basis of other perceived racial differences. So, for example, in the USA, swimming is not taken to be a recreational activity much pursued by black people or black families. There are absurd explanations for why this is so, including claims that "black bones" are denser, or that black people are naturally less buoyant. But even among the better explanations of why this kind of apparent behavioural difference between the *races* should exist, we still find recourse to somatic or bodily difference. One good candidate explanation is that black parents have not learned to swim and so cannot teach their children, hence there are lower numbers of black participants in recreational swimming. Further pressing on why this should be so sees "hair" or "black hair" as a frequently cited factor. While the allusion to racial differences in hair type (and the related difference in required maintenance of that hair) will be familiar to most people, the point here is merely that in such a case we can only cite such simple bodily differences as explanations of complex social differences because there is an underlying assumption that these bodily differences are key to marking racial differences.

---

2. See Telles (2004) for a commentary on the various skin colour classification in Brazilian race categories.

Race is something that we inherit from our parents, grandparents, and so on

Our ordinary concept of *race* also seems to rely on the notion of inheritance – we assume that an individual's *race* is dependent upon the *race* of that individual's biological parents and ancestors. Again, this is a fairly non-contentious claim about our uses of the concept of *race*. And again, there are plenty of obvious instances showing just why, in our ordinary talk and thought, we assume that heritability and/or genealogy is crucial to *race*.

The most obvious evidence for our ordinary assumption of racial inheritance comes from examining our likely responses to questions about the respective *races* of parents and children – asked about the possible *race* of a black person's parents, we are unlikely to entertain seriously any answer other than "black". However, we can see the assumption of racial inheritance in other ways too. For example, our consternation and surprise at, and explanations for, atavism – instances where, for example, black parents give birth to white children, or white parents give birth to black children – all highlight our assumption of racial inheritance. First of all, we simply do not expect to see parents give birth to children who appear to be racially different to them, and so we find such cases fascinating. Second, we often assume that a more likely explanation is that we are not really seeing racial difference between parents and children, but instances of cuckoldry and concealed infidelity. In such instances, our assumption of racial inheritance is preserved of course – the absent or concealed parent explains the apparent anomaly and *race* is inherited just as we suspect. And finally, even where our assumption of racial inheritance cannot be maintained by suspicion of concealment (because cuckoldry is ruled out, say), the whole notion of atavism, the "evolutionary throw-back", relies upon the idea that some ancestor buried deep in the genealogy has the racial trait which the child has now manifested. Inheritance lies at the heart of this.

A further example worth mentioning is the use of genealogy and family trees by Nazi researchers for finding workable definitions for classifying individuals as "Gypsies". The problem faced by those charged with the task of giving a ready definition of "Roma", "Sinti" and "Gypsies" that would enable the easy classification and removal of these racial groups was that, unlike other racial groups, the somatic and bodily markers of racial difference were not so clear or prominent. The next best thing, it was decided, was to make use of long and elaborately researched family trees, genealogies, and ancestral histories – a key marker of being racially Roma was being the offspring of someone who was racially Roma. This, of course, is an extreme case, but nonetheless, it shows that in circumstances where readily useable markers of racial difference are needed, among the first to be called upon are racial inheritance and ancestry.

Racial differences are tied to geographical origins

The claim that our ordinary *race* talk and thought takes *race* and *racial differences* to be tied to differences in geographical origins is the familiar idea that *races* are somehow linked to particular areas of the Earth – white people tend to originate in Europe, black people in Africa, and so on. Of course, such a claim is mostly interconnected with the first two markers mentioned – contemporary black people and white people in the USA, for instance, need never have set foot outside North America, but we perceive the somatic markers of their *race* to be inherited from their forebears who did originate in other geographical locations.

Again, we can see this underlying assumption about *race* in our everyday talk and behaviours. We talk of African-Americans, British-Asians or Anglo-Australians for instance, and such categorizations, which explicitly draw *race* and geographical location together, even find themselves included on official census forms in many countries. And there are, of course, less pleasant examples which illustrate just how we tie racial differences and geographical origins in our ordinary thought and talk – an oftcited (but ludicrous) sentiment arising from racial anger and resentment is that racial minorities should "go home". The idea that members of *races* perceived to originate in some other geographical location should be relocated is absurd of course. Nonetheless, the specious assumption that the geographical origins of *race* should not be transcended reflects an underlying assumption that *races* do, in fact, have geographical origins. This idea features powerfully in our notion of *race*.

Different *races* have different physical and mental capabilities

The notion that racial differences are somehow captured in different physical or mental capabilities, dispositions, strengths and weaknesses is, again, a fairly easy idea to grasp – being of a certain *race* automatically endows us with various strengths and weaknesses by virtue of different *races* manifesting different physical and mental attributes. Particular examples of how this assumption plays out are found in frequent assertions about the relative IQs of different *races*, or the differences in sporting ability across *races*. Indeed, we have already mentioned the notion that the lower numbers of black recreational swimmers is explained by recourse to the physical unsuitability of the black body to swimming. Similarly, the preponderance of black basketball players, sprinters and boxers is often explained by appeal to presumed black racial characteristics of "natural" athleticism, strength and aggression.

The notion that *races* are characterized by particular physical and mental capabilities has been aired in plenty of recent famous cases – Herrnstein and Murray's (1994) assertion that apparent differences in IQ between black and white males is due to racial inheritance, or Jon Entine's (2000) claim that black sporting ability is due to black racial traits, for instance. Indeed, the ubiquity of these ideas about *race* is amply illustrated by the following observation from sports columnist David Halberstram:

> [T]he contemporary White perception, both in the media and among fans, [is] that Black athletes are natural athletes, doing night after night what comes quite readily to them. This is an ironic update to the earlier myth, which was that Blacks were faster than Whites but could not play in difficult positions ... because they lacked both the guts and talent. Whites, by contrast, are seen as less gifted but headier athletes who practice and perfect their skills. (Halberstram 1987: 38)

Different *races* have different cultural and attitudinal behaviours

Closely related to the claim that racial differences are marked by differences in physical and mental capabilities is the notion that racial difference is marked by ingrained or not easily suppressed cultural behaviours or attitudes. For example, there are many widely held beliefs which tie particular character traits to racial identity – whites are industrious, blacks are lazy or welfare-dependent, Jews are studious, east Asians are docile and entrepreneurial, and so on.

We can find evidence that this idea is a common feature of our notion of *race* in many places:

Quarrelsome, quick to anger or laughter, they are unthink-
ingly but not deliberately cruel. Loving bright colours they are
ostentatious and boastful but lack bravery. They have little idea
of time, proportion of measurement and are superstitious about
childbirth, fertility, food and sickness. ... Believing in charms and
curses, they admit the falsity of their fortune telling. They betray
little shame, curiosity, surprise or grief and show no solidarity.
(Entry for "Gypsies" in Garvin and Hooper 1956: 43–4)

Even though such explicit racial characterizations are less prevalent
than they used to be, formal studies show that such ideas as natural and
ingrained racial attitudes and behaviours are still widespread. For example,
the University of California at Berkeley's 1991 National Race and Politics
Survey found that 31 per cent of white respondents thought most blacks
were lazy, 50 per cent thought that blacks were aggressive, and 60 per cent
thought blacks were ill disciplined (Survey Research Centre 1991). A recent
survey further endorses these findings (Survey Research Centre 2004).

And finally, we find that some of these ideas even surface in policy making. So widely held is the view that Asian communities in the USA have
assimilated into American mainstream society through a natural propen-
sity for hard work, self-sufficiency, and respect for authority and family
that they are almost always excluded from academic programmes and
scholarships aimed at under-represented minorities – often by fiat.[3] The
assumption is that natural Asian characteristics have made them *model
minorities* who have assimilated and become academic high-fliers in many
instances – no additional help is required.

Races are more or less pure

The final common idea about *races* and racial difference that we will turn to
here is the notion that "purity" is a feature of racial identity. Again, the idea
is easy to grasp and readily apparent in many everyday contexts – we can
be more or less purely of one *race* or another such that if I have three black

---

3. See Ostriker *et al.* (2009) as an example of how the National Research Council's assessment
   of research doctorate programmes in the USA in 2009 used among its assessment variables
   racial and ethnic diversity of both faculty and graduate students. However, Asian minorities
   were explicitly excluded from this data. Also interesting on this topic is Bascara (2006).

grandparents and you have only one, I am more black than you. However, depending on the context, the notion of purity also manifests itself in terms of impact upon behaviour – the presence of certain "racial blood lines" can lead to certain outcomes in terms of behaviour. Consider:

> I do realize now the strong white influence that was in my family, and I want [my daughter] to be raised like that. Like for instance, the difference between me and my boyfriend ... he's Black and I'm mixed. And he doesn't feel like you should say yes ma'am and no ma'am to people. I was raised to do that, okay. And I want her to be raised that way ... But it's really becoming a problem especially considering the fact that my daughter is more Black than I am.
>
> (Quoted in Rockquemore and Brunsma 2002)

The respondent here worries, if only tacitly, that the greater degree of "blackness" had by her daughter means that she will manifest a greater number of the behaviours associated with blackness. Indeed, this kind of thinking can also be seen as further confirmation of the notion that different races have different cultural and attitudinal behaviours (see above).

As additional support for this more everyday thinking about the purity of *race*, we can find official policy reflecting these ideas. For example, the notorious "one drop rule" that emerged from various Jim Crow Laws in antebellum USA stated that blackness was conferred upon any individual with a single black ancestor. Here the notion of white purity is such that it is permanently tainted by contact with black blood. Or we might think of Australia's 1901 Immigration Restriction Act, which led to a series of policies and objectives that, "based upon the maintenance of racial purity", resulted in widespread removal of bi-racial white/aboriginal children from their aboriginal homes. The idea, developed and accommodated in law by statesmen and state appointed "protectors" such as Neville Cook, was that mixed-*race* children would still have some of the positive features of their white forebears, and the negative black characteristics could be bred out within five generations. A different notion of purity from the "one drop" hypo-descent thinking of course, but reflective of the idea all the same.[4]

---

4. For details of these "white Australia" policies see Manne (2001).

MAKING OUR EVERYDAY CONCEPT MORE PRECISE

That the preceding six notions commonly feature as part of our ordinary *race* and thought talk should now be quite clear. There may be other notions, but I take these six to be the most common and clear-cut. What this gives us, then, is a rough and ready characterization of the pre-theoretical notion of *race* that underpins our everyday thought and talk about *race*. Roughly speaking, *race* is a matter of particular physical or somatic traits; involves genealogy or inheritance; is tied to geographical origin; involves certain physical or mental traits; involves certain cultural and attitudinal behaviours; and is subject to considerations of purity. For example, the notion of "blackness" in the USA is a matter of having black skin, coarse hair, and full lips, of having black ancestors, of being part of a bloodline that originates in Africa, of being more physically robust but less intelligent than most non-blacks, of being less inclined to hard work than most non-blacks, and of having a claim to blackness (or no genuine claim to whiteness) by virtue of having at least some "black blood". This, of course, is very simplistic, and very simplified. The notion of a geographical origin in Africa, for instance, comes with many suppressed provisos and caveats: there are plenty of white people who can claim to be Africans, and given current orthodoxy about the origins of humankind, we might all be part of a bloodline originating in Africa. Nonetheless, we have, I take it, a good sense of our pre-theoretical notion of *race* here.

However, this pre-theoretical notion that we find underpinning our ordinary thought and talk about *race* is merely a starting point. After all, our intention in this chapter is to subject our notion of *race* to some philosophical scrutiny. What this means is that having uncovered a pre-theoretical notion of *race* in our everyday thought and talk, we must now attempt to make it more robust. But why worry about making this pre-theoretical notion more robust, or more precise?

Recall that our aim in this chapter is to find out if our ordinary talk and thought about *race* is drawing on a concept which has any claim to being real – hence our starting question, *is race real*? However, if we are going to take the question seriously we have to make sure we are working with the most robust and precise version of the concept underpinning our everyday *race* thought and talk. Put simply, if we draw philosophical conclusions that lean heavily on a more tenuous, weaker and less central feature of our ordinary concept, then those conclusions are at best less compelling or interesting than we might have hoped. At worst they are simply wrong.

Developing some robustness in our pre-theoretical notion allows us to gather the central, core and non-negotiable features together and make stronger philosophical claims about them as a result.

In terms of an example, suppose we examine what sort of notion underpins our everyday thought and talk about water. It turns out we all seem to believe that water is a liquid found in rivers, streams, oceans and seas, is crucial to life on Earth, and so on. However, it turns out that a few of us also believe that water has its own form of consciousness. Suppose this latter feature leads to some philosophical contradiction and is also completely unsupported by science. If we then conclude that everyday thought and talk of water is underpinned by an empty concept, we appear to have said something simply incorrect. And the reason is obvious – the idea that water is conscious, in this example, looks to be a marginal feature of the ordinary notion and strong conclusions based on it simply aren't compelling. After all, most ordinary talkers and thinkers don't hold this to be a feature of water.

On the other hand, had we managed to illustrate that science shows the content of rivers to differ from the content of streams, which in turn differs from the content of seas and oceans, and further that none of these substances are crucial to life, then our claim that ordinary "water" talk latches onto an empty concept would be more compelling. The reason being that these commonly held ideas about water are much more central, and far more crucial to the ordinary concept of *water*. The lesson, of course, should be obvious – by removing those ideas that are not crucial and retaining those that are, we can make our concepts more precise and more robust, and our philosophical conclusions more compelling and more interesting as a result.

The only question that remains, then, is how to make the notion of *race* that underpins our ordinary thought and talk more robust and more precise. And this question is not without philosophical interest in its own right, since there are various ways of going about this.[5] Here, we shall use a simple thought experiment based on what we might call a *method of disagreement*. The idea is that we can take two individuals who disagree wildly about *race*. Indeed, they disagree on these matters about as wildly as it is possible for any two people to disagree. What we then do is pass each of

---

5. The most philosophically interesting, by some margin, is Joshua Glasgow's use of Putnam's Twin Earth argument (Glasgow 2009a). In many ways, the method we are about to use is very similar.

the features we have identified as underpinning our ordinary thought and talk about *race* before these individuals, and see which, if any, it is impossible for them to disagree about without apparently talking about two entirely different things altogether.

To illustrate, suppose that two people, Rheneaus and Skarlowey, disagree about whether an Oreo is a cookie or a cake. Suppose that this seems to be due to a disagreement about what does and doesn't count as a cookie. If we can get right about just what the core features of a cookie are, perhaps we can settle this vexed question. For Rheneaus, Oreos have a key feature of other cookies – they are small. Skarlowey points out that he can buy cookies with a diameter far larger than many straightforward examples of cake. Rheneaus objects that at this point Skarlowey has merely noted he can purchase cakes that look like cookies – they are no more a cookie than a novelty graduation cake is a roll of paper and mortarboard. Size, then, begins to look as though it isn't a crucial or core feature of *cookie*.

Further, suppose that Rheneaus points out that Oreos are edible and, at the very least, a cookie must be edible, but Skarlowey objects that some cookies can be eaten and some can't. Further probing reveals that Skarlowey thinks that cookies could be made from wood, rubber, inanimate carbon rods, and indeed, that there could be no edible cookies at all. At this point we might begin to suspect that Skarlowey is talking of something else entirely and his disagreement here is due not to the non-centrality of edibility for *cookie*, but rather to his perverseness. Now, just as *acceptable disagreement* – as in the matter of size – is a good indicator of a non-core feature, *perverse disagreement* – as in the matter of edibility – is a good indicator of a core feature. It seems that parties cannot disagree over such features without appearing to have a perverse understanding of the concept in question – Skarlowey's notion of *cookie*, for instance, seems quite far removed from our ordinary thinking on such matters. This example is, of course, contrived, but it is nonetheless a good illustration of how the method we are about to use works: if we look at the possibilities for disagreement for each of the six proposed features of the concept underpinning our ordinary thought and talk of *race*, which of them allow acceptable disagreement (and are thus non-core), and which of them lead to perverse disagreement (and are thus core)? The core concepts, of course, form our robust and more precise ordinary concept of *race*.

How, then, does applying this method to the six common features of our ordinary concept of *race* work? Which features allow for acceptable disagreement, and which make for perverse disagreement? Which form the core of our ordinary concept of *race*, and which are non-core? The way we shall proceed is to take the six features outlined above in reverse order and see just what kind of disagreement they allow for.

Purity

Recall that the idea that *race* is a matter of purity forms part of the concept of *race* underpinning our ordinary thought and talk of *race*. Is it possible for there to be acceptable agreement about this, or would disagreement seem to lead to at least one party having a perverse notion of *race*?

Let's take two people, Penelope and Persephone. Penelope maintains that racial purity is a crucial feature of the notion of *race*. Persephone, on the other hand, does not; she thinks the idea of purity in respect of *race* is simply bizarre. Discussing the example of Ryan, who appears white, self-identifies as white, and is widely assumed to be white, but has a distant black great-great-grandfather, they disagree about Ryan's *race*. Penelope maintains that regardless of what Ryan may feel about his own racial identity, or what society may assume from surface appearances, he should probably count as black, but at the very least does not count as white. The presence of a black ancestor ensures that this is so.

Persephone on the other hand cannot see why this black ancestor, whom Ryan has never met and does not identify with, has such a decisive influence over Ryan's *race*. After all, many people who we would identify as white, who would call themselves white, who would quite legitimately declare themselves as white on census forms and who identify with white culture still have a reasonably recent black ancestor. Some studies, for instance, suggest as many as 30 per cent of white Americans have a black ancestor (see, for example, Shriver *et al.* 2003). As far as Persephone is concerned, it would be simply ludicrous to say that these people aren't white.

The interesting thing about this debate for us though is this: is the disagreement between Penelope and Persephone here one which is acceptable, or is it due to some perverse reading of the concept of *race*? And I think the answer is clear enough: the disagreement is quite acceptable. There is some core idea that they seem to both have in mind with regard to *race*, but in thrashing through the finer details of what this concept comes to they find themselves at loggerheads in respect of *purity*. What is also apparent, though, is that nothing in what either Penelope or Persephone maintains here seems to be due to some wildly idiosyncratic view of how we find *races* in the world. For example, it's not that Persephone, in addition to her denial of the role of purity, also thinks that *race* is something for which we must obtain vocational training (with different *races* requiring different qualifications), that we can retire from in later life, and can change should our qualifications and inclinations allow. This would, of course, still allow her to maintain her denial of the relevance of purity, but it would also lead us to suspect that she was perhaps confusing what we, Penelope, and lots of others call "race", with something that we would all probably call "profession" or "career". In short, there is no apparent perverseness underlying the disagreement between Penelope and Persephone.

It should be clear what I take this to mean for our discussion here. Purity looks to be a non-crucial feature of the concept that underpins our ordinary concept of *race*. It appears we can disagree completely about the relevance of purity to our ideas about *race*, and at the same time still be talking about the same thing. Purity, then, is not a core feature of the ordinary concept of *race*, and will not form a part of our more robust account.

Culture and behaviours

Recall that the fifth common idea underpinning our ordinary thought and talk of *race* was that *race* is tied to different cultural and attitudinal behaviours. Particular examples were that black people were lazy or aggressive, that Asians were docile and subservient, and so on. Could this idea that different *races* display different characteristics be a core notion in our ordinary concept of *race*? Is it possible for there to be acceptable agreement about this, or would disagreement seem to lead to at least one party having a perverse notion of the concept of *race*?

Again, take Penelope and Persephone. Penelope, like many of the respondents to the ~~Berkeley University~~ 1991 National Race and Politics Survey, thinks black people are lazy, aggressive and ill-disciplined. For her, black people who manifest these features do so by virtue of their blackness. She also suspects that those black people who do not manifest these features are having to work especially hard to suppress them, and in the right circumstances are more likely to show such characteristics than a white person. Persephone, again, thinks this is simply nonsense. Besides the overwhelming number of everyday examples of hard-working, disciplined, peaceful black citizens, just why should we think that characteristics such as these tie themselves to *races*? As far as Persephone is concerned, even

UC Berkeley

25

if we could show convincingly that there was a higher preponderance of such nebulous and difficult-to-measure things as laziness or docility among particular *races*, we would still be a long way from showing that such things were due to the inherent characteristics of *race*. For example, suppose we can show that voluntary unemployment (taken as a measure of laziness) is higher among black aboriginals than whites in Australia. Does this mean that black aboriginals are lazy because they are black aboriginals? Or does it mean they are lazy for some other reason? For instance, we might suppose they are part of a long under-privileged part of society offered only badly paid, dead-end work, and for whom employment offers no clear advantage or benefit. Here our assumed measure of laziness has not shown laziness due to *race*, because it cannot exclude laziness due to long-standing social structure, class and lack of opportunity. For Persephone, until we can sort through these kinds of possibilities, Penelope's assumptions about racial characteristics are a long way short of convincing.

Again, the question for us is whether the disagreement between Penelope and Persephone here is acceptable – are they disagreeing about the details of something that in other respects they have a common grasp upon? Or is their disagreement perverse – is one or other of the parties working with a concept completely removed from the common notion? And again, I take it to be that, understood straightforwardly, the disagreement here is acceptable rather than perverse. Penelope and Persephone know who they and most others would count as black, white, Asian and so on, and although they disagree it is clear that there is a common element forming the basis of their debate – this suggests that different cultural and behavioural attitudes as a feature of *race* is not a core part of the concept of *race* and will not form part of our more robust account.

Physical and mental attributes

Recall that the fourth common feature of the concept underpinning our ordinary thought and talk of *race* was that different *races* manifest different physical and mental capabilities. For example, black people are thought to be more athletic and better at sports (of a certain kind), while white people are more intelligent. Could this idea be a central feature of our ordinary concept of *race*? Would disagreement about this be acceptable or perverse?

Again, taking Penelope and Persephone, we can say that Penelope finds herself in strong agreement with the idea that *races* manifest particular physical and mental capacities. In particular, she finds herself in broad agreement with the assertion that significantly lower IQ test scores of black people are due to their being black – it is a feature of their *race*. She also finds herself sympathetic to some of the conclusions drawn from this about the irremediably lower IQs of blacks meaning that many ameliorative social programmes are simply wasted money. She is also convinced that certain sporting and cultural achievements associated with black people are due to their *race*.

Persephone on the other hand thinks that talk of particular *race*-related physical and mental capacities is completely wrong. As far as she is concerned, the kind of phenomenon that work on IQ test disparities seeks to explain is not even clearly established. For Persephone, to go from lower scores on IQ tests to claims about the basis of intelligence in racial propensities and genetic inheritance is just too troubling. As is well known, when IQ tests were first adopted a large number of results suggested that American soldiers of the First World War were for the most part simpletons, that the majority of immigrants to American shores were feeble-minded, and the only intelligent people in the USA were rich, urban English speakers. Unsurprisingly, this was simply the upshot of an IQ test that judged correctness by using the answers likely to be given by rich, urban English speakers as the standard. For Persephone, before any assumptions about *race*-related intelligence can be drawn from such a notoriously troubling measure as IQ tests, standards of correctness which advantage some *races* but disadvantage others need to be ruled out. And even if this could be done, the well-known spectre of "stereotype threat" would need to be excluded too.[6] As for the notion of natural black athleticism contrasted with white players' sports related intelligence, the influx of competitive, athletic white basketball players from the former Soviet Bloc into the US National Basketball League is enough for Persephone to think this is more a matter of perception than fact.

As before, we can see that this disagreement is not a matter of perversity – neither Penelope nor Persephone are using some odd and idiosyncratic notion of *race* to ground their particular attitudes to the idea that *race* involves particular physical or mental capacities. There is a core of agreement around which their disagreement centres, which makes it quite clear

---

6. See for example Steele and Aronson (1998) for a study showing that when black students knew they were being tested in the context of their race, their anxiety increased and their test scores decreased. This reduction in scores once racial stereotypes were activated is called "stereotype threat".

that, once again, this feature of our underlying ordinary concept of *race* is not a central or core feature. Disagreement about whether different *races* manifest different physical and mental capacities (by virtue of being that *race*) is what we've been calling acceptable disagreement, and consequently this feature will not form part of our more robust account of the ordinary concept of *race*.

Geographical origins

Recall that the third common feature of our ordinary concept of *race* was that *races* and racial difference are somehow tied to geographical origin. The blackness of certain people is a marker of their ancestral origins somewhere in Africa; the whiteness of certain people is a marker of their ancestral origins somewhere in Europe; and so on.

Suppose that Penelope thinks this idea of geographical origin makes perfect sense – there is a large community of people in the city where she lives who look east Asian. If you ask them where they are from, they will say that they are Australian, but they may qualify this by saying they are Chinese-Australian or *ABC* (Australian-born Chinese). And the reason they look the way they do, and are the *race* they are, is that their origins, either in recent generations or from generations far removed in the past, are traceable to a particular part of the world where people look just as they do. Indeed, if you ask Penelope about *races* generally, she will tell you that there are certain kinds of *races* and that they look as they do because they come from different parts of the world.

Persephone, on the other hand, thinks about these matters rather differently. For Persephone looking at a black person tells us nothing about the geographical origin of them or their ancestors. Indeed, it would be quite likely, on Persephone's view, for us to find numerous black people for whom every ancestor is black yet who are indubitably northern European. Or numerous white people for whom every ancestor is white yet who are indubitably African. Moreover, if I learn that I am about to meet a person for whom every single ancestor was a native of the southern Indian subcontinent, I can draw no sensible conjectures about that person's *race*. In short, *race* and geography are disconnected and the latter is irrelevant to the former.

The question here, again, is whether such disagreement is acceptable or perverse. And it should be clear, I hope, that this is beginning to look perverse. It seems as though Persephone has some ideas about *race* that

28

aren't common or widely held. Her ideas look more like nationality, perhaps. Indeed, it is quite likely that in a discussion about how best to secure
racial equality, if our interlocutor revealed that they thought someone
without any ancestral connection to Africa was black in contemporary
USA, we would quite likely conclude that our discussion had better take a
pause while we work out whether we are using the same key concepts. This
makes it look as though geographical origin is a central or core feature of
our underlying ordinary concept of *race*. Disagreement about whether different *races* have different geographical origins is what we've been calling
perverse disagreement, and consequently this feature *will* form part of our
more robust account of the ordinary concept of *race*.[7]

Inheritance

Recall that the second common feature underpinning our ordinary thought
and talk was that *race* and *racial difference* are somehow tied to inheritance. In particular, the assumption was that an individual's race is somehow
related to the *race* of their ancestors such that if, say, white people produce
offspring, those children will be white too. Similarly, if black people produce offspring, those children will also be black. And so on.

Suppose that Penelope thinks this notion makes perfect sense. As far
as she is concerned the idea that parents and children share *races* because
race is inherited from one's parents is part and parcel of the idea of *race*.
If we were to tell Penelope that two people of the same *race* were having a
baby, she would be quite certain that we could tell the *race* of the child well
ahead of time – it will be white if its parents are white, black if its parents
are black, and so. Further, if we were to tell Penelope that in fact the child,
now born, had all the appearances of being of a different *race* to its parents,
she'd attempt to explain that difference in ways that still relied on the idea
of inheriting our *race* from our parents – perhaps there is an ancestor of
the same *race* as the child about which the parents were ignorant; perhaps

---

7. It may be worth showing some caution though. As will become clear in Chapter 2, the socio-
historical aspects of race are such that our concept of race could have arisen in a context
where geographical origin became irrelevant to racial formations. Indeed, in some racial classifications, such as those found in rural Haiti, "whiteness" depends on being foreign more than
it depends on being from Northern Europe (see Labelle 1978, for example). So saying that
geographical origin is a core feature of our racial concept, we may have to bear in mind that
our particular social context will play some part in this.

the putative father is not really the father and the *race* of the *real* father will explain the *race* of the child.

Persephone, on the other hand, thinks of matters rather differently. As far as she is concerned the idea that we inherit *race* from our parents makes no sense at all. If we told Persephone about two people of the same *race* having a baby, she would be quite certain that no predictions about the *race* of the child were open to us. If pushed further on why, she would not cite the possibility of a lost ancestor of different *race* (or cuckoldry, etc.), she would simply say that she is not asserting that we might be unsure about the *race* of the parents, but rather that the *race* of the parents has *absolutely no bearing* on the *race* of the child. Indeed, for Persephone, it is quite acceptable for parents and children to have entirely separate *races*, for children of the same parents to have different *races* and so on. Moreover, in such cases, our common quest to find out why parents and children differ racially in terms of some lost ancestor is to entirely miss the point – *race* is not inherited from parents!

Again, we are not interested in who is right, but in what we are to make of this disagreement – is it acceptable or is it perverse? And just as with the issue of geographical origins, it should be clear that this is beginning to look perverse. Had Persephone's point been that we can't be sure about parental or ancestral *race* – there's always the chance that we do not know of someone in our familial line who is of a different *race* to the *race* we take ourselves to be – we might have thought the disagreement was an epistemic one, and acceptable. Indeed, we might have thought that there was no disagreement at all. However, given that Persephone's refusal to countenance the idea that *race* is inherited is not an epistemic point but a constitutive one, it looks as though our first conclusion has to be that Persephone's idea of *race* is quite divorced from that held by the rest of us and we should spend some time making sure she is talking about the same thing as the rest of us. This makes the disagreement look perverse, and as we noted, perverse disagreement means that this feature *will* form part of our more robust account of the ordinary concept of *race*.

Somatic markers

Recall that the first common feature behind the ordinary concept apparent in our thought and talk was that *race* and *racial difference* are somehow tied to certain somatic markers and bodily differences (e.g. skin colour, facial features, hair texture). Again, the idea is simple. What makes a black person the *race* they are is that they have certain bodily features common to black people – primarily darker skin colour, but also things like coarse hair, a broad nose and so on. What makes a white person the *race* they are is that they have certain bodily features common to white people – primarily white skin, but also things like fine hair, a thin nose and so on.

Suppose that Penelope thinks this notion makes perfect sense. As far as she is concerned black people have exactly the set of bodily features that we identify with that *race*, the same with white people, the same with Asians. Indeed, she is so committed to the idea that racial difference is deeply connected to somatic markers that she also thinks we can extend this notion to other racial and ethnic groups – Jews, Romany Gypsies, Arabs – and even within broad ethnic groups: southeast Asians have some bodily differences to Chinese Asians, northern Europeans have some bodily differences to southern Europeans. Moreover, for Penelope, if she is presented with a person who is said to be, say, black, but who has all the physical characteristics of a white person, she would think something was wrong. Either we were wrong about this person's *race*, or there is something over-riding the ordinary physical traits of their blackness (vitiligo, albinism, make-up, etc.), or their claim to be the *race* they are is dependent on a distant ancestor, and so on. Either way, without the obvious physical traits of blackness, the claim to blackness here needs to be investigated.

Persephone on the other hand sees no connection between physical characteristics and *race*. For her it seems ludicrous that someone has to have black skin, coarse hair, a broad nose and so on, in order to count as black. The same holds for any claim about the characteristics of *races*. When pushed further on this it becomes clear that Persephone does not mean that there are people who have a claim to blackness or whiteness and so on, who nonetheless don't show the supposed traits very strongly. What she means is that *race* has nothing to do with physical characteristics. So irrelevant are the supposed physical markers of *race* on Persephone's view that it is quite possible for two physically identical people to be entirely different *races*. Indeed, when meeting someone with very black skin – the kind of person Penelope would, without a moment's hesitation, unequivocally declare as black – Persephone would consider us to have absolutely no physical evidence upon which to hazard a guess at *race*. Appearance is irrelevant and so tells us nothing about *race*.

And as with our examination of disagreement for all the other characteristics that form part of our ordinary concept of *race*, the question for us

31

is not who is right, but whether the disagreement is acceptable or perverse. And I would hope that this disagreement, perhaps more than any other, is obviously perverse and could not be tolerated in any ongoing discussion about *race*. Penelope and Persephone would clearly be talking about two unrelated things. Indeed, while we might think Penelope takes the somatic criterion of *race* a bit far, we would obviously think that Persephone was entirely divorced from anything ordinary people considered to be *race*. And again, remember that Persephone's point was not that physical markers about *race* aren't always reliable, or universal, or obvious, it was that they had nothing to do with *race* at all. Presented with a paradigm physical case of some *race*, Persephone would openly say she hadn't the slightest clue what *race* this person could be if physical appearance was all she had to go on. This makes the disagreement look perverse, and as we noted, perverse disagreement means that this feature *will* form part of our more robust account of the ordinary concept of *race*.

Summary – what is our ordinary concept made precise?

Using the idea of acceptable and perverse disagreement, we have taken the six most common characteristics found in our everyday thought and talk about *race* and refined it into something that identifies the most central features. The idea was that those characteristics about which there can be no acceptable disagreement are non-negotiable features of our ordinary concept of *race*. In particular, it means that only three of our original six concepts look non-negotiable – *race* is marked by somatic differences, is inherited, and is tied to certain geographical regions. More importantly, it means that our ordinary, more robust account of *race*, as recovered from our ordinary thought and talk, is broadly as follows: *race* and *races* are marked by particular physical markers, such as skin colour; are inherited from earlier generations; and connect particular *races* to particular geographical areas in terms of origin.

At this point, then, we have worked extremely hard at getting a robust account of our ordinary *race* concept; that is, the notion of *race* as it appears in our everyday thought and talk. We identified a series of characteristics and shaped those characteristics into a concept with three core elements – *race* is manifested through certain somatic markers, it is inherited, and it ties us to certain geographical regions of the Earth. I am "black" because I have certain somatic markers of that *race* (I have black skin, coarse hair, a broad nose, etc.), because my parents and ancestors were black, and because my ancestry is tied to Africa. You are "white" because you have certain somatic markers of that *race* (you have white skin, fine hair, a thin nose etc.), because your parents and ancestors are white, and because your ancestry is tied to Europe. The question that faces us now, though, is the very question with which we began – is *race* real?

RACE AND SCIENCE

There are a host of ways in which we might understand our guiding question,[8] but the most obvious and fitting one, and the reading we shall consider here, is whether our concept of *race* corresponds to anything in the natural world. Put another way, is our concept of *race* a fit subject for science? Is it given any credibility by the best of our natural sciences? And the answer is a clear and resounding "no, it doesn't". Below we shall spend some time looking at reasons why. In particular, we shall examine some reasonably simple biological facts and observations that tell against the kinds of characteristics that form the core of our *race* concept also forming a coherent concept for scientific study.

The refusal of somatic markers to cluster

The first interesting thing that we shall note here is that the somatic markers that we think of as demarcating one *race* from another do not cluster into the kinds of groups that we would need them to if they were to be markers of our ordinary *race* concept. Consider the characteristic that we've mentioned most and which would certainly feature in any ordinary notion of *race* – skin colour.

Skin colour is what is known as a cline. The British biologist Julian Huxley introduced the term "cline" in the 1930s to describe the gradual

---

8. For example, we might ask whether we experience treatment and behaviors in terms of this "race" concept, and of course we do. This is something we shall explore further in Chapter 2. We might even be asking some variant of the Cartesian concern with sceptical doubt. But of course, these aren't the obvious readings that we are exploring here.

change in particular biological characteristics of a species over a geographical area (see Huxley 1938). An interesting example is tooth size. The tooth size of early human groups would depend very much on diet – larger stronger teeth were required for a predominately raw diet while smaller teeth were sufficient for a predominantly cooked diet. And of course, the need for a cooked diet increased the nearer a group lived to a climate where food might be frozen – that is, the further one lived from the equator. Consequently, tooth size gradually changes from larger to smaller as one moves from the equator to the poles.[9] And skin colour behaves in a like manner – the nearer one is to the equator, the darker one's skin tends to be. We shall return to the question of why this is so shortly, but what this shows is that skin colour is a cline. But if skin colour is a cline and the subject of scientific and biological study[10] then why does this count against our ordinary concept of *race*?

The reason is quite simple – the clinal distribution of a characteristic like skin colour does not match the putative racial distribution of that characteristic as suggested by our ordinary concept of *race*. For example, the skin tone of people from north Africa, southern Europe and east Asia all form a rough group under clinal distribution. This obviously groups together peoples who, by our ordinary racial categorization, should not form part of the same group. Moreover, people grouped together under the same *race* would be separated if we were genuinely treating somatic markers as manifesting race – east Africans have more in common with the *races* of the Indian sub-continent under the clinal distribution of skin tone than they do with west Africans. Our assumptions about skin colour, then, do not seem to divide people in the right way to make our notion of *race* match up to anything like a scientific study of those somatic markers.

We could, of course, object that we are selecting a single somatic marker in isolation here and that what we tend to do is group a host of somatic markers together – that is what we mean when we say bodily difference marks racial difference. However, once we start to introduce other somatic markers it makes matters even more intractable. For example, assumptions

---

9. There are other complicating factors, of course, and there are even local clines in places such as Australia where cooking food was introduced to indigenous populations only relatively recently, and slowly spread across the continent. See Brace (2005) for extended treatment of the connection between race and clines.
10. There are lots of examples of scientific work on clines – see, for example, Livingstone (1962), Post (1962) or even Taylor (1981).

about the relation of *races* to nose size are no more clear-cut than those about skin colour. Nose size isn't clinal in quite the same way as skin colour, but it can be gradated in some similar ways. However, the key point is that nose size and shape does not match our ordinary racial divisions – the typical nose shape in east Africa is very similar to that of northern Europe. This means we have black people and white people with the same somatic characteristic. Further, the typical nose shape in southeast Asia is broader and flatter than the typical nose shape found in China. This means we have Asian people with different somatic markers. Combine these factors with other characteristics – skin colour, say – and things begin to get very messy indeed, and the resulting groups certainly look nothing like the putative racial groupings suggested by our ordinary concept of *race*. An east African will be classified as "black" under our ordinary concept but this person shares a skin colour with people from India and a nose shape with people from northern Europe. This makes our ordinary concept of *race* look to be in bad shape as an object for scientific study – it fails to divide the world up as it suggests it should. Moreover, its nearest scientific concept – *clines* – looks too different to our ordinary concept of *race* for us to treat the latter as the scientific counterpart to the former.

The lack of genetic basis for *races*

A common assumption about *race* is that the various characteristics that we want to gather together under our ordinary concept are explained by some deeper biological fact – primarily genetics. Indeed, this is exactly how many of us in our pre-theoretical thinking about *race* might attempt to give scientific coherence to our *race* thought and talk. We might reason, for instance, that our bodily traits are something that we get from our genes – our racial markers are the physical manifestation of our genetic codes. Further, our racial inheritance is something we get from our genes – genes are passed down from earlier generations. The geographical notions of *race* are just meant to capture the idea that, for whatever reasons, those people isolated in Africa had particular traits which were compounded and enforced by the interbreeding of people in that area, the same for Europeans, the same for Asians and so on – breeding is just a matter of genetics, right? However, genetics lends little weight to this kind of thinking.

Take, for example, the geographical notion. There is much very deep analysis of genes, genetic make-up and human migration out of Africa into

Europe and Asia and what this might mean for notions of *race* (see, for example, Cavalli-Sforza *et al.* 1994).[11] However, we can examine how genetics simply fails to give any endorsement to the geographical characteristic of our *race* concept without delving too deeply into the literature here by looking at some simple disanalogies between *race* and its nearest workable scientific concept – the idea of a breeding population or sub-species.

If we are to treat *races* as breeding populations in the way that the geographical assumptions of our ordinary *race* concept seem to suggest – black people are tied more closely to the breeding population that established itself in Africa, Asians are more closely tied to the breeding population that established itself in Asia and so on, then certain things follow from this. First of all, let's grant some assumptions implicit in this view, namely that the geographical divisions we tie to *races* do represent some broadly discrete divisions among the breeding populations of our ancestors such that early humans in Africa did not interbreed much with the Asians and Europeans at the geographical borders of these putative *races*, and so on. We shall return to this assumption shortly, but let's grant it for now. Second, let's grant that the notion of a breeding population in biological science corresponds quite closely to our ideas of *race*. Scientifically, relatively discrete breeding populations represent something like sub-species. Where a species might be thought of as a group of individuals that can interbreed and produce fertile offspring, a sub-species is a group of individuals within that species that forms a breeding population and shows some genetic differences as a result of that interbreeding. Our idea of *race*, and the notion of geographical ties seem to be a folk-realization of just this sort of idea. However, even with these things granted, this can't give any scientific credence to our ordinary concept of *race* for a few reasons.

First, our treatment of relatively discrete breeding populations as *races* is not in the least bit consistent. Consider that we are treating the geographical notion in our ordinary concept as an expression of the idea that racial groups are tied to discrete breeding populations – the geographical notion is just an expression of how the world has divided people in the past. It turns out that in contemporary society all kinds of social reasons and practices divide people into relatively discrete breeding populations. Religious differences, especially in less secular societies and ages, have enforced quite

---

11. For a more philosophically useful and thorough dissection of the connection between science and our race concepts see Naomi Zack's outstanding *Philosophy of Science and Race* (2002).

strict rules about intermarriage with those of a different religion. Yet we do not think of Protestants, Catholics, Hindus or Muslims as *races*.[12] Similarly, some groups have managed to keep some marked distance between themselves and other elements of society through careful social rules about marriage and material inheritance – think of the British aristocracy at its height, governed by concerns about primogeniture and good marriages. Yet we do not think of aristocratic classes as *races*.[13] This makes it look as though our treating some breeding populations as *races*, but not others, is completely arbitrary.

We might argue that not any old social division of people into breeding groups will do for *races*, and that we are thinking specifically of geographical divisions for quite precise reasons, which rule Protestants and aristocrats out of our racial categories. In particular we are thinking of older populations that had a significant amount of time to breed separately and form clear genetic differences – the continental divisions between peoples show that these are *foundational* breeding populations rather than current or recent ones. Indeed, we might allow that if Protestants and aristocrats were to form discrete breeding populations for a significant period, they might form *races* in the far-off future. However, even this kind of qualification is not enough to mean that we can make sense of this geographical element of *races* in terms of genetics.

To begin with, even allowing geographical divisions to represent discrete breeding populations and allowing breeding populations and sub-species to be the best potential scientific counterpart to *race*, there are insufficient genetic differences between the groups posited as *races* under such a division to give any weight to this idea. For example, Richard Lewontin's famous study of genetic variation between and within *races* showed that variation *between races* was not as great as that *within races* (Lewontin 1972). Lewontin found that around 85 per cent of genetic variation between individuals could be found within sub-groups of a *race*. That is, 85 per cent of genetic differences were found to exist between people classified not only as of the same *race* (for example, Asian), but also as of the same racial

---

12. Of course, there are some connections between religion and races that are worth noting – Jewishness can be seen both as a matter of faith and of genetic inheritance. Indeed, there is even some evidence that Islam is taking on the features of racial division within some societies.
13. Intriguingly, however, the term "race" may well have its historical roots somewhere in the description of aristocratic lineage (see Fredrickson 2002: 53).

axolotl genome is 10x the size (32g base pair) of the human genome

loblolly pines, about 7x (22g base pars

sub-group (for example southeast Asian). Of the remaining 15 per cent of genetic differences, around 8 per cent were found to exist between individuals of differing racial sub-groups (for example between southeast Asians and northern Chinese). Finally the remaining 7 per cent was between different *races* (between Asian and European Whites, for example). When we also consider that human beings are 99.8 per cent genetically similar, we can see just how small the difference that is supposed to explain racial variation would be. Consider that the genetic variation of chimpanzees within the *same* sub-species can be as much as six times greater than within human populations (see, for example, Kaessmann *et al.* 1999, Kitano *et al.* 2003 or Stone *et al.* 2002) and we can see just how unlikely it is that different *races* are genetically discrete enough to form a coherent scientific subject based on genetics. It is hard to see how we could motivate a call for sub-species of humans on the basis of less genetic variability than is tolerated *within* sub-species for chimpanzees – if a certain degree of genetic variability cannot justify greater sub-specific division for chimps, an even lesser degree of variability certainly cannot justify it for humans.

Additionally, none of the genes that might be thought to mark racial differences remain exclusively within the putative racial groups that our geographical assumptions about *race* suggest. For example, the b-globin gene in human beings can be manifested in various ways, called *alleles*.[14] One particular allele of b-globin – sickle cell – is particularly associated with people who our ordinary *race* concept would treat as “black”. Indeed, a related genetic disorder, sickle cell anaemia, where individuals inherit two sickle cell alleles, is widely considered to be a “black disease”. In the popular imagination, then, the genetic basis for *race* might be found here in apparently *race*-specific alleles. However, it turns out that sickle cell, like all putative *race*-specific alleles, is not *race*-specific at all. Instead, it tracks the presence and frequency of the malaria parasite since the sickle cell confers malaria resistance upon its carriers. Interestingly, this means that the sickle cell allele is commonly found in Africa, but also in populations in the Mediterranean, the Arabian Peninsula, the Indian sub-continent and

---

14. To see just what we mean by saying that *alleles* are simply the various ways in which a gene is manifested consider a fictional example of genes that determine the location of flowers on plants. Let's say that there is a single gene, *F*, which determines flower location. However, *F* has two varieties: one which determines that flowers appear at the top of the stem – we'll call this allele *T* – and one which determines that flowers appear in the middle of the stem –which we'll call allele *M*. So, gene *F* has two alleles, *T* and *M*.

southeast Asia. So this allele, like many of those accounting for human genetic variation, is in some sense dependant on geographic differences, but unfortunately for those looking to ground the racial differences suggested by our ordinary concept of *race* on genetics, it depends on the *wrong* geographical elements.

So far we have concentrated quite heavily on the assumptions about *race* and geographical origin present in our ordinary concept of *race*, but genetics also fails to underpin other elements of our ordinary concept of *race*. In terms of the somatic markers of *race*, for instance, the lack of support from genetics is quite dramatic – especially since somatic markers are by far and away the most crucial element of our ordinary concept of *race*. To see why our notion that somatic difference marks racial difference is unsupported by genetics, let's use some simple observations and examples, and introduce some terminology to begin with.[15]

In talking about somatic markers of *race*, primarily skin colour, and resting on the assumption that there is some underlying genetic reason for these markers that varies between the *races*, we are relying the concept of *phenotypes*. Phenotypes are the physical and physiological traits of an organism determined by its underlying genetics. So, eye colour is a phenotype, but hairstyle isn't.

For phenotypes such as skin colour to be supported by genetics in a manner that allows for the scientific treatment of our ordinary concept of *race*, however, it would have to be clear from genetic make-up just what the phenotypic outcome would be. So, for example, we need to be able to look at the genes for skin colour and see that in this case we have the "black skin" allele, and in this case the "white skin" allele, and so on. However, the relationship between phenotype and genotype is not clear-cut enough to allow this.

Consider the example of eye colour. Our eye colour is determined by genetic material inherited from both parents. To have blue eyes, however, one must ordinarily inherit a "blue eye" allele from both parents. This is because the blue eye allele is recessive, meaning that when combined with a "brown eye" allele, the blue eye allele will be dominated and the brown eye allele will be manifested at the phenotypic level. To see why this

---

15. Throughout what follows we will omit lots of details about genetics, including notions such as epistasis and polygenic inheritance since, though crucial to the nature of certain phenotypes such as skin colour, they are not crucial to understanding the mismatch between genetics and our ordinary assumptions about race.

matters, consider that we could have two individuals with brown eyes but the alleles inherited from their parents could be different. Individual A, for instance, might have inherited a brown eye allele (*br*) from one parent and a blue eye allele (*bl*) from the other parent. Individual B, on the other hand, might have inherited a brown eye allele (*br*) from both parents. What this means is that we have two individuals with the same phenotype – brown eyes – but different genetic make-up. Individual A is (*br/bl*) whereas Individual B is (*br/br*). This is a very simple example, but it shows that a unified phenotype need not tell us anything about the underlying genotype.

What is more, the genotypes for skin colour are much more complicated than this. After all, unlike our eye colour example, it is known that there is no single gene responsible for skin colour. Moreover, the interactions between alleles are much more complicated in the case of skin colour than in the simple dominant/recessive relation between alleles for eye colour. Nonetheless, it is worth looking at a somewhat simplified example for skin colour since it illustrates just how complicated the underlying genetic factors can be and just how far our simple assumptions about phenotypic differences between *races* are from mapping onto a simple genetic corollary of *race*.

For our example of skin colour, there are three things to bear in mind. First, let us assume there are three interacting genes that determine skin tone, *A*, *B* and *C*. Each of these has two alleles: one that determines dark skin tone *(d)*, and one that determines light skin tone (*l*). Second, rather than the simple dominance relationship that we saw with eye colour, where inheriting a dominant allele means showing that allele at the phenotypic level, here a different relationship holds. For skin colour, the alleles are *weakly dominant* – at the phenotypic level the characteristics coded for appear to blend.[16] For example, cross-pollinating some white and red flower varieties yields a pink variety – the red allele is clearly not dominant, but neither is it recessive. And third, the relationships between the alleles for skin colour are such that they are accumulative: the more (*d*), the darker the skin colour; the more (*l*), the lighter the skin colour.

With this in mind, consider the following chart where two parents both have the following alleles for skin colour: A(*d/l*) B(*d/l*) C(*d/l*). Each parent contributes half of the alleles to its offspring. The sixty-four potential

---

16. Its important to note that this is not really blending since the separate traits are recoverable in later generations, but we can omit this detail here for the sake of simplicity.

combinations of these light and dark alleles for skin tone, then, look as shown in Table 1.1.

Just looking at the possible combinations listed in this chart for what is an extremely simplified view of the genotypic factors behind the phenotypic marker of skin colour makes its clear just how very complicated it really is to treat phenotypic traits as underpinned by genotype. All the same, there are certain things that we can note here that show just why somatic markers of *race* cannot tell us anything important about the genotype that lies beneath.

First of all, note that there are seven different types of skin tone that could emerge from these combinations. But of course, we certainly don't have seven notions of *race* drawn from a somatic marker like skin colour. Indeed, we have more in some contexts. What this means is that our ordinary notion of *race* breaks open the groupings in charts like these in a rather arbitrary fashion – or rather, if this is a scientific breakdown of a somatic marker, it certainly doesn't match our ordinary non-scientific breakdown.

Second, notice that because all that matters for skin tone is how many (*d*) or (*l*) alleles one has, individuals with very different combinations of alleles will look the same. Look at the skin tone that results from having three light alleles and three dark alleles – there are twenty alternative combinations of alleles in this category. If we are going to group together those individuals that look the same in terms of skin colour and call them a "race", the lack of underlying genetic uniformity is going to make this look as though it is not a scientific enterprise.

And finally, note something that is interesting not just for how it undermines any claims to support from genetics our ordinary ideas about *race* might have, but also because it makes our claim that *race* is a matter of inheritance or ancestry look scientifically unsupported too. Recall that we said both parents for these possible combinations had three (*d*) alleles and three (*l*) alleles. And note that while twenty of the combinations will give the same skin colour at the phenotypic level, many of the offspring will show phenotypic differences to these parents. Most interesting is that the parents might well be classified as black on our ordinary *race* concept in the USA or Europe, but at least one of the offspring (the one with all six (*l*) alleles) will be classified as white and share genotypic as well as phenotypic similarities with individuals classified as white. Our claims about *race* coming directly from our parents begin to look at odds with the scientific underpinning we are seeking out here.

Table 1.1 Skin colour and underlying genotype

Possible gene/allele combinations			Resulting skin tone
Six (*l*) light alleles, zero (*d*) dark alleles			
1. A(*l/l*) B(*l/l*) C(*l/l*)			
Five (*l*) light alleles, one (*d*) dark allele			
2. A(*d/l*) B(*l/l*) C(*l/l*)	3. A(*l/l*) B(*d/l*) C(*l/l*)	4. A(*l/l*) B(*l/l*) C(*d/l*)	
5. A(*l/d*) B(*l/l*) C(*l/l*)	6. A(*l/l*) B(*l/d*) C(*l/l*)	7. A(*l/l*) B(*l/l*) C(*l/d*)	
Four (*l*) light alleles, two (*d*) dark alleles			
8. A(*d/l*) B(*d/l*) C(*l/l*)	9. A(*d/l*) B(*l/l*) C(*d/l*)	10. A(*l/l*) B(*d/l*) C(*d/l*)	
11. A(*d/d*) B(*l/l*) C(*l/l*)	12. A(*l/d*) B(*d/l*) C(*l/l*)	13. A(*l/d*) B(*l/l*) C(*d/l*)	
14. A(*d/l*) B(*l/d*) C(*l/l*)	15. A(*l/l*) B(*d/d*) C(*l/l*)	16. A(*l/l*) B(*l/d*) C(*d/l*)	
17. A(*d/l*) B(*l/l*) C(*l/d*)	18. A(*l/l*) B(*d/l*) C(*l/d*)	19. A(*l/l*) B(*l/l*) C(*d/d*)	
20. A(*l/d*) B(*l/d*) C(*l/l*)	21. A(*l/d*) B(*l/l*) C(*l/d*)	22. A(*l/l*) B(*l/d*) C(*l/d*)	
Three (*l*) light alleles, three (*d*) dark alleles			
23. A(*d/l*) B(*d/l*) C(*d/l*)	24. A(*d/d*) B(*d/l*) C(*l/l*)	25. A(*d/d*) B(*l/l*) C(*d/l*)	
26. A(*l/d*) B(*d/l*) C(*d/l*)	27. A(*d/l*) B(*d/d*) C(*l/l*)	28. A(*d/l*) B(*l/d*) C(*d/l*)	
29. A(*l/l*) B(*d/d*) C(*d/l*)	30. A(*d/l*) B(*d/l*) C(*l/d*)	31. A(*d/l*) B(*l/l*) C(*d/d*)	
32. A(*l/l*) B(*d/l*) C(*d/d*)	33. A(*d/d*) B(*l/d*) C(*l/l*)	34. A(*l/d*) B(*d/d*) C(*l/l*)	
35. A(*l/d*) B(*l/d*) C(*d/l*)	36. A(*d/d*) B(*l/l*) C(*l/d*)	37. A(*l/d*) B(*d/l*) C(*l/d*)	
38. A(*l/d*) B(*l/l*) C(*d/d*)	39. A(*d/l*) B(*l/d*) C(*l/d*)	40. A(*l/l*) B(*d/d*) C(*l/d*)	
41. A(*l/l*) B(*l/d*) C(*d/d*)	42. A(*l/d*) B(*l/d*) C(*l/d*)		
Two (*l*) light alleles, four (*d*) dark alleles			
43. A(*d/d*) B(*d/l*) C(*d/l*)	44. A(*d/l*) B(*d/d*) C(*d/l*)	45. A(*d/l*) B(*d/l*) C(*d/d*)	
46. A(*d/d*) B(*d/d*) C(*l/l*)	47. A(*d/d*) B(*l/d*) C(*d/l*)	48. A(*l/d*) B(*d/d*) C(*d/l*)	
49. A(*d/d*) B(*d/l*) C(*l/d*)	50. A(*d/d*) B(*l/l*) C(*d/d*)	51. A(*l/d*) B(*d/l*) C(*d/d*)	
52. A(*d/l*) B(*d/d*) C(*l/d*)	53. A(*d/l*) B(*l/d*) C(*d/d*)	54. A(*l/l*) B(*d/d*) C(*d/d*)	
55. A(*d/d*) B(*l/d*) C(*l/d*)	56. A(*l/d*) B(*d/d*) C(*l/d*)	57. A(*l/d*) B(*l/d*) C(*d/d*)	
One (*l*) light allele, five (*d*) dark alleles			
58. A(*d/d*) B(*d/d*) C(*d/l*)	59. A(*d/d*) B(*d/l*) C(*d/d*)	60. A(*d/l*) B(*d/d*) C(*d/d*)	
61. A(*d/d*) B(*d/d*) C(*l/d*)	62. A(*d/d*) B(*l/d*) C(*d/d*)	63. A(*l/d*) B(*d/d*) C(*d/d*)	
Zero (*l*) light alleles, six (*d*) dark alleles			
64. A(*d/d*) B(*d/d*) C(*d/d*)			

The sensitivity of genotype to environment

One final issue that we shall look at in showing how our ordinary concept of *race* fails to ground itself in scientific reality is that our underlying natures, our genes, are shaped by and interactive with our environments in very important ways. Before looking at just why this is important, though, let's illustrate it with a very simple example of how environment influences the things we think are important to *race*.

We have already looked, albeit in a very simplistic way, at the kinds of genetic factors underlying skin colour. An additional factor, however, is how our environments affect us and our reproductive fitness, and the influence that this has over skin colour. For instance, consider the following well-known facts about skin colour and how its determination is influenced by environmental factors (see, for example, Jablonski 2004). Both vitamin D and folic acid are crucial to reproductive fitness, and influenced by the presence of natural sunlight – vitamin D is crucial to bone growth and strength, and needs lots of natural light for synthesis; folic acid is crucial for embryonic development and correct spinal tube growth, but is depleted by lots of natural light. The influence on skin colour, however, is interesting. What these factors mean is that the human skin must allow in enough UV light to allow the synthesis of vitamin D while not greatly depleting folic acid. In a low light setting no one would need to worry about the depletion of folic acid, but the synthesis of adequate vitamin D would require lighter skin. Those with darker skin in such environments would be at a reproductive disadvantage – although they would have adequate levels of folic acid they would be more prone to vitamin D deficiency, have weaker and smaller bones (crucially including the bones of the pelvis), and thus be less successful at reproducing than those with lighter skin in this environment. Conversely, in a high light setting no one would need to worry about the synthesis of adequate levels of vitamin D, but preventing the depletion of folic acid would require darker skin. Those with lighter skin in such environments would be at a reproductive disadvantage – although they would have adequate levels of vitamin D they would be more prone to folic acid deficiency, have increased numbers of foetal anomalies and spinal tube defects, and thus be less successful at reproducing than those with darker skin in this environment.

This makes obvious sense of the putative distribution of *races* across the world: white *races* predominate in areas towards the poles, where light levels diminish in increasing levels and reproductive success is more likely to be had by those with lighter skin; black *races* predominate in areas around the equator where light levels are at their highest and black skin confers reproductive advantage on the individual. As we noted earlier, skin colour is a cline. But why does this tell against our ordinary concept of *race* being underpinned by biological science?

The first thing to note is that a key somatic marker of *race* – skin colour – is massively dependent on environment, not on some deep genetic feature. Indeed, this ties in with our talk about the genetic elements of skin colour above and we can see that particular alleles might come to predominate in a group for environmental reasons. Should the environment change, so will the pressure affecting which alleles come to bear, and so the predominant skin colour will change too. But with skin colour being such a malleable and changeable feature, clearly dependent on environment, it is not at all obvious that somatic markers are stable or fixed enough to really fill the role they are supposed to in our ordinary concept.

The second thing to note is that this undermines our thinking about the ancestral element of our ordinary *race* concept. For instance, we could, hypothetically, relocate a breeding group of people from one environment to another and see the change in UV light levels lead to a change in skin tone in that population over time. What this means is that my ancestors may not have been the same *race* as me at all in terms of skin colour. Indeed, it would be remiss to conclude that our ancestors had the racial traits that we now use to divide people with our ordinary *race* thought and talk – despite the clinal nature of skin colour and our confidence that equatorial regions would produce different environmental pressures to regions closer to the poles, we lack the evidence to rule out other environmental factors or variables. A ready and plentiful source of folates or the presence of thick hair covering, for instance, would diminish the pressure on those most at risk of losing folic acid in a high UV light environment. We simply have no evidence about our ancestors' racial characteristics, and the openness of markers such as skin colour to environmental factors means we are in no position to draw scientific conclusions about the *race* of our ancestors.

The final thing to note is that this adds further weight to our earlier observation that the somatic markers of *race* do not cluster in the way our ordinary concept suggests they should. As we noted, skin colour is a cline. However, we can also extend that observation to undermine the geographical assumptions of our ordinary *race* thought and talk. As we've noted, the clinal nature of skin colour means that a key marker of *race* is not divided along the lines it would need to be to make our ordinary concept a genuine scientific class. But the implications of this for our geographical marker are worth emphasizing here. In particular it means that the somatic markers of *race* track environmental conditions rather than discrete geographical locations such that similar environmental pressures are likely to mean similar somatic markers. Geography is, of course, implicated in this, but it is certainly not a necessary feature and is not neatly divided in the way our ordinary concept would need it to be. Moreover, as the relationship between our somatic markers and environmental change suggests, geography need tell us nothing about *race* at all. Were massive environmental changes to occur in a given location then the putative marker of *race* in that geographical location could easily change under those changed pressures (e.g. from black to white skin). We would then have a single location but two potential markers of *race* in that location. It would look as though any choice about which marker was the important one for our current thinking would be completely arbitrary.

When we consider all these factors, and the factors about somatic clustering, and the general mismatch between our ordinary concept and the genetic evidence, *race*, as we have recovered that concept here, looks to be completely without support from science.

CONCLUSION

Although this detour through some of the scientific matters of *race* might seem complex to some, or too cursory to others (indeed, discussion of the scientific evidence for *race* is quite massive and often very complex), I hope it is clear just why our ordinary concept of *race* has no support within science. We spent much of this chapter getting clear about just what our ordinary, pre-theoretical concept of *race* was, and we identified six loose characteristics of our *race* thinking – somatic markers, ancestry, geography, physical capacities, cultural dispositions and purity. We then refined this loose cluster into a more robust concept comprised of the most crucial and important characteristics – somatic markers, ancestry and geography. Having reached this hard-won position, we put the resulting ordinary concept of *race* to the test by examining if it was, as our ordinary uses suggest we take it to be, scientifically credible. In particular, we were interested to see if our concept of *race* mapped on to any nearby scientific categories (such as breeding populations, or clines), and whether genetics gave any support to our ordinary views on *race*. Most importantly, we saw that they did not: the somatic markers that we tend to treat as racial do not cluster together in the right way to be markers of a scientifically credible concept; the putative genetic evidence does not support the kind of racial divisions we have in mind; concepts like breeding populations and sub-species make no sense as racial categories because they are either arbitrarily selected at the ordinary level as being equivalent to *races*, or the genetic variation between "racial" groups is insufficient to suggest genuine sub-species status. And so on.

The general conclusion from this chapter has to be this: our ordinary concept of *race*, judged by the standards of science and scientific study, is not real. In some ways, the conclusion that *race* is not real may seem shocking. After all, when we asked about the reality of *race* at the start of this chapter it seemed incontrovertibly obvious that there was such a thing as *race* – we experience it all the time in our everyday interactions with people. If it turns out that we are all completely mistaken and *race* is an empty concept, then maybe matters are closed and we should close the book on *race*. That is quite a remarkable idea to take on board. To discover that the concept underlying our everyday concept of *race* has no scientific credibility whatsoever is, quite understandably, something that many baulk at.

From a philosophical point of view, though, such a discovery turns out to be deeply interesting. Far from requiring that we close the book on *race*, the lack of scientific credibility for our ordinary concept opens up a whole range of philosophical questions. As we shall see in the following chapters, the discovery that *race* isn't real opens up philosophical discussion rather than closes it down, and calls for more questions, not fewer.

CHAPTER TWO

Is *race* social?

Given that we have seen that the concept of *race* that underpins our ordinary talk and thought about *race* is not real if judged by science – science suggests there is no biological kind that could be all of the things our ordinary concept of *race* would require it to be – it looks as though we must conclude that *race* is not real. However, for many this is too hasty a conclusion; we have certainly not exhausted the questions we can ask about the nature of *race* now that we have shown that our ordinary concept of *race* does not latch on to one of the "natural kinds" studied by physical scientists. Indeed, if we were to leave matters there it would seem as though we had missed something crucial to our *race* thought and talk – regardless of its scientific underpinnings, it is a robust social phenomenon bound down in our socio-historical practices, behaviours, conventions and institutions. If we bypass this feature of our concept of *race*, then we have clearly bypassed something important.

In this chapter, then, we shall spend some time looking at the relationship between our concepts of *race* and the socio-historical practices, behaviours, conventions and institutions that give rise to them. In particular, we shall begin by looking at how to make sense of the interactions between socio-historical practices and *race* concepts by briefly examining the rise of *race* thought and talk, and looking at two examples of how particular racial categories and practices involving *race* thought and talk were formed – one for contemporary USA, and the other for contemporary Brazil.

With this in place, we shall then look at three ways of reading this socio-historical aspect of our *race* concept in terms of what it means for the reality of *race*. The first is what we shall call *strong social constructionism*.

Proponents of this idea treat the socio-historical practices surrounding *race* thought and talk as making *race* real – *race* may not be a biological kind, but it is a social kind and thus real. The second is what we shall call *weak social constructionism*. Proponents of this view see our engrained social practices as explaining the existence of *race* thought and talk, but do not think this commits us to the reality of *race* as a social kind as a result. The third and final area we shall examine is what we shall call *reconstructionism*. Proponents of this view treat *race* thought and talk as crucially dependent upon our social practices, but think that the interesting social practices for grounding *race* thought and talk are not those of history and of our predecessors, but those of our present and future selves. We shall examine the detail of these positions and attitudes towards the social aspects of *race* in greater detail below, but first, let us begin with a brief examination of the socio-historical picture that gives rise to *race*, and two examples of how such practices give rise to particular racial classifications.

A BRIEF HISTORY OF *RACE*

In the vast literature on *race* and *racism* we often find the assertion that *race* is a modern idea (for example, Isaac 2004). While there are a variety of ways to explain the rise of *race* thought and talk, the standard picture is that in the ancient world, people were not classified along anything that we would now think of as racial lines, and there simply appeared to be nothing that we would call "race" (see, for example, Snowden 1983). Moreover, such notions as *race* only arose in the socio-economic climate of late medieval European trade expansion and the building of empire through colonial acquisition. These notions were then further consolidated by the new authority of science with Enlightenment classifications of people along these racial lines.

For example, we famously find the Swedish botanist Carl Linnaeus in his 1758 tract *Systema Naturae* classifying the Human species into forms with particular characteristics, as summarized in Table 2.1 (Linnaeus [1758] 1997).

While the idea that this is a genuinely scientific classification of *race* seems absurd to us, it is interesting that some of the key features we identified earlier as part of our ordinary ideas about *race* are in use here too. What we identified as physical and somatic markers of *race* are identified

Table 2.1 Linnaeus's classification of *races*

	African	Asian	American	European
Colour	Black	Yellow	Red	White
Temperament	Sluggish, lazy	Melancholy, stern	Irascible, impassive	Hearty, muscular
Face	Black kinky hair, silky skin, short nose, thick lips	Black hair, dark eyes	Thick straight black hair, broad nose, harsh appearance	Long blond hair, blue eyes
Personality	Sly, slow, careless	Strict, contemptuous, greedy	Stubborn, happy, free	Sensitive, very smart, creative
Ruled by	Caprice	Opinion	Custom	Law

as colour and face type for Linnaeus; what we identified as perceived *race*-specific abilities and attitudes are identified as temperament and personality for Linnaeus. More importantly though, given our current discussion, such classifications of *race* as these were the by-product of the Age of Enlightenment and the notion that new sciences such as biology could be subject to formal taxonomic projects.[1] The division of *races* and the ascription of particular properties in this manner conferred the newly accepted authority of science upon pre-existing notions of *race* – such "scientific endorsement" ossifies the "folk" ideas of *race* upon which such classifications are based.[2] But given the lack of racial concepts in the ancient world, just how did these folk ideas arise during the age of empire building in order to become endorsed by science?

We can gain a reasonably clear picture of the socio-historical background to the advent of *race* concepts by looking at the changing economic climate

---

1. There are plenty more. The most pernicious and influential was, perhaps, Blumenbach's ([1795] 1997) *On the Natural Variety of Mankind.*
2. With Linnaeus's classification for example (see Linnaeus [1758] 1997), the physical descriptors for *African* also include the claim that African females have a "genital flap". This is a clear case of Linnaeus's giving formal scientific endorsement to the long-held and popular myth of what became known as the "Hottentot Apron". See for example Fausto-Sterling (1995), or Gould (1982) for more on the Hottentot Venus.

of European countries in the late medieval period, and the beginning of the Age of Empires. As countries such as Spain, Portugal, Holland, France and England began to expand into the Americas, new sources of wealth began to present themselves, and growing mercantile classes began to need justifications to divide and exclude people. On the one hand, the need to protect certain positions of influence and power for ruling elites meant that certain classes, for example converted or settled Jews and Muslims, needed to be excluded from public office. A useful notion to enable this was the idea of inherited characteristics and "bad blood" – no matter how long ago one's ancestors had given up their non-Christian ways, inheritance of bad blood meant one was debarred from positions of power and influence regardless of current beliefs. As central as ideas about blood and inheritance were, the more important need was the justification of enslavement of black Africans in increasingly large numbers.

Portuguese and Spanish trade with the northwest African coast meant that European powers had long been in contact with the slave trade. However, as Portugal in particular began to develop sugar-producing colonies in the Atlantic and the Americas, the need for labour increased. Unable to send Portuguese nationals to labour in these new ventures in any great numbers, the need for other workers was greatly increased. However, sensibilities held against using European slaves – even in the fifteenth and sixteenth centuries there was some distaste at the idea of enslaving other Europeans. Further, using native workers was difficult. First, there were similar sensibilities in some quarters and the belief that the Americas were filled with "noble savages" not meant for slavery. More pressing though was the practical issue posed by the appalling decimation of indigenous populations by imported diseases. This meant that the use of native workers was not a viable solution to shortage of labour in the colonies. Instead, the Iberian powers relied on slave labour purchased on their trade routes and connections in Africa. And given the particular trade routes used to expand the new ventures in the Atlantic and Americas, the west African slave markets became particularly used.

The New World ventures, and especially the Portuguese sugar plantations on the Brazilian coast, proved to be immensely profitable and the need for workers increased, but with such increased involvement in the slave trade came an increased need for justification, especially where the Christian sensibilities of the European countries dictated that enslavement must be a means to redemption for the non-believer. And indeed, the justification for the enslavement of black Africans was found in that

Christian sensibility too. The darker skin of black Africans, especially west coast Africans with whom much of the Portuguese and Spanish slave trade began, was explained by reference to a supposed Biblical curse placed upon Ham, the son of Noah, who witnessed his father drunk and naked. As punishment for this, Noah cursed the children of Ham to servitude:

> And Noah awoke from his wine, and knew what his younger son had done unto him. And he said, Cursed be Canaan; a servant of servants shall he be unto his brethren. And he said, Blessed be the Lord God of Shem; and Canaan shall be his servant. God shall enlarge Japheth, and he shall dwell in the tents of Shem; and Canaan shall be his servant.   (Genesis 9:20)

It was also a commonly held belief that the curse blackened the skin of Ham's descendants, and this was the origin of the people of Africa. This, though tenuous, was considered justification enough for treating a class of people as marked as lesser by God, and thus irredeemable from Christian mission and salvation regardless of their religious conversion.

The pressure behind slavery was, of course, economic, but the justification was cultural and religious and compounded the particular practice of taking west African slaves. And of course, once the profitability of these practices was observed in a world where competition for the riches and resources of the New World was increasing, other European countries – Britain, France and Holland especially – engaged in and furthered the practices of taking black African slaves from the west coast of Africa to work in the American colonies. Once the practice of taking slaves from this region of Africa was established and propagated by economic concerns, justified by religious authority, and promulgated among ordinary "folk", its continuation was all but assured. Indeed, by the eighteenth and nineteenth centuries, the natural connection between slavery and blackness, though an accident of the original trade connections of the Spanish and Portuguese, was almost completely unquestioned. It seemed as though slavery was the natural upshot of *races*, when in fact *races* were the accidental upshot of slavery. When put this way, it is clear that slavery as an economic requirement of colonizing nations plays a key part in the birth of *race* as we tend to think of it, but that *races* are really born from the justification of such practices. Indeed, once practices such as slavery were justified by recourse to supposed natural differences such as "blood lines", ancestry and somatic markers, the pseudo-scientific endorsement of these views by Enlightenment taxonomists was enough to ensure that something very like what we now think of as "race" was born.[3]

Racial formations in the USA

The development of *race* and racial notions that we have just outlined seems to suggest a relatively global account of *race* and racial difference. And in contemporary Europe and the Americas at the very least, this history is hugely influential in our thought and talk about *race*. Indeed, as the social anthropologist Michael Winnant notes, "colonialism in the age of capitalism differed from previous imperial systems in that it came to encompass the entire world ... Racial groups are the outcome of relationships that are global and epochal in character" (Winnant 2001: 37). And of course, notions of racial hierarchy, broad categories of black, white, yellow, and so on, are common the world over. However, an important feature of understanding the social aspects of *race* is seeing that there are differences in how *race* is identified, thought of and talked about in different societies and social settings. And in particular that the legal, political and economic organization of societies can have huge influences on how *races* are classified, and thus how they are formed.

Given the history behind the rise of *race* concepts we can see much of the foundation for the notions of *race* and racial thinking in contemporary USA. After all, the massive importation of slave labour into the Americas meant that by the time of foundation the USA had a sizeable black slave population. Imported along with these slaves was the attitude that the division of peoples into *races* was both natural and scientifically endorseable. Moreover, the view that that *races* could be seen hierarchically with the white *race* considered superior to the black *race* was similarly endorsed. However, the particular socio-political and economic climate of the USA has made a distinctive contribution to how *race* is seen in that country.

First, consider that by the time of nation founding and when the question arose of how to integrate slave classes into society, America was already well established with white immigrants of various classes. Whites were in positions across various social ranks and the only clear or desirable economic and social role to be allocated to slaves was that of menial

---

3. Useful work in this area is Fredrickson (2002) and Williams (1944).

slave worker. Consequently, early social and political organization was such that it was designed to disempower and disenfranchise black Americans and enable white Americans to retain control over black lives. In particular, non-whites were denied citizen rights, property rights, religious freedom, the right to control their own labour, the right to education, and so on. These socio-political practices allowed for discrete racial categories of black and white. And of course, once these practices were in place, they became self-compounding in that anyone classified as black had shared socio-political interests and experiences with anyone else classified as black, and acted and behaved in accordance with them.

However, as the categories became harder to police in antebellum USA, new categories were introduced, removed, reclassified and legislated for. For instance, post-abolition racial categories attempted to account for the degree to which one's ancestry was black or white. However, since an octoroon (someone with one black great-grandparent) might be physically indistinguishable from a white American, the threat of those from lesser racial categories (a partly black group) passing as members of a more highly regarded racial category was increased. Since the rights to resources were allocated on the basis of *race*, and blacks were no longer legally enslaved, the threat to the socio-political interests of white Americans required action. Indeed, in 1918, the American Census Bureau suggested that three-quarters of black Americans had some white ancestry and posited that the category of "black" would eventually become obsolete. The response was to introduce the now famous "one drop rule" and to drop "mulatto" categories from the census in 1920. From that point on, any black ancestry was enough to count as black. The effect of this was to keep in place a strict division between the two racial categories of "black" and "white". The socio-political pressures and choices, and the practices they enforced and the divisions they compounded are clear. The USA was a nation of black and white racial categories.

Of course, this is very simplistic, and other ideas about *race* and racial categories play a part in racial formation in the USA too. For instance, as a growing constituency of Hispanic Americans have begun to assert their identity and to lobby for recognition within the USA, they too are beginning to find themselves part of the racial make-up of the USA. In 1970, for example, a Latino/Hispanic category was added to the census. Moreover, there are clear signs that the legacies of the "one drop rule" and hypodescent thinking are beginning to lose their grip on *race* thought and talk in the USA. Even in the 1960s, when racial self-identification became more prominent, the idea of blackness being conferred by a single black ancestor was still a strong folk idea about *race*. However, as separate categories of bi-racialism and multi-racialism have come to be recognized – such a category was included on the US census in 2000 – and work on what multi-racial identity in the USA means increases (see, for example, Rockquemore 2002 and Rockquemore and Brunsma 2002), it is clear that "one drop" thinking is waning and the nature of *race* thought and talk is becoming more multi-faceted. All the same, just how social and political needs and pressures go towards making up *race* in the USA should be obvious.

Racial formations in Brazil

The creation of racial categories in Brazil, as a contrast to the USA, is interesting and highly illustrative of how social pressures and economic interests contribute to the making of *race*. In particular, the connections between *race* and the west African slave trade are broadly the same for both the USA and Brazil. However, a crucial difference lay in the relative numbers of blacks and whites, existing infrastructures, and so the needs and interests of the ruling white elite in each country. In the United States as much as 80 per cent of the population was white, with pre-existing white labouring classes acting as intermediate social groupings between the ruling and slave classes. In Brazil though, this was not the case – it is estimated that upon achieving independence from Portugal in 1822, as many as three million of a population of four million was of African or mixed African descent. The socio-economic pressure that this brought was that the intermediate classes found in the USA were lacking in Brazil. There were no obvious candidates to take the role of military personnel, foremen or guards for slave plantations, farmers for the many enterprises needed to supply sugar plantations, or any of the jobs and tasks forbidden to slaves; there were simply too few white Portuguese and European immigrants. Consequently, it served no one to follow the simple black/white racial bifurcation that was witnessed in the United States. The upshot of the peculiar economic needs of a young Brazil, and especially its need for a range of intermediary social classes between white rulers and black slaves was an elaborate colour based system of racial classification. Brazil has had as many as twenty-eight different racial categories at any one time ranging from *blanco* (white) to *negro* (black), but including groups such as *branco*, *preto* and *moreno*, which acted as intermediary groups between the two racial poles, taking the various social roles that whites were too few to fill and blacks were too socially restricted to be allowed access to.

Depending on the social pressures at any given time, the particular groups that have existed or been used in Brazil has varied. However, what is clear is that, for the most part, the "one drop rule" thinking about *race* that had been so prevalent in the USA has no real purchase in Brazil. In a 2000 study of the DNA profiles of Brazilians, it was found that while 97 per cent of those who considered themselves to be *blanco* did in fact have white European ancestors, a full 61 per cent of them also had non-white ancestors. Again, the socio-historical context of Brazil explains this – of the few Portuguese and European immigrants to Brazil, only a small minority were women – but more importantly, it explains just why a hypodescent rule would be so unwelcome in Brazil. If almost two-thirds of the potentially white population turned out to be black by virtue of "one drop rule" thinking, then the positions of power and influence over the social mechanism that preserve white privilege would be threatened by sheer dint of numbers.

One final point about racial classification and the socio-historic pressures that contribute to notions of *race* in Brazil is worth noting. Just as the grip of hypodescent in America is begin to loosen and ideas about mixed racial identity and self-determination are beginning to find some purchase, it seems that some economic and social pressures are beginning to lead to the rise of racial bifurcation and "one drop rule" thinking in some areas of Brazilian life. While Brazil has long considered itself to be a racially well-balanced and open society, there is a growing awareness of the social, political and economic disparity between white and non-white Brazilians. Recent studies have found that non-white Brazilians have worse educational and occupational opportunities, and are paid less, than white counterparts. A shared experience of discrimination has tended to unite many non-white Brazilians behind a common and increasingly used banner of *Afro-Brasiliero*, or even simply *negro*. Moreover, as government programmes are introduced to help alleviate the social injustices experienced by non-whites, more Brazilians are beginning to rely on the presence of any black ancestor in order to claim and gain access to affirmative action initiatives. Such actions appear to be the beginning of "one drop" style thinking about *race*.[4]

---

4. Particular useful views and an account of the climate of race and racial classification in Brazil can be found in Skidmore (2003) and Telles (2004).

WHAT SHOULD WE MAKE OF THE SOCIAL NATURE OF *RACE*?

As the preceding section suggests, there is a significant socio-historical aspect to our concept of *race* and our *race* thought and talk. In particular we can see how quite specific socio-economic pressures and requirements led to the rise of the concept of *race* that we currently have. Moreover, by looking, albeit very briefly and in a simplistic manner, at the way *race* concepts were formed, compounded, changed and developed in different socio-economic settings, we were able to see just how different needs, different practices and different conventions have shaped different ideas about what *race* is and the number and nature of *races* that exist. Hopefully what this means is that at this point we have a richer and more detailed understanding of what we are really saying when we say that our *race* concepts and *race* thought and talk have a strong socio-historical grounding and that to bypass this is to bypass something very important about *race*. The history of *race* concepts is crucial to seeing how we can have such a deeply impacting phenomenon despite the lack of scientific foundation for our ordinary concept. And an exploration of how different social pressures, requirements and structures can shape and alter our ideas about *race* in such varied ways shows just how crucial social behaviours are to the nature of *race*. Now, all of this may seem more like a history or sociology lesson than a philosophical exploration of *race* thought and talk. However, with this background in place, we are now in position to ask a series of interesting questions about just what this social element amounts to for the reality of *race*.

The key and central philosophical issue which we shall now explore is simply this: while our *race* thought and talk may have no firm footing in science, it is quite clear that it does have a firm foundation as a social phenomenon. But what does this really mean for the reality of *race*, or rather, what are we to make of this social element of *race* in ontological terms?

For some, this social reality is enough to confer an ontologically robust status upon our *race* thought and talk and the key questions are to do with how we should understand this social construction of *race*. For others, the social elements of *race* certainly explain the felt phenomenon of *race*, but this observation falls a long way short of conferring ontological robustness on *race* thought and talk. The key questions for these philosophers concern just why the social elements of *race* are not reality conferring. For others, the social elements of *race* are philosophically interesting not so much because they tell us about how *race* has come to be, but because they tell us how we, as social agents, can change and reconstruct *race*. The key questions for these philosophers become how such reconstruction might be enacted. In the rest of this chapter, then, we shall examine these three philosophical reactions to the social elements of *race*. However, some of the questions which concern these three positions will carry over into our third chapter in obvious ways – what one thinks *can* be done with *race* given the scientific evidence and its social elements will obviously influence what one thinks *should* be done with *race* thought and talk. So, while we shall explore what these positions amount to, some of the detailed answers to the questions they raise will be deferred until Chapter 3. Let us begin, then, with those philosophers who see the social elements of *race* thought and talk as conferring some ontological robustness upon those concepts.

Race as socially constructed – the strong notion

If we accept that the core of our ordinary thought and talk about *race* – the concept that we spent so much time examining and developing in Chapter 1 – is not supported by the natural sciences and so does not latch onto a genuine biological kind, then it might seem that we should also accept that *race* is not real. However, the strong socio-historical component of *race* and the manner in which it comes to depend upon social practices and behaviours in order to be the way it is leads some philosophers to draw different conclusions. Consider, for example, Charles Mills's position:

> [T]here is conceptual room for a view of race as both real and unreal, not "realist" but still objectivist. This position is *racial constructivism*. ... Racial constructivism involves an actual agreement of some under conditions where the constraints are not epistemic (getting at the truth) but *political* (establishing and maintaining privilege) ... [A]n objective ontological status is involved which arises out of *inter-subjectivity*, and which, though it is not naturally based, is real for all that. Race is not foundational: in different systems, race could have been constructed differently or indeed never have come into existence in the first place. Race is not essentialist: the same individuals would be differently raced in different systems. Race is not "metaphysical" in the deep sense of being an eternal, unchanging, necessary, part of the basic furniture of the universe. But race is

> a *contingently* deep reality that structures our particular social
> universe, having a social objectivity and causal significance that
> arise out of *our* particular history. For racial realism, the social
> metaphysics is simply an outgrowth of a natural metaphysics;
> for racial constructivism, there is no natural metaphysics, and
> the social metaphysics arises directly out of the social history.
> Because people come to think of themselves *as* "raced," as black
> and white, for example, these categories, which correspond to
> no natural kinds, attain a social reality.   (Mills 1998: 47–8)

The idea is simply that while *race* may not be a biological kind and something that we find as "part of the basic furniture of the universe", it could nonetheless be real by virtue of the social practices that surround it. As Mills says, *race* could have an objective ontological status because of the inter-subjective practices and agreements which give rise to it – that is, *race* could be real because we all act and think as though there are *races*.

At first blush the idea that, though there is no deep *scientific reality* behind our *race* concepts, there is a *social reality* that confers a significant ontological status on our *race* thought and talk may seem strange. However, the idea that something is not real in a manner independent of social contingencies but is objectively real just the same may not be quite so odd or alien as all that. Consider, for example, the idea of nations or nationhood. It is undeniable that there are nations and nation states in the world. Indeed, their very existence dictates so much of what we can and cannot do – where we can go, what rights we have, the direction of world affairs, even down to placing constraints and allowances on the sports I play (assuming I am good enough to be considered of international standard). Nations are very real and any denial of this would surely be met with outright incredulity. However, it does not seem incumbent upon us that by holding nations to be real we must also hold that they are part of the "basic furniture of the universe". Nations and the idea of nationhood clearly depend on shared human practices and agreements, conventions, and agreed upon malleable contingencies. And yet we take them to be real. Moreover, we take them to be real by virtue of the particular practices, conventions and agreements we have in place – we are prepared to accept that their make-up and even existence depends on the international conventions we have in place concerning the recognition of nationhood. Nations are real because of social practices – they are a social reality. But to describe the concepts of nation and nationhood thus is not to patronize them.

To extend social constructionism to the notion of *race* is to make similar assertions about the reality of *race*. Our examination of science tells us that *race* will not be one of the basic ingredients of the universe, and nor does it latch onto some basic ingredient in a simple or isomorphic way. Nonetheless, there is a rich history that explains the rise of *race* concepts and *race* thinking. And various socio-anthropological investigations, such as those underlying the examination of racial formations in the USA and Brazil given above, show us just how variations in conventions, contexts, human needs and concomitant practices can alter the exact realization of our *race* concepts. *Race* is clearly as dependent upon social conventions, practices and malleable contingencies as *nation*. And just like *nation*, *race* is a robust felt phenomenon that directs our lives, constrains us in certain respects, and affords us opportunities in others. Put like this, it becomes clear just what the social construction of *race* amounts to, and why it is not strange to think of *race* as real even if it is construed as a social reality rather than a biological kind.

Some worries – passing and travelling

Hopefully it should be clear that treating *race* as real by virtue of its being created, maintained and constituted by socio-historical factors is not so strange as it might initially seem. And for many this basic idea forms the core of their claims that though *race* is a myth in biological terms, the rich social elements that surround our *race* concepts mean that *race* is not empty – it is a biological myth, but a social reality, and thus part of the objective ontology of our world. Whether this really is the best conclusion to draw is something we shall leave for a short while, and we shall grant, for the sake of argument, that the social elements of *race* are best read as conferring an objective ontological status. However, even granting this, there may be some issues that such a reading will need to address. We shall look at the two most prominent of these: the phenomenon of "passing", and the refusal of *race* to "travel".

Passing

Part of the social phenomenon of *race* is the notion of "racial passing" or simply "passing". *Passing* is the idea that members of one *race* can pass as members of another *race* either knowingly or entirely unwittingly. There are well-known fictional explorations of racial passing – for example Mark Twain's 1894 novel *The Tragedy of Pudd'nhead Wilson* tells of a white-looking slave-born child who is swapped with his master's child, with the two being raised in complete ignorance that they are occupying racial categories that they should not have filled. Similarly, Philip Roth's 2000 novel *The Human Stain* features a black character who knowingly "passes" in his professional academic life as white and Jewish. And of course there are several well-known real cases: Archibald Belaney, a native Briton who passed as an aboriginal Canadian Anishinaabe named Grey Owl; or the black American and one time NAACP leader Walter Francis White, who was able to pass as white during his investigations into racial lynching in the American South during the 1920s. But why should racial passing pose any sort or problem for the idea that *race* is real by virtue of its being socially constructed?

The idea is simply this: if passing is a genuine phenomenon, and it seems to be so, then treating *race* as socially real would need to allow for that. However, it may be that social constructionism about *race* cannot allow for passing. Consider a case where someone in the USA looks white, acts white, is treated as white, is afforded the benefits of being white, and may even consider themself to be white, but has black heritage or a black ancestor. This should count as a case of racial passing if anything should – a black person (by the hypodescent thinking about *race* in the USA) seems to have spent their life believing, acting, sharing in the experience of, and being taken as, white. However, if *races* are socially constructed then being a particular *race* is to live within and experience the social conventions and practices that direct the social lives of that particular class of people. For example, if being black in the USA is to be subject to a particular set of social conventions, and to take on particular behaviours and attitudes as a result of experiences that are brought about through inter-subjective agreement and accordance with those conventions and practices, then it looks as though anyone who has these experiences or adopts these practices simply *is* black. But of course, the experiences of the individual who passes are just those of the members of the *race* they are said to pass for. In which case the individual who is said to pass for white is not passing at all. Rather, this individual, by virtue of inhabiting the social role constructed for those who are white in this society, is simply white. Passing looks like a real phenomenon, but if social constructionist ideas are enough for us to think that *race* is socially real, and then it seems hard to make sense of what racial passing could be.

This of course is not the end of the matter. There are several ways that we might develop our social constructionist views so that they can overcome this problem.[5] In essence though, the problem is that social constructionism as construed here seems to leave no room for error. If being a member of a *race* is merely a matter of filling a socially constructed role, engaging in practices deemed to be those of that *race*, or of sharing the experience of a racial group from "the inside", as it were, then it is hard to see how any individual meeting these conditions could fail to be a member of the *race*. The task for the social constructionist wanting to accommodate the passing phenomenon is to provide ways in which, despite filling social roles constitutive of particular *races* and so on, we can still be wrong about whether we, or others, are members of the *races* they appear to be.

Travelling

The second potential worry facing this reading of the social aspects of *race* is what is frequently called "the travelling constraint". According to this view of *race* and racial construction, it seems as though the *race* assigned to someone in one society or at one particular juncture will not be transferable or transportable to a different time or a different society. And many philosophers who are committed to this strong social construction of *race* take this to be the case. For example: "*Race* does not travel. Some men who are black in New Orleans now would have been octoroons there some years ago or would be white in Brazil today. Socrates had no race in ancient Athens, though he would be a white man in Minnesota" (Root 2000: 631–2). Indeed, given what we have seen about how the concept of *race* arose and how different societal pressures create different racial formations, claims about the failure of *race* to travel may seem uncontroversial. The types of social pressure in Brazil are clearly different to those in the USA so it is unsurprising that the societal roles that constitute *races* in the USA are not the same as those in Brazil. Consequently, the racial roles one would fill in one place could not be carried across to another. Similarly with transporting *races* across time – if there were no social roles that constituted *race* at a particular time, then I could hardly have filled the racial role

---

5. Indeed, this is precisely what various social constructivists do (for example Mills 1998; Sundstrom 2002), and what several contributors to the passing/traveling debate do (for example Mallon 2004; Glasgow 2007).

that I fill here and now had I lived then. I could no more have been black in ancient Britain than I could have been a computer programmer – there was simply no social construction of such roles. However, things may not be quite so simple as this initial plausibility may suggest.

Consider the following question – do black people in the USA have better rights and better lives compared with the period before the abolition of slavery? I am guessing that even if you are unsure about the answer, you do not think the question ill-formed. Yet if the apparent refusal of *race* to travel on the *strong social constructionist* account has any weight, the question should be wrong headed – the racial categories and social conventions surrounding *race* thought and talk simply do not match up, and we would have no single group to hold fixed across our comparison. To further illustrate, consider the following quote:

> Empirical studies dating back to the 1940s indicate that, all other things being equal, racial minorities, particularly African-Americans, are disproportionately more likely to receive the death penalty for murder than are convicted whites. The U.S. General Accounting Office conducted a comprehensive review of the relevant studies in 1990 and concluded that ... racial disparities in the "charging, sentencing, and imposition of the death penalty" persisted. ... State and federal government studies conducted since 2000 largely confirm these findings.
>
> (Cholbi 2006: 255)

If the refusal of *race* to travel is really so compelling, then we should simply find Cholbi's claims here spurious – the racial category (and thus the *race* that it constitutes) that received the death penalty disproportionately in the 1940s simply cannot be the same category that suffers similar treatment in the 1990s. But in truth, even if there are reasons why we are not compelled by Cholbi's appeal to historical facts about the punishment of black Americans in comparison to their white counterparts, the refusal of *race* to travel is highly unlikely to be amongst them. Rather, the idea that *race does* travel seems perfectly acceptable to us and underpins all manner of everyday generalizations and anthropological, social and political comparisons between different societies, times and social contexts.

Of course, just as with passing, this worry need not mean that *strong social constructionism* is wrong about how to understand the socio-historical aspects of *race* thought and talk. The conflict between the *strong social constructionist*'s commitment to a non-travelling *race* and our ease with generalizations and comparisons in which *race* seems to travel perfectly well may actually be apparent rather than real. For example, it may be that the constructionist's description of *race* as resistant to travel is better described in another way – that *races* are realized relative to contexts for example, and that any individual will have numerous *races*, since there are numerous racial roles they would fill depending on context. So, for example, let's take the three racial contexts of the USA, Brazil and Haiti,[6] and one individual – say, Barack Obama. If we treat *race* as constituted relative to a context, then we can see that Barack Obama's *race(s)* is/are respectively black$_{USA}$, moreno$_{Brazil}$ and blanc$_{Haiti}$. Viewed this way, we can perhaps make better sense of what the claim that *race* refuses to travel means – one's *race* does not travel, because one has multiple *races* which are either foregrounded or backgrounded depending on the society one finds oneself in. And this might help us to make sense of issues of cross-cultural generalization and racial comparisons too. When we are making comparisons of the educational opportunities afforded to black people in the USA and in Brazil, for example, what we are interested in could be any number of things – how are those citizens classifiable as black in both places likely to fare in each country (i.e. we are interested in people whose *race* is black$_{USA}$/black$_{Brazil}$)? Or how are those classifiable as black in the USA likely to fare in the Brazilian system (i.e. we are interested in people whose *race* is black$_{USA}$/any$_{Brazil}$)? The results, and the individuals we are interested in, would clearly vary depending on how we frame our interest, but it is not immediately obvious that there is a clash between our account of how *races* remain tied to particular social practices and the possibility of comparing *races* across times and places.

There may still be problems here, of course, and this is not the only way in which the travelling constraint might be cashed out by the *strong social constructionist*, but the potential for both questioning this way of reading the socio-historical aspects of *race* and for developing the position are clear.[7]

---

6. For an especially useful guide to race and racial formations in Haiti see Labelle (1978).

7. There are various debates and positions around both the passing and travelling constraints and how they impact on the strong social constructivist position. I direct the interested reader to the best literature in these debates in the guide to Further Reading at the end of this book. However, Glasgow (2007) is worth reading for various ways in which the travelling constraint can be cashed out and their related implications.

Race as socially constructed – the weak notion

The strong notion of social construction that we have just surveyed is not the only way we could read the social aspects of our *race* concept. It may be that issues with passing and travel constraints push us into thinking that there is something deeply wrong with the idea, and thus to abandon it. However, the view we are about to examine, what we are going to call *weak social constructionism*, takes the strong view to be unsatisfactory for entirely different reasons. Before we examine just why that is, however, let us try to get a better idea of how *weak social constructionists* think we should read the social aspects of *race*.

To take a *weak social constructionist* position on the social aspects of *race* is, in very many respects, to cover similar ground to the *strong social constructionist* position. For example, the *weak social constructionist* is perfectly happy to take the socio-historical background and impact of *race* very seriously. It is clear to see from this perspective that our ways of thinking and talking about *race* have emerged through a process of economic pressures, pseudo-scientific endorsement and socio-political protection of dominant group interests within certain societies. Moreover, the *weak social constructionist* is quite happy to hold with their *strong constructionist* counterpart that *race* is a felt phenomenon – it has a massive impact in our daily lives and governs our actions. A child born in the USA who is, for whatever reason, assigned to the racial category of "black" will have a markedly different set of experiences, and be afforded a markedly different set of opportunities, than a child assigned to the racial category "white". There is no denying this. However, where the *weak social constructionist* parts company with the *strong social constructionist* is in thinking that this robust social presence is in any way *reality conferring*. The *strong social constructionist* believes that socio-historical and socio-political categories that are bound up with *race* concepts are constitutive of *races* in an ontologically robust way; the *weak social constructionist* thinks of these social categories differently, believing we must stop short of treating the social aspects of *race* as reality conferring. Instead, we must think of *races* and racial categories merely as labels, or badges, conferred upon different peoples and groups by broader societal agreement and practice. We shall examine just why we might reject the *strong social constructionist* claims about the reality of *race* shortly, but it is worth pausing to see just what the *weak social constructionist* reading of the socio-historical elements of *race* thought and talk really amount to.

The reason this is pressing here is that denying that the social aspects of *race* are reality conferring is made more acceptable if we can suffer no loss of explanatory power as a result. And to describe the socio-historical and political elements of *race* as labels or badges, as the *weak social constructionist* claims we should, looks as though it will owe us an explanation of something that the stronger constructionist position explains well – namely just how impacting, dominating and pervasive our *race* thought and talk is. That *races* are real – albeit as a social kind – has explanatory bite when it comes to understanding how the lives of millions can be, and have been, so affected by racial thinking and *race* concepts. The claim that *races* are simply labels or badges invented and applied according to various political and economic agendas looks, at first blush, like a far more anaemic explanation of such a powerful and dominant thing as *race*. Nonetheless, the *weak social constructionist* can garner some evidence that the organizing power of labels and badges is highly influential and might have a radically strong impact upon our lives. Consider the following example:

Let's say that most people think of university professors as having certain kinds of characteristics. Asked to describe what they might expect were they to meet a university professor, they might give the following list of characteristics: male, white, old, intelligent, shabby, absent-minded, eccentric, not good at practical things, and so on. And we can often give these characteristics more detail too: "intelligent" might often be qualified as "deeply informed about some highly esoteric subject"; "shabby" might be qualified as "wears unfashionable glasses, tweed jackets with worn elbow patches and comfortable brown shoes"; "not good at practical things" might be qualified to mean "so distracted by their thoughts that the everyday practicalities of food shopping or programming a washing machine are beyond them". And so on.

In addition to this, we have other expectations about the experiences a professor might be privy to in the right context – on campus, say, where being a professor has particular salience. Perhaps students are deferential, polite, and formal in conversation with the professor, rather than casual and informal. The professor will presumably get different treatment from librarians, administrators, and campus security than from students. Indeed, the professor may well expect to be afforded certain treatment and privileges by virtue of being a professor, and to be declined or constrained from others. It would be unreasonable for a professor to expect to receive the student discount at the campus bookshop, for instance. But why does any of this matter?

Well, obviously this idea about what professors are like, and the experiences they might have, can inform our behaviours. If I am a professor who fails to meet any of these expectations – I look young, dress in clean fashionable clothes and wear contact lenses say – then it is also quite likely that I will not experience some of the things I expect to as a professor. Campus security will question me and ask me for ID when I return to my car after working late; students are relaxed and call me by my first name; librarians don't seem to treat my requests as seriously as they do some of my older, more "stereotypically" professorial colleagues. It seems then as though one thing I can do is take on whatever elements of this odd collection of social assumptions about professors that I can in order to receive the expected behaviours. I can't make myself old, but maybe I can wear a jacket with elbow patches, or wear serious-looking glasses instead of my contact lenses. I can take on the social role; I can live up to the label.

The point, I hope, should be reasonably clear. Our notion of "professor" is bound down with certain kinds of expectations and ideas about what a professor is, how a professor behaves and so on. And all kinds of practices and social conventions exist around this idea. If we say that "professor" merely acts as a label for these assumptions, practices, and so on, we certainly don't detract from the power of this label to significantly affect peoples' lives. We have seen from the descriptions just given how the label could affect peoples' behaviour towards professors, and even how professors themselves could adopt the behaviours attached to the label. And we should be able to see how this kind of idea can be extended to the notion of *race*.

Our socio-historical construction of *race* and racial categories function to label and badge particular categories and determine which particular people fall into them depending on the political, legal and economic interests of dominant groups. But the power of these labels should not be underestimated – it clearly meets a certain class of interests for dominant groups if they act in accord with these labels and adopt behaviours towards themselves and others as a result. And even groups who are on the negative end of such practices can find empowerment by embracing these labels and badges to organize their own behaviour. For example, the socio-historical practices which characterize blackness in the contemporary USA might well seem to involve negative and disenfranchising behaviours – and it is not hard to see how the socio-political climate creates negative experiences for black Americans. We might also think that no-one would want to embrace or adopt a label which would lead to such negative experiences – in the example we gave of "professor" it is clear why we might embrace the constructed identity given the supposed privileges of the label, but if the effects of embracing that identity were negative, it is less clear why we would take on that label willingly. However, racial labels can allow individuals to predict their likely experiences, or to identify with others who fall under that label within our society. These can be positive or empowering things. We shall return to such issues as the positive and negative features of *race* and racial identities in our next chapter. For the time being, though, we can see that denying that the socio-historical elements of *race* are reality conferring and asserting that they are merely labelling certainly need not lead to an inability to explain the power and pervasiveness of *race* and racial concepts as a felt phenomenon in our lives.

At this point, then, having seen how we might acknowledge the socio-historical aspects of our *race* concepts without thinking that *race* is thereby made real, it is worth turning to the question of just why the *weak social constructionist* parts company with the stronger position and thinks that *race* is not a social kind.

Why the social reality of race does not make it really real

There are various reasons why one may not buy into the *strong social constructionist* claim that the socio-historical aspects of *race* are constitutive of *races* and thus reality conferring, and opt for a weaker claim instead. To begin with, we might simply deny that there are such things as social kinds. However, we shall not explore that idea since it would take us too far off course and into debates which, though related, are not necessary for us here. Instead, we'll examine a different kind of argument, one that leaves the existence of social kinds to one side.[8] The kind of argument we shall explore here is especially important for some of the issues we raise in our next chapter, in which a closer examination of its merits will be undertaken.

One reason we might not take our reading of the social aspects of *race* as far the *strong social constructionist* is that while there may well be such things as social kinds, *race* does not purport to be one of them. By treating

---

8. Those interested in work on social kinds may refer to Searle (1995) and Mallon (2007).

it as a social kind and conferring reality on it, we are doing a disservice to the ontological intent behind the concept. *Race* is indeed bound down in social practices and conventions, and in this respect it is like our concepts for "nation" and other social kind terms. However, *race* thought and talk also has the additional feature of purporting to be a biological kind, or at the very least, of latching on to a deeper biological and non-social fact about the world. In this respect it is entirely unlike "nation" and related social kinds that do not purport to be a feature of a deeper non-social ontology. Indeed, it is quite clear to those of us who engage in talk of nations and related ideas that the social reality is front and centre in our use of such concepts and any aspiration to a deeper non-social reality would be delusional – we know that nations would not be revealed during a complete examination of the underlying natural make-up of the universe. Instead, it is our agreements, international laws and conventions and shared practices that gives *nation* its friction with the world. *Race* thought and talk, however, is not like this – it purports to report a fact about the world over and above our social practices, in particular it purports to report a fact about underlying human biology. This is enough, so the claim goes, to mean that *race* cannot be a social kind. ①

There are two elements of this argument that need drawing out – the claim that *race* thought and talk purports to be about biological, natural and scientific facts, not social conventions or historically and politically ② grounded practices; and the claim that this disqualifies *race* from being a social kind. The first of these – that the aspiration of *race* thought and talk is to report some biological and scientific fact – should be reasonably straightforward, especially after Chapter 1. For us ordinary language users, there seems to be an implicit assumption that our concept of *race* does latch onto some deeper biological reality. And notice that in Chapter 1 we looked at notions like inheritance, "natural" characteristics and endowments, and so on. These are all ideas that, if only implicitly, rest on ideas about genetics and biology. Our ordinary thought and talk makes it look as though we do think of *race* more as though it were a natural and scientific thing, at least in part, rather than merely and solely a social thing.

Moreover, we can see from the socio-historical details given earlier in this chapter that the racial thinking of European powers in the Age of Empires sought consolidation from Enlightenment science. Indeed, Linnaeus's taxonomic categorization of *races* was merely an opening gambit in the "scientific" treatment of *race* and there is an active history of scientific analyses and projects since the seventeenth century.[9] It looks, then, as though there is some mileage in the claim that our *race* concept purports, at least in part, to be underpinned by biology and science. But why does this mean that *race* cannot be a social kind? Why does the *weak social constructionist* take this to lead to their second claim?

The reason, again, is relatively straightforward, but is perhaps best illustrated with an example. Take, for example, a religion that is, of course, bound down with all manner of social practices and conventions – it has a priesthood, ceremonies for birth, death and union, rituals of gratitude and so on. And it is clear that we can talk about the rise and nature of those practices in socio-historical terms – the make-up of the priesthood at one time was thus, but for socio-political reasons say, is different at another time. However, the practitioners of this religion (and let us assume that it is a widespread institution with very many followers), while recognizing the socio-historical descriptions we might give of their practices, do not think that their religion is *constituted* by these social practices. They reject the claim that their faith *is* the set of conventions and practices mentioned. Rather, they believe that their religion rests upon some fundamental facts about the way the universe is and that the practices in which they engage are tied directly to these natural facts.

Notice how unlike the "nations" example of a social kind introduced earlier this is. With the notion of a social kind like "nation" we can argue and discuss various issues – which practices give rise to nations, what other related notions come about as a result (trade protection, or patriotism, for example), why one set of conventions is nation-constituting but another not, and so on. What we cannot debate in any meaningful way, however, is whether or not nations are part of the natural world – that is whether or not in carving apart nature at the joints we find ourselves with "nation" somewhere among the socially independent constituents of reality. After all, we have agreed from the outset that "nation" and "nationhood" is the product of social practice and conventional agreement. With the kind of religion we are talking about, however, the debates take on a very different feel – no practices give rise to this religion, the religion is taken to give rise

---

9. For example, the monogenesis/polygenesis debates of the eighteenth century, the craniological and social Darwinist projects of the nineteenth century, and the eugenics studies and social programmes of the early twentieth century all suggest that race has been perceived as a fit subject for scientific study. Even into the twenty-first century, the Bell Curve controversy and similar related myths about race purport to use scientific evidence to support their case.

to these practices; no set of conventions is "religion" constituting because the religious "facts" which underpin it are just a part of the furniture of the universe, and so on. Moreover, we can debate the kind of things that are off the table in discussions about "nation" – we really can ask how the facts behind this religion will show themselves among the socially independent constituents of the world. And of course, this is all because we take the religion in question to be socially independent at root, rather than socially constituted. With all this in mind, if we were then to say that the socio-historical aspects of this religion mean that it is a social kind and thus made real, it looks as though we would be missing the point.

The extension to *race* should be obvious. *Race* is not intended to be a merely social reality and to have its objective status conferred upon it by social facts. Rather it is intended to latch on to some underlying physical and biological reality about the world. To bypass that assumption about *race* is to fail to take the concept seriously on its own merits. And more importantly, it alters the way we should read the socio-historical aspects of the concept. For some concepts, the socio-historical elements that surround them are explicitly reality conferring – this is an intended feature of the concept. In such a case it seems quite appropriate to call that notion a social kind. It wears its social reality on its sleeve, as it were. For other concepts though, while there may be a range of socio-historical practices surrounding it, those practices and conventions are not intended to be reality conferring – the assumed reality is supposed to run deeper. This alters how we should think of, and describe, those concepts and how we should read the socio-historical aspects connected to the concept in question.

The points here can seem subtle, and indeed, it is not obvious that this argument runs very straightforwardly without the additional weight of arguments about what we want to do with *race* concepts once we find out they are biologically empty. This is something we shall turn to in Chapter 3. But it is worth briefly making a clarifying point. The pull of an argument such as this is more obvious when we remind ourselves that we are simply asking what we should make of the socio-historical aspects of *race*. On the *strong social constructionist's* view, we are saying that there are myriad social and historical facts, and that we can muster these interesting and powerful social, legal, political and economic aspects into something which constitutes *race* – *race* is given reality by these facts. On the *weak social constructionist's* view we can look at these same facts and the same socio-historical elements of *race* and remind ourselves that while one *can* do this for concepts we might do well to pull shy of that when the concept openly purports to obtain its objective status from some other non-social source – in the case of *race*, its biological and scientific underpinnings. Notice that the power and impact of this argument will be felt differently depending on whether we are allowing the emptiness of the biological underpinnings to form part of the question we are asking. That is, if we were asking, "given the biological emptiness of *race*, what should we make of the socio-historical aspects of *race*?", we would view this argument differently. And as we shall see in the next chapter, we would see the argument differently if we were allowing other normative elements to come into play too – "given the biological emptiness of *race*, should we make the socio-historical aspects of *race* reality conferring?". But here we are asking a simpler question, "what should we make of the socio-historical aspects of *race* considered in and of themselves?". And for the *weak social constructionist* the answer is, "nothing so strong as reality conferring".

Reconstructionism

To close this chapter we shall look briefly at a position that we shall call *reconstructionism*. We will explore *reconstructionism* in much greater detail in our next chapter, where we will ask just what we should do with *race*. Nonetheless, it is still worth introducing the rudiments of this position at this point since we can see it as an alternative way of thinking about our question of what we should make of the social aspects of our *race* concepts and *race* thought and talk.

In what have seen so far, we acknowledge the socio-historical elements of our *race* concepts. And we have seen that some read these elements as meaning that *race* is a social kind; that the social facts about it are such as to confer reality upon it. Others are more reticent about reading the social facts in this way – in order to declare a concept to be a social kind, the path to its social reality must be clear of any pretensions to a more natural or socially independent objectivity. For the *reconstructionist*, however, the socio-historical aspects are interesting for reasons that are, at least in part, separate to questions about the objectivity of *race*. In fact, one can be a *reconstructionist* and also be a social kind realist, or a social kind sceptic, or think that *race* is a social kind, or think that *race* cannot be a social kind because of its assumed socially independent objectivity. Indeed, one can be committed to that idea that *race* must be a biological category and still be a *reconstructionist* (see for example Andreason 1998, 2004 or Kitcher

1999). We shall explore some of these ideas further in Chapter 3, but the point here is simply that the thing about the socio-historical aspects of *race* that impresses itself most directly upon *reconstructionists* is not the kind of ontological concern of the *strong* or *weak social constructionist*, but rather something else – namely the way in which we can press concepts and notions into serving some particular social processes.

For the *reconstructionist*, as with any right-thinking individual in the contemporary world, the use of *race* in many of the social, political and legal projects in which it has appeared are lamentable. However, if we can learn anything from these processes, it is that racial concepts are malleable – depending on the kind of social projects we have, or the kind of outcomes we want, we can change, adapt, or reinvent our *race* concept. Consequently, the most interesting philosophical questions for the *reconstructionist* are not so much what our socio-historical processes have given rise to – these are sociological and anthropological inquiries from which the philosopher of *race* can learn much – but rather, which socio-historical processes we can use to change our concepts, and what our concepts of *race* could become. The way to read the socio-historical aspects of *race* thought and talk, for the *reconstructionist*, is as evidence of a malleable concept open to our future projects concerning *race* or some very nearby concept.

To give a quick illustration of the idea here, think about a society for whom education is realized in a very particular way. Suppose that the whole point of education in this society is that it is presumed to be about the improvement of an individual's character and betterment of their soul. The society and social pressure surrounding such a view is that a supposed natural social hierarchy requires that certain individuals are well educated in order to fulfil the roles that they naturally occupy at the top of this social structure. This will shape the nature of educational institutions in this society, such that the subjects studied and the individuals with access have a particular character. For instance, perhaps only religious texts, legal texts, and items deemed to be "improving" are studied. Maybe only first-born males of wealthy families are sent to school.

If we notice just how much this institution is shaped by perceived social and historical practices and conventions, we may decide that it can be changed if other practices and pressures are bought to bear. Indeed, we may decide that this system is entirely out of step with the kinds of social projects and practices we think important. We might think that the religious tracts about hierarchy are dated and others emphasizing the equality of all in the eyes of God are more important. We might also think that education should be useful for improving the practical skills and abilities of people, especially since our economy relies more on manufacture and production now than on working the land. As such, we could shape our idea of education and the institutions related to it to reflect these social needs and pressures. If we then begin to purposefully promote the idea of *"education"* as something that is about the acquisition of useful skills and abilities that aid us in our working lives, and that all who need it should have access to it, we can see how the subjects studied and those given access might change to suit our needs as and when this idea takes hold. Perhaps the religious tracts taught would change (assuming they were taught at all), there would be little need to teach legal tracts since the skills and abilities required by most would be more basic – simple literacy and numeracy, some practical craft skills and so on. Indeed, we might still retain certain schools for those for whom the skills and knowledge required to govern are still relevant, thus having a spectrum of educational institutions. And perhaps, since our society sees males as being those in need of access – we treat them as the primary workers and rulers, and see the domain of the female as solely domestic – we extend the right to education to all males, not just first-borns.

This is very simple, but we can see how, from one understanding of a particular concept, we can help to promote and develop that concept into something else depending on the social projects and ambitions we might have for that concept. We can reconstruct this concept by pressing different social projects and practices into service. And this, or something very like it, is how the *reconstructionist* sees *race*. The really interesting things about *reconstructionism* are the kinds of social projects they think are important, what they think about our current concept of *race* and how it would relate to any reconstructed concept and so on. These are things we shall spend time exploring in Chapter 3. However, here it is enough to see that for the *reconstructionist*, the socio-historical aspects of *race* are philosophically interesting, but we should view them not only, or even primarily, as concerned with what *race* is, but as the tools for shaping what *race* could become.

CONCLUSION

In this chapter we have spent some time looking at the socio-historical aspects of *race*. In particular, we have seen that our modern view of *race* is deeply rooted in a particular period of history – the Age of Empires gave rise to an especially large-scale slave trade, and this slave trade clashed with so many moral sentiments it called for justification; that justification relied on a *race* concept and the authority of Enlightenment science gave weight and endorsement to that concept by treating *races* as an apt and legitimate subject of scientific study. Moreover, we saw that the formation of *races* and racial categories depends heavily on the socio-political and socio-economic climate in a given context – in our examples, the needs of the USA, both from foundation to the contemporary age, have been quite different to those of Brazil and as a result very different racial formations have arisen in those places.

From a philosophical point of view, we have also seen that there are various ways of reading these socio-historical aspects of our *race* concept and *race* thought and talk. In particular we looked at three broad attitudes one might take to such phenomena. First, we looked at *strong social constructionism* – the view that the social facts behind *race* are reality conferring. The idea was that certain concepts look as though the social realities surrounding them are constitutive in that they generate a socially dependent reality. These *social kinds* may not be part of the basic furniture of the universe, but they are real nonetheless. *Race*, by virtue of these socio-historical elements, looks to be a social kind. Second, we looked at *weak social constructionism* – the view that the socio-historical elements of *race* are not best read as meaning that *race* is a social kind, but that the power of *race* to affect lives by virtue of its socio-historical elements is in no way diminished by this. Instead, we should see the socio-historical elements of our *race* concepts as creating labels, badges and particular racial identities that, for all the lack of a socially independent objectivity, are still deeply powerful and impacting. And finally, we looked at *reconstructionism* – the view that the most interesting feature of the socio-historical element of *race* is that it highlights the malleability of the concept and its fitness for change according to future projects and practices. This view assumes that the most philosophically fruitful way to look at *race* is not so much in terms of what our socio-historical practices have done to create the *race* concepts that we have now, but how the *race* concepts we would like to see in the future might be best realized in the social and political projects we can generate now.

The interesting thing about these positions is that they have important ramifications for the topic of our next chapter – what should we do with *race*? We shall explore a whole series of questions and approaches that in many ways take off directly from the questions and answers we have explored in this chapter. Consequently, we shall refer back to the positions explored so far quite frequently: we shall make more fine-grained distinctions within them; we shall expand upon them; we shall raise more pressing arguments against them; we shall raise more compelling arguments for them; and we shall, I hope, come to a deeper understanding of what they are.

CHAPTER THREE

What should we do with *race*?

In our last two chapters we have covered much ground on the question of *race*. In particular, we have spent time getting clear about what our ordinary concept of *race* comes to; what its most central features are. We have also seen that our ordinary concept can make no claim to scientific reality – none of the appropriate scientific concepts seem to lend it credence, and a host of biological evidence suggests that most of the assumptions we make about *race* are unfounded. The take-home message of Chapter 1, then, was that, in terms of biological science and biological kinds, *race* is not real. In Chapter 2, however, we spent much time examining the socio-historical background to our concept of *race* – how it arose, and how various categories and racial notions are shaped by the socio-political pressures in any given context. We also saw that quite what we make of these socio-historical facts will vary. We might think these social facts make *race* a candidate social kind, and thus real. Alternatively, we might think these social facts make for interesting explanations of our racialized behaviours, but at the same time not see this as necessarily reality conferring; or we might see these social facts as suggesting a way to move forward with our concept of *race*.

Lurking in the background of these various observations, however, are a set of concerns and questions that are especially alive, not just for philosophers of race, but for everyone. And all these questions concern just what we should do with *race*. For example, if *race* is not biologically real, we might begin to wonder whether we should simply stop talking about it as though it were – it is ridiculous of us to carry on acting, thinking and talking about a phenomenon known to be an empty concept as though it did latch on to some genuine facts about the world. But if *race* is a fit candidate for categorization as a social kind, then maybe it is fine to keep *race* talk. However, given the frequently negative and damaging nature of *race*, should we continue with such social practices? After all, we don't have to. But assuming we can drop our current social practices surrounding *race*, which practices, if any, should we take up? And so on.

What should be obvious about these questions, and many like them, is that they are all concerned with more *normative* issues than those we have focused on so far. Chapters 1 and 2 concerned themselves more centrally with a descriptive question – what *is race*? Or more properly, what *is our thought* and *talk* of "race" about? The questions that concern us now, though, are focused on a much more prescriptive concern – what *should* we do with *race*? In this chapter, then, rather than leave this normative concern lurking in the background, we shall bring it to the fore and look at the various approaches and answers that philosophers of race give. In particular, we shall look at three general ways in which we might approach this normative concern.

First we shall look at what we shall call *eliminativism* – the view that we should do away with *race*, purge it from our linguistic and cognitive landscapes. We shall look at the various reasons that might motivate such a position, but as we shall see, this view relates strongly to the *weak social constructionism* that we saw in the last chapter. Second, we will look at what we shall call *preservationism* – the view that we should retain the notion of *race*, or at least the central, core features of it. Again, we shall look at various reasons why we might adopt such a position, and again we shall see that such a view relates strongly to a position outlined in the last chapter – namely *strong social constructionism*. Moreover, we shall see that the various considerations that stand in favour of *eliminativism* are meant to be considerations that count against *preservationism*. And likewise, the various considerations that are supposed to count in favour of *preservationism* are also meant to count against *eliminativism*. Finally we shall look at a series of positions that we shall gather under the banner of *reconstructionism*. As the name suggests, *reconstructionist* answers to the question of what we should do with *race* are basically extensions of the *reconstructionist* reading of the socio-historical facts about *race* that we examined at the end of Chapter 2. When we come to examine *reconstructionism* we shall, of course, note the various positions that one might take under this broad heading, since there are various differing issues motivating those positions. However, what all have in common is that they see both a need and a mechanism to change our concept of *race*, and with it our *race* thought and talk.

ELIMINATIVISM

In the broadest possible terms we can think of *eliminativists* as arguing that we should abandon our *race* thought and talk for three connected reasons. First, the scientific failings of our ordinary concept of *race*, as discussed in Chapter 1, show that *race* cannot be a biological kind. Second, the socio-historical practices surrounding our concept of *race* and racial categorization are not enough to be reality conferring – in short, *race* is not a social kind either. Finally, the various *race* labels and racialized practices that we generate and live by, although not reality conferring, are divisive, negative and socially destructive. Take these things together and we can see that there is no such thing as *race*, and no reason to want there to be. In the interests of intellectual honesty and social prudence, then, we should rid ourselves of *race*.

This is a rather short summary of the position and one need not buy into each of these observations in order to be an *eliminativist* – one *might* think that *race* is scientifically or socially real, for instance, yet still think the damage done is enough for us to eliminate our *race* thought and talk. However, we are interested in the kind of *eliminativism* summarized here. And put like this, we can see that there are two general elements to this *eliminativist* argument: first that some motivation for elimination is found in the lack of scientific and social reality of *race*; and second, some motivation for elimination is found in the negative social impact of *race*. We shall examine these two elements in greater depth in what follows.

Race as lacking scientific or social reality

The first main element of the *eliminativist* argument is that since *race* is neither a biological nor a social kind, we should eliminate *race* thought and talk from our lives. The argument here rests on a rather straightforward idea about how we should conduct our cognitive and linguistic lives. Put simply, we think it important that whenever we take ourselves to be talking and thinking about the way the world is, our thoughts and words should latch on to some truth about the world. If it becomes apparent to us that the things we take ourselves to be talking and thinking about are not, in fact, features of the world, it seems that the correct thing to do is to stop talking and thinking about those things as though they were real. Indeed, we should perhaps stop talking and thinking about those things at all.

In slightly different terms, our beliefs and assertions aim at, or aspire to, the truth. My belief that my dog is a Boston Terrier rests on my taking it to be true of my dog that he is of that particular breed. Similarly, when I assert "Wooster is a Boston Terrier", I do so because I take myself to be stating a truth. If, however, I find out that I am wrong about Wooster's breed and all the experts agree that he is, beyond any possible doubt, a French Bulldog, then it seems that I should no longer entertain my previous beliefs, nor continue to espouse my previous assertions. Indeed, I should alter both my beliefs and my assertions to take account of the newly revealed truth. Moreover, if I were to continue to believe and assert that my dog was a Boston Terrier, even while acknowledging and accepting the stated conclusions of the experts, we would feel I was doing something very strange – I am not deluded, I acknowledge the truth, yet I continue to talk and think as though some now disproved idea were a fact about the world. We would think that what I should do is to stop believing and asserting that my dog is a Boston Terrier – I should change my doxastic and assertoric practices so that they accord with the facts. My words should mirror the world.

In many ways, what seems to be wrong is that our thought and talk is supposed to be sensitive to how the world is. When we discover that the way the world is differs from the way we take the world to be, it is up to us to alter our words and thoughts accordingly. If we acknowledge the difference between our words and the world, yet refuse to alter how we talk and think, this looks at best intellectually remiss, and at worst perverse. When we apply this kind of thinking to *race* thought and talk, it becomes obvious how things stand for the *eliminativist* – the very point of thinking and talking about the world requires that upon discovering that the world does not contain any of the things our ordinary concept of *race* suggests, we should abandon those ways of thinking and talking. It is incumbent upon us, as agents sensitive to the connections between words and the world, to be *eliminativists* about *race*.

All of this, of course, rests on the dual denial of the reality of *race* – *race* is neither biologically, nor socially real. And these arguments are familiar to us from earlier chapters. In Chapter 1, we saw that our ordinary concept of *race* is given no scientific support from biology, or by latching neatly on to nearby scientific concepts such as clines or breeding populations. In Chapter 2 we outlined what we called a *weak social constructionism*, part of which involved the view that the socio-historical aspects of *race* cannot be reality conferring because *race* aspires to biological and scientific integrity. We shall leave the lack of scientific support for our ordinary concept of *race* uncontested here, but we shall look more deeply into the connections between *eliminativism* and *weak social constructionism*.

As we saw in Chapter 2, the *weak social constructionist* does not see the socio-historical facts about *race* as being a reason for treating it as a social kind. As we have noted, this is because our ordinary concept of *race* purports to be a biological kind and to be underpinned by scientific fact. For the *weak social constructionist*, to ignore this fact is to refuse to take the concept of *race* on its own merits. As we noted, a social kind, such as *nation*, is supposed to be constituted by the practices and conventions surrounding its use – its objective status was always assumed to rely upon its social reality. *Race*, however, is not like this – we assume that racial membership relies on some deep biological feature of individuals, and that racial differences rely on differences between these essential biological features. For the *eliminativist*, we can take this *weak social constructionist* point even further. When we look at social practices and conventions, which, like *race*, purport to be grounded in scientific fact or to latch on to some deeper metaphysical fact about the world for their objectivity, something interesting happens when we discover that there is no non-social reality underpinning the concept – namely, we stop using that concept.

Consider, for example, *humours*. From Galen onwards, but especially prevalent in medieval Europe, it was assumed that four basic elements called humours – *blood, phlegm, black-bile* and *yellow-bile* – made up the fluids of the human body and were produced by particular body parts – the head, the lungs, the spleen and the gall bladder. These humours were taken to be key factors in human health and temperament. In particular, ailments and illness were due to these elements being out of balance, and such ailments were remedied by encouraging the humours back into alignment. And of course, many social practices and conventions existed around this notion of humours. For example, doctors would blood-let to rebalance an excess of blood, or prescribe lungwort to induce coughing and rebalance an excess of phlegm. Similarly, the humours were associated with temperaments and particular human characteristics – people were described as *sanguine, choleric, melancholic* or *phlegmatic*. And such things were even assumed to affect dreams:

> Certes this dreem, which ye han met to-nyght,
> Cometh of the greete superfluytee
> Of youre rede colera, pardee,
> Which causeth folk to dreden in hir dremes

Of arwes, and of fyr with rede lemes,
Of rede beestes, that they wol hem byte,
Of contek, and of whelpes, grete and lyte.
Right as the humour of malencolie
Causeth ful many a man in sleep to crie
For feere of blake beres, or boles blake,
Or elles blake develes wole hem take,
Of othere humours koude I telle also.[1]
      (*The Nun's Priest Tale*, Chaucer 1974)

Though some of the language of the humourist age remains – we still describe people as "melancholic" or "phlegmatic" for instance – we no longer believe or assert anything about humours. Consequently, we no longer let these assumptions guide our social practices or conventions surrounding discussions of health, medicine or temperament. And the reason for this is simple: we discovered that our social practices surrounding "humours" were not underpinned by scientific fact. Since this was a crucial feature of the concept – after all, we had assumed humours to be tied to biological features of human beings and thus to be useful in managing health – we simply jettisoned the concept and looked for something better to perform the task required.

For *eliminativists*, then, *race* is more like *humour* than *nation*. Our concept of nation does not purport to obtain its objective reality from non-social facts about the world, and so it is a fine candidate for a social kind – discovering that nations are not part of the basic furniture of the universe should have no impact on our use of *nation* thought and talk. *Humour*, on the other hand, did purport to latch on to some non-social fact about the world and so, when we discovered that it did not, it made no sense to suddenly start treating it as though it could be a social kind with reality-conferring practices and conventions – its job was to describe a non-social reality and govern practices accordingly. When it was found wanting in that regard, the right and only thing to do was to jettison it. And that is what we did. For the *eliminativist*, then, *race* is simply the *humour* of the twenty-first century.

---

1. Roughly translated, this is: "It is certain that your dream tonight came from an excess in your choleric temperament, which causes nightmares of fire, and red beasts and red wheal marks. Just as being excessively melancholic can cause a man to cry in his sleep from nightmares of black bears, black boils, or of being taken by black devils, I could speak of the other humours too".

The negative social impact of *race*

We might argue that, even granting the *eliminativist* arguments about the lack of scientific or social reality, we still need to be sure that there is no reason to retain *race*. After all, we can quite easily imagine a social category which we take be underpinned by biological or scientific fact turning out not to be so on closer inspection, yet it still benefiting us to retain the concept and embrace its social reality. Consider, for example, the notion of *parenthood*.[2] This is a notion that is bound up in many social and historical practices and conventions – we take parents to be morally and legally responsible for their children, we have different expectations for parents than we have for non-parents, and so on. Also, we tend to think *parent* is biologically grounded and so perhaps subject to scientific study and so on. However, closer inspection reveals that our notions of *parent* and *parenthood* are much more complex than this. We often find people applying the terms indicating parenthood and parental relationships – "father", "mother", and so on – to those with whom they have no biological connection. It is common to hear people describe step-parents as "mother" or "father" while using a prefixed term, such as "biological father" or "birth mother" to explain their relationship to others with whom a qualified parental relationship holds. This, of course, does not show that our concept of parent has no biological component, just that those whom we are prepared to treat as parents on a personal, moral and legal level need have no biological relation to their child at all.

The way that such an example applies to the *eliminativism* we are looking at here, then, is as follows: here we have a notion, *parent*, which is scaffolded with a multitude of social practices and conventions, which impacts on lives, and which changes and directs behaviours. Moreover, pushed to explain what "parent" means, most of us would lean on biological notions such as *ancestor, offspring* or *progenitor*,[3] but closer inspection reveals that we are happy to forgo these elements in many of our everyday applications of *parent*. It looks, then, by *eliminativist* lights, as though we have a concept

---

2. Sally Haslanger discusses "parent" in a very similar context to this in her 2006 paper "Philosophical analysis and social kinds: What good are our intuitions?". We shall return to some of the points made by Haslanger later in this chapter.

3. Indeed, look at our description of "race" in Chapter 1 – we quite explicitly pressed a biologically endowed notion of "parenthood" into service there to explain the idea of race involving a notion of ancestry and genetic inheritance.

that is not essentially biological in the way we thought it was and so does not tie up with non-social reality in the way we had assumed it did. It seems as though, by *eliminativist* lights, we should dispense with it – it is neither biologically grounded, nor a social kind (since it purports to rest on a biological notion). But this is not what we have done, and nor are we likely to. And the reason seems clear: *parent* is a useful notion that serves an important purpose in our personal and social lives. To dispense with the notion on these grounds looks as though it passes too quickly over some reasons worthy of consideration – if we are wrong in our assertion that some concept relies on non-social facts for its reality, we might perhaps do better to pause before moving immediately to jettisoning that concept. After all, we might have reasons for retaining a concept that override its failure to report a deep fact about the world. What this means is that we have to be sure that there is no social utility in retaining our concept of *race* before we concede to the *eliminativist* argument and jettison *race* thought and talk.

The *eliminativist*, of course, has lots of reasons for thinking that, on the whole, our concept of *race* has none of the positive or useful elements that stand behind keeping a concept such as *parent*. There are, of course, numerous facts we could point to in order to show many atrocious things that have been done under the assumption that *race* is real: the notorious slave trade which gave rise to our *race* concept in the first place, or the segregationist Jim Crow laws of antebellum USA, or South African apartheid, White Australia policy, genocide and so on. These are all reasons to be suspicious of any claims that *race* is a useful concept to keep.

Of course, we might accept that these are genuinely appalling things, but note that these kinds of event can also be cited against other concepts, notions and categories – *class, ethnicity, nations* – which we are nonetheless happy to retain for other reasons. However, the *eliminativist* can cite what look like a series of limitations and negative outcomes that occur on a personal level too.

Consider, for example, the kind of labelling behaviours that we used to characterize the impact of various social practices when we outlined *weak social constructionism* in Chapter 2. We talked there about how one might adopt certain behaviours and attitudes as a result of the kind of social label or badge by which one lives. There are various ways of thinking how this might be negative. For instance, our social practices surrounding gender are such that we expect those who are gendered "female" to have specific body types, perform particular social roles, have particular tastes and so on. Moreover, females often act in accord with these expectations by, for example, abstaining from certain kinds of masculinized activities or ways of carrying their body, expressing an interest in feminized subjects and careers, and avoiding masculinized topics and careers, and so on (see Saul 2003: chapter 5). It should be clear how such things are limiting and negative – women exclude themselves from whole areas of life (and this is aside from other restrictions imposed externally).

In terms of *race*, the effects are similar. Consider, for example, that part of the labelling of Romany Gypsies in Great Britain is that they are largely illiterate and refuse education, mostly as a consequence of nomadism. Despite the obvious limitations that taking up illiteracy as part of adopting a racial label would impose, we nonetheless find this happening. For instance, the social anthropologist Judith Okely reports "Sometimes a completely negative attitude to literacy burst out. A 14-year-old girl picked up a magazine in my trailer and without any apparent provocation, tore it to shreds exclaiming, 'only Gorgios read!'" (Okely 1983: 162).[4] Or even:

> Travellers recognise that a place on a site or the offer of a council house meant greater pressure to send their children to school. Resentment was sometimes voiced:
>
> "They say that you've got to send the kids to school on these sites. I don't want my child going anymore. I don't want her to have one of those jobs pushing a pen in an office, what's the good of that to my girl?"   (Okely 1983: 161)

Given the nature of *race* and the very many negative characteristics that we find circulating around the central features identified in Chapter 1, it is unsurprising that racial labels can be negative and limiting. Given the scope for such negative impacts on those individuals falling under our *race* labels, it seems obvious that we should do without them.

Of course, we may recall that when we discussed *weak social constructionism* in Chapter 2, we mentioned that there might be some positive reasons for taking up or acting in accordance with *race* labels. Recall that we mentioned such things as shared experiences, being able to anticipate likely obstacles and opportunities which arise as a consequence of acting under a certain *race* label, and so on. However, even these kinds of positive,

---

4. "Gorgio" (pronounced gor-ja) is the Romany word for non-Romanies.

"group-based" effects of racial labels might be seen as too negative. Consider, for example, Kwame Anthony Appiah's discussion of racial labels:[5]

> It seems to me that they are not so much labels of disability as disabling labels ... "Race" disables us because it proposes as a basis for common action the illusion that black (and white and yellow) people are fundamentally allied by nature and, thus, without effort; it leaves us unprepared, therefore to handle the intraracial conflicts that arise from the very different situations of black (white and yellow) people in different parts of the economy and of the world.   (Appiah 1992)

Appiah, a committed *eliminativist*, is making a very simple point here. The concerns and interests of individuals, even of sub-groups, become consumed by and subsumed within the needs, objectives and interests ascribed to an entire group falling under a racial label. Clearly, we can see how individuals might suffer here if their own concerns are not neatly aligned with the racial interest as a whole. Additionally, we can see how the interests of the group as a whole are threatened or made weaker by having a racial label gather such disparate (in other non-racial respects) groups together. When a label such as *race* has effects like these, we can again see more reason to live without it and jettison *race* thought and talk from our lives.

Summary

The *eliminativist* argument, then, is quite straightforward. The imperative that our thought and talk accord with the way the world is dictates that we should do away with *race*: the lesson of Chapter 1 tells is that there is no scientific reality underpinning *race*, and the *weak social constructionist* position of Chapter 2 tells us that there are no good grounds for treating *race* as constituted by social facts either. Moreover, even if we are to think that we might have reason to keep hold of an empty concept on grounds of utility, by *eliminativist* lights *race* would still need to be jettisoned – the massively destructive political and social injustices performed on the basis

---

5. Kwame Anthony Appiah is perhaps the clearest example of a race *eliminativist*, and the description of *eliminativism* used here leans very heavily on the account of race and racial labelling that he gives. See Appiah (1996) in particular.

of *race*, along with the limitations that racial labels help us to impose on others and ourselves, mean *race* is too dangerous and negative a concept to retain.

Although in the process of getting clear about just what *eliminativism* comes to, we have hinted at some considerations that might count against the *eliminativist* arguments, we shall, in our next section, examine some more detailed concerns. In particular, we shall examine some concerns raised by those who think not only that *eliminativist* arguments are wrong, but also that *race* should be retained.

PRESERVATIONISM

As should be obvious from the name, *preservationists* think, unlike *eliminativists*, that we should retain our concept of *race*. The kind of *preservationism* that we are going to look at here takes the lessons of Chapter 1 to be clear – there is no scientifically respectable underpinning for our ordinary *race* concept.[6] In this respect, then, there is a point of agreement and some common ground with the *eliminativists* about the lack of non-social facts surrounding our ordinary *race* concept. However, where *preservationists* disagree with *eliminativists*, and thus find room for their own claim that *race* should be retained, is in how best to read the socio-historical elements of our *race* thought and talk, and in the claim that *race* has no social utility. In particular, *preservationists* tend towards *strong social constructionism* and are keen to deny the claims made in favour of the *eliminativists'* preferred *weak social constructionism*. Additionally they deny that the case made by *eliminativists* for the negative social impact of *race* is as straightforward as it seems. In what follows we shall examine the *preservationists'* arguments against *eliminativism* in these two areas and see just how far they go towards helping establish that we should retain our ordinary thought and talk of *race*.

---

6. As we have mentioned before, however, there are those who see ways in which science could be used to generate a non-social reality for our ordinary race concepts, for example Andreason (1998) and Kitcher (1999). Whether these views could properly be called *preservationism* is less clear. The point, however, is merely that while we shall treat the denial of scientific reality for *race* as a point of agreement between *eliminativists* and *preservationists*, it certainly need not be.

Defending the social reality of *race*

Recall that the *eliminativist's* denial of the reality of *race* is two-pronged: *race* has no scientific support and so is not made real by any non-social facts; and *race* cannot be made real by any social facts, that is, it cannot be a social kind, because it aspires to objectivity from non-social reality. The *preservationist* accepts the lack of scientific support for *race*, but thinks that the *weak social constructionist* arguments about the lack of social reality for *race* are incorrect. For the *preservationist*, there are grounds for thinking that the socio-historical elements surrounding our *race* thought and talk are reality conferring. In short, one way of making sense of *preservationism* is to argue against *eliminativism* by undermining the *weak social construction-ism* upon which part of its argument rests. There are numerous ways that one might argue against this feature of *weak social constructionism*, but we shall examine just two of the most interesting cases. These views both hold that social kinds can and do include physical and biological elements within them and so can realize the aspirations of our concept of *race*. However, they differ on just how social kinds might achieve this.

Social kinds and biological elements

The starting point for the kinds of *preservationism* that we shall look at here is basically the same: argue against the *weak social constructionism* that the *eliminativist* makes use of by acknowledging that our concept of *race* does have biological aspirations, but also argue that this does actually form part of our socially constructed notion of *race*. Indeed, many *strong social constructionists* think that biological notions are key not only to our ordinary concept of *race*, but to the very possibility of socially constructing *race*. Bernard Boxill, for example, urges:

> [T]he belief that people are members of a biological race, with all this implies, is essential to the social construction of races. Without such a belief, cultural, ethnic or class prejudice may result in the social construction of certain classes of individuals, but these classes will not be races. (Boxill 2001: 32)

At first blush a claim such as this may seem to concede to the *weak social constructionist* and, by extension, to the *eliminativist*, exactly what is

88

needed to deny that *race* is a social kind, and, again by extension, to call for the jettisoning of *race* thought and talk. However, the point is subtler than this and trades on the idea that the construction of *races* is a social phenomenon, but it is a social phenomenon that knowingly rests upon and interacts with a series of biophysical factors. Moreover, this interaction is ongoing, evolving and developing in such a way that the kinds of biophysical factors that are central to *race* are far more fluid than the rather fixed notion of *biological kind* that the *weak social constructionist* suggests is central to our ordinary concept.

However, to acknowledge that our concept of *race* is supposed to latch on to some biological facts, and to assert boldly that we can allow this and retain our *strong social constructionist* sensibilities (assuming we have any) is one thing. To show how this might work more thoroughly is another matter entirely, and this is where the two *preservationist* views we shall look at part company: the first, which we shall call *social naturalism*, is due primarily to the philosopher Lucius T. Outlaw (Jr); and the second, which we shall call *pragmatic realism*, is due primarily to the philosopher Paul C. Taylor.

Social naturalism

The *social naturalist* view that we are interested in here takes the biological elements of *race* to be crucially central to our social construction of *race*, in that categories are constructed on the basis of biological difference and those categories then become culturally embedded and biologically self-realizing. In short, we identify some perceived biological difference, normally a phenotypic difference such as skin colour, and on the basis of that we identify *races* and build all manner of social convention and practice around this. These differences then become engrained in various ways, rather in the manner that people take up the labels and badges we noted in Chapter 2. Most importantly, though, our perception of physical and bodily differences has a profound effect on sexual preferences and mate choices. In particular, endogamy (that is, intraracial marriage and mate choice) is very much higher than exogamy (that is, interracial marriage and mate choice). For instance, in 2005 around 96 per cent of white people in the USA were married to other white people; around 90 per cent of black people; were married to other black people; and so on. (For a breakdown and analysis of the various statistics on racial, religious and educational endogamy in the USA, see Rosenfeld 2008.) The phenotypic differences that we initially used to divide *races* then form the basis for social institutions and practices, which help to compound and ossify those divisions by creating what are effectively breeding populations. Consider, for example, Lucius Outlaw's view:

> Human populations and their sub-groupings are better understood as *social-natural kinds*: that is groupings of humans that are formed and named under contingent socio-historical, cultural conditions, according to social conventions … groupings of biologically and socially evolving living beings who are part of socially conditioned natural histories. For important reasons we should understand races … as *natural*: that is as particular types of bio-social collectivities that develop or evolve, as do all things in the natural world, but in ways that are characteristically human. (Outlaw 1996b: 12)

For Outlaw, these *social-natural kinds* are simple facts about the way human beings organize themselves:

> I want to inquire into … humans forming themselves into bonding, self-reproducing social collectivities that are distinguished by biological and socio-cultural characteristics that are shared by the members of each collectivity. These groupings … form a relatively distinct, self-reproducing breeding population constituted as such by shared socio-cultural systems. … The complicated processes (biological, socio-cultural, historical) by which such populations and population sub-groups are formed and maintained are what I refer to as *raciation* … I will argue that raciation … [is a] fact of human evolutionary histories. (Outlaw 1996b: 4–5)

For *social naturalists*, then, the interacting biological and social elements of *race* are such that we see an evolving, ongoing process, which constitutes *races* in terms of breeding populations. These groupings are not simple biological kinds. But neither are they simple social kinds in the manner suggested by the *strong social constructionist* position of Chapter 2. Instead they are *social-natural* kinds. However, because this category tracks facts about "human evolutionary histories" we can see that it is real and reality conferring – facts about physical make-up generate social categories, which in turn compound or reinforce the physical facts, which further inform social categories, and so on.

Intriguingly, this rethinking of the biological elements of our ordinary *race* concepts seems to take some of the steam out of the *weak social constructionist's* position. If the idea is that our socio-historical notion of *race* aspires to scientific credibility by having our core notion of *race* latch on to the defining and necessary elements of a biological kind, then clearly there is a problem in saying that *race* is made real by social factors alone. If, on the other hand, we think that our notion of *race* is always socially constructed by an ongoing evolutionary process of interacting social elements and bio-physical factors, things seems less straightforward – perhaps we can allow for social construction without ignoring the biological aspirations of our ordinary *race* concept. There are, however, some concerns that we might have about *social naturalism*. We'll examine just two here.

First, *social naturalism* relies on a couple of biological notions that we have already raised some serious doubts about, namely, phenotypes and breeding populations. In Chapter 1 we noted that if our ordinary concept of *race* aspired to scientific credibility by being a biological kind, it could not do that by latching phenotypes onto genotypes, and it would certainly find no headway in treating *races* as breeding populations. We might note that in the evolving process behind *social-natural* kinds, phenotypes such as skin colour are merely the starting point, and we have no need for there to be a genuine biological kind underpinning this. However, since part of the notion is that through social conventions these categories form breeding populations, thus maintaining and self-realizing the divisions, we have to pause and ask whether this is really the right idea of *race*. And as we noted in Chapter 1, breeding populations are not good candidates for explaining *race*, or at least, not the kind of thing our ordinary concept of *race* purports to be.

Second, we might have some worries about the central role that endogamy seems to play in such a picture. It is certainly clear that for the most part people are more likely to breed with and form life partnerships with those of the same *race* – however, there are many factors that make such simple readings of census data seem incautious. The waters here are murky. For instance, in the USA it is well known that in what is known by sociologists as "the marriage market", black women have to compete with other black women against a supposedly well-recognized black male preference for lighter-skinned women, indeed, potentially a preference for white females (see, for example, Rockquemore 2002 and Bond and Cash 1992).

Similarly, if various surveys and Gallup polls are to be believed, interracial union is increasingly seen as acceptable.[7] Further, the apparent rise in individuals who want to actively identify as bi-racial led to the US Census Bureau adding a bi-racial category to the 2000 census. Now, consider that in the USA at least, the legal status of interracial marriage was questionable until famous cases such as the 1967 *Loving vs Virginia* Supreme Court decision, and we can see that we only have one generation of even moderate legal freedom for people to explore exogamy. Such factors might not be by any means decisive in undercutting the *social naturalist* position since much still needs to be clarified. However, the assumption that endogamy is the result of a basic and inherent human condition from which *race* as a *social-natural* kind arises – something that Outlaw calls an "anthropological necessity" to organize and draw differences between ourselves – seems too hasty.[8]

Pragmatic realism

An alternative way of acknowledging the biological elements of our race concept while retaining our *strong social constructionism* is to adopt *pragmatic realism*. This is a position endorsed most prominently by Paul C. Taylor (see, for example, Taylor 2004a: chapter 3 and 2004b) and draws heavily on some of the insights of the classical pragmatists. In particular, the more practical elements of classical pragmatism emerge in this kind of *preservationist* position, and it is through these ideas that we might best see what *pragmatic realism* amounts to.

The central pragmatist idea in play here is that we get to know whether a term or concept is real and what it means by looking at whatever genuine friction or difference it makes in the world.[9] A concept that has no practical

---

7. Let's be clear, though, "acceptable" in a Gallup poll often turns out to be a long way from "accepted" in our everyday lives and interracial couples invariably face numerous negative attitudes against their union.

8. As Ronald Sundstrom (2002) points out, there are reasons to suspect that Outlaw's notion of "anthropologically necessary" does not lead where he thinks it does. In particular, why must the notion of anthropological necessity be realized through "race" and not, say, eye colour, or tooth size? And even granting that the *social-natural* kind of *race* does arise this way, why must this be an argument for the preservation of race?

9. This idea of knowing the meaning of a term by knowing the practical difference it makes in the world is a particularly Peircian and Deweyan take on pragmatism, and Taylor (2004b: 167) is quite explicit in taking this view into his account of race.

effects or makes no difference is empty. If we look at *race* we can see that as a concept it does have genuine friction – that is, it is a tangible difference-maker in the world. In short, we know lots of things about how things stand in the world if you are of one *race* rather than another. Moreover, by tying some of the things that we initially identified as behind our ordinary concept of *race* – somatic markers, ancestry, geographical locations – to these different ways of experiencing the world, we have the core of a socially constructed but biologically serious enough notion of *race*. To see this, consider the following example.

In Australia, in the second decade of the twenty-first century, we can outline some pretty detailed experiences, expectations, and ways the world might be for those classified as Indigenous Australians. For instance, if you are an Indigenous Australian male you can expect to live until you are fifty-nine, and a female until sixty-five. A non-Indigenous male can expect to live to seventy-seven, and a female until eighty-two. Indigenous families can expect their children to be three times more likely to die before the age of five than non-Indigenous children, and for 83 per cent of those deaths to occur before the age of one. Indigenous children can expect to have only a 68 per cent chance of attaining national standards for reading by the time they are eight – compared with 93 per cent for their non-Indigenous counterparts. They can also expect to have only a 45 per cent chance of still being in secondary education by the time they are seventeen compared with 86 per cent of non-Indigenous Australians. When they leave school they can expect to have a 48 per cent chance of gaining employment, 24 per cent less than non-Indigenous Australians. An Indigenous Australian over thirty-five is five times more likely to suffer from diabetes that a non-Indigenous Australian. An Indigenous Australian is twice as likely to be the victim of physical or threatened violence than their non-Indigenous counterpart. And there are very many more statistics we could introduce here (see Australian Bureau of Statistics 2008). To be able to give these kinds of detailed accounts of the difference *race* makes when one is classified as an Indigenous Australian rather than a non-Indigenous Australian is certainly enough to show that *race* is not simply empty in a pragmatic sense – it has real effects and we can judge it by those effects.

We might, of course, object that those kinds of experiences and expectations are the result of interweaving and complex conditions including gender, class and, in the case of Indigenous Australians, whether one is from an urban or remote rural location. Perhaps we can get at those effects without positing that *race* is real. However, for the *pragmatic realist*, if we follow the *eliminativist* and remove *race*, we have lost something very important in our ability to explain what is going on. For instance, we might drop talk of *race* and simply talk about the tribal ethnic communities that the subjects we are interested in are from. However, once we start to talk about the rates of school completion among the Darug, Kuringgai or some other group, we begin to lose something from our explanation. Certainly the tribal group differences are worth acknowledging, since they too will be a factor (among many) in explaining the way the world is for a certain group of people. However, the decreased chances of employment experienced by a member of the Pindjarup are due not simply to their being a member of that group, but to the Pindjarup being one of the many groups of Indigenous Aboriginal peoples in Australia. When we drop *race* from the picture here, we lose the ability to explain that fact and note something that unites the experiences of whole groups of people. Cast in these terms, then, *race* looks to be crucial to explaining the way the world is – we cannot account for the difference made unless we include *race* as a difference-maker here.

A further objection that we might raise against this picture, and one that draws out a useful additional element of this *pragmatic realist* account, is that just because there are differences in behaviour, that doesn't mean the posited difference-maker is genuinely real. For instance, think back to the point we made earlier about *humours*. That certainly used to be posited as a difference-maker – it helped to explain health, temperament and even dreams. And people acted in accord with such beliefs: it should be of no surprise to me as a "melancholic" that I dream of black bears, but were I "choleric", I should be concerned about such dreams as they are out of kilter with my natural temperament and may require a rebalancing of my humours. But of course, we don't think that humours are real, at least not in any genuinely robust sense. And after all, the *pragmatic realist* is trying to counteract the *eliminativist* position here and show how we might have a *strong social constructionist* picture that allows *race* to be real in a more robust sense than just as a simple social kind – its biological pretensions have to be taken seriously. However, the *pragmatic realist* has an answer here.

A good pragmatist lesson over and above looking to the practical is to be aware that our questions do not have one simple answer. Instead, the answer will be relative to the interests of the inquirer. This can have a marked effect on just what we think we are doing in raising questions and embarking upon inquiries, and more importantly, on just what we take as an acceptable answer.[10] Consider, for example, the question "is my work desk flat?". The answer depends on who is asking. For my daughter who wants to build her train set where the smooth running of her trains will not be compromised by uneven joins in the tracks, the answer is "yes, perfectly flat". For my partner, who is investigating the micro surface features of common objects, the answer is "no, not in the least bit flat". Clearly we have different answers, each one acceptable given the inquiry in hand. For the *pragmatic realist*, this has an impact on questions about the reality of *race*, and by extension, the need for preservation or elimination.

When we ask "what should we do with *race?*", the inquiry turns, as we have seen, to some deeper questions. And the question we are focusing on is "is *race* real?". It is quite acceptable for everyone to agree that, considered as a quest for a biological kind, the answer is "no". Considered as a quest for a wholly social kind, that is, one which we knowingly construct as a kind whose objectivity is given by only social facts, we can also concede that the answer is "no". However, for the *pragmatic realist*, it is a mistake, and a mistake the *eliminativist* makes, to stop there. Considered as a fact about how we can use physical markers and ancestry as predictors and guides which we connect to experiences and felt differences in peoples lives, *race* is clearly real – it is a fact that certain skin colours and certain ancestries are used in the construction of social realities that have profound effects and genuine friction in the world, and are real difference-makers. To ignore this is to ignore something real and, from the *pragmatic realist* point of view, to knowingly pass by these difference-makers as though they were not real is to miss something important about *race*. A final worry that we might raise is whether the *pragmatic realist* is really doing justice to the biological aspirations of our ordinary *race* concept. After all, it seems that we are talking primarily about surface-level features of *race* and how they are used in predicting practical experiences. Now, in many ways we might concede that the *pragmatic realist* way of finding common ground between the *strong* and *weak social constructionist* positions is better than the *social naturalist's* in as far it doesn't lean quite so heavily on worrying and discredited notions such as breeding populations.[11] However, we

---

10. Taylor, for example, calls this *contextualism* (Taylor 2004b). However, it is a standard observation of Peircian and Deweyan pragmatism that inquiries are not free of the interests of inquirers.

11. Taylor is, nonetheless, keen to include many of the issues about endogamy among the various differences that race makes, and while his *pragmatic realism* has many affinities with the *social naturalism* of Outlaw, the two are quite distinct in this regard.

might still be concerned that the kind of "real" element that the *pragmatic realist* identifies is not that which our ordinary concept of *race* purports to have. Of course, the *pragmatic realist* is trying to draw a connection between bodily features, ancestry, and so on – the very things we identified as forming the core of our ordinary concept of *race* – and the social construction of *race*. However the worry here is that there is an assumption that a deeper, more unified biological feature underlies and unites these features and that *pragmatic realism* does not seem to speak to these. The *weak social constructionist* worry is that *race* aspires to be a biological kind, and even though we can agree with the *pragmatic realist* that the physical markers of *race* have real friction with the world, that does not mean that we have satisfied the demand for scientific credibility – we have already seen that our ordinary concept of *race* cannot have that. By moving away from a notion like breeding population, as we find it in the *social naturalist* version of *strong social constructionism*, and towards something closer to the surface-level markers of *race* used by ordinary speakers, the *pragmatic realist* moves further away from the kinds of things which could bestow biological credibility on our *race* thought and talk.

The *pragmatic realist* could, of course, respond to this by suggesting that this will only seem worrying to us because we are reading the apparent aspirations of *race* to be a biological kind far too strictly. Perhaps all that our social constructions are intended to do is to make sense of what seems to most people to be clear and tangible surface-level differences. After all, if we asked most people what really divides one *race* from another, we would be more likely get an answer that talks of the surface-level physical markers than of deeper essences or biology – that is, we are more likely to be told "black people look black, white people look white, yellow people look yellow" than we are to be told "black people form one distinct biological group, while white people form another biological group". This is all much closer to the looser *pragmatic realist* reading of how the non-social element of *race* construction is supposed to work than it is to the *weak social constructionist* construal of *race's* biological aspirations.

Nonetheless, we might worry that we have already seen enough evidence of how ordinary speakers use and interact with the concept of *race* to suggest that despite the likelihood of such a response, the real assumption about *race* is one of a deeper, non-surface-level kind. For example, when we talked earlier about the concept *parent*, it seemed obvious that when asked how we are supposed to characterize *parent* or *parenthood*, most people would invoke biological notions such as progenitor and offspring (although perhaps not using such terms). However, when pushed harder or when going about the world, they would be more likely to include people and relationships that are not biological, but which have a status involving caring and legal responsibility. What appears to be happening is that we can characterize the concept in terms of the reflective descriptions given by ordinary people, and we can characterize it in terms of the everyday practices of ordinary people – that is, we can look at what they say, and we can look at what they do.[12]

Ultimately, of course, we are interested in both of these things, but we can see how this is important for our discussion of *race*. In Chapter 1 and in the background to the *weak social constructionist* claim about the non-social aspirations of our *race* talk is the idea that we must look at what people *do*. And what people do is allow that one can *look* white but be black, or that one's long-lost distant ancestors can pass on something that re-emerges and determines our *race*, or that our skills and capacities are biological endowments. This looks like an assumed biological essentialism about *race*. For the *pragmatic realist*, however, we must look at what people *say*.[13] And what people seem to say about *race* frequently depends on the surface-level markers of *race*. As the *strong social constructionist* Ronald Sundstrom notes:

> I do not think, frankly, that to say race has a presence and impact ... is to make a fantastic, startling, or anyway exciting claim. It is the most obvious and banal of claims ... It is enough that we open our eyes and take a good look around.
>
> (Sundstrom 2002: 100)

When asked what is meant by "race" people say "take a good look around" – the non-social facts about *race* are there to see. And if this is so, then the *pragmatic realist* looks to be on reasonable ground in saying that the *weak social constructionism* which the *eliminativist* relies on is only compelling if

---

12. These kinds of ideas are drawn from work by Sally Haslanger (see Haslanger 2000, 2004), which notes that there are *descriptive definitions* – what we are saying is drawn from what people say – and there are *manifest definitions* – what we are saying is drawn from what people do. Haslanger thinks making these distinctions (and others besides) are crucial to our understanding of the metaphysics of concepts such as race and gender. We will look a little more at Haslanger's work in the next section.

13. And of course, we must look at what they do on the basis of this – this is the practicalist upshot of the *pragmatic realist* position.

we think that the non-social facts our *race* concept aspires to *are* the *deeper biological kind* that would confer scientific credibility. If, however, the non-social facts that our *race* concept aspires to are something closer to making sense of, and taking seriously, the macro-level physical differences we see around us, then we seem to have good grounds for rejecting *weak social constructionism*, and by extension *eliminativism*. And of course, if we have no reason for eliminating *race*, then we have grounds for preserving *race*.

Defending the social impact of *race*

In many ways the arguments for *preservationism* that we have just looked at only give us half the story. What we saw was two ways in which the *preservationist* might show that *race* is real by counteracting the *eliminativist* arguments that rely on *weak social constructionism*. However, showing that we need not be compelled by the *eliminativist* arguments against the reality of *race*, that is, showing that do have grounds for treating *race* as a social kind, isn't enough to show that we *should* adopt *preservationism*. As philosophers are fond of saying "you can't derive an 'ought' from an 'is'". Or more specifically, just because we *can* construct *race* as a genuine social kind, that doesn't automatically mean we *should*. For *preservationist* arguments to work, then, we need to show that there are reasons for wanting to persist with *race* thought and talk. And we shall turn to these arguments now.

When we looked at *eliminativism*, we noted that there seemed to be an awful lot of reasons for not wanting a *race* concept. *Race* was implicated in huge social evils such as slavery, the holocaust and apartheid. Moreover, the kinds of restrictions that *race* labelling placed upon people at an individual level made it hard to see why we would want to retain *race* thought and talk, even if we could make sense of how it could be real. For the *preservationist*, however, to focus on this is to miss some very positive and prudential reasons for keeping hold of our *race* concept.

To begin with, although lots of negative effects come from racial labelling, there are many potentially positive outcomes to be had too. For instance, there is much pride and individual self-esteem to be had from identifying with one's particular racial group. Indeed, the kinds of self-esteem to be had from identifying positively with one's racial group can be useful in countering the kinds of negative self-labelling that we noted earlier. For example, we mentioned the apparently limiting effects of labelling Romany Gypsies in the UK as illiterate, in as much as it seemed

only if you live in a system of hierarchically ordered races to lead to an increased negativity among Romany Gypsies towards literacy, and a resistance towards mainstream education. It should be obvious, however, that positive images about the nature and value of Romany art, culture and literature can easily counteract these negative ideas. But of course, such positive messages require the presence of a *race* in order to be coherent.

What's more, there may be good grounds for thinking that the kinds of positive effects on personal identity to be had here are only achieved by retaining a concept of *race*.[14] Consider, for example, someone who is very positive and has a well-developed sense of self-worth and self-respect. Among the very many positive things that they feel is a sense of self-esteem due to being a member of a particular *race*. But how are we supposed to explain these feelings? The self-esteem and positive feelings might be had by taking pride in the achievements of one's racial group – when one hears that an Olympic champion, or a Nobel Prize winner, or a particularly respected musician shares one's *race*, one might feel a peculiar sense of pride – but this cannot be due to any personal achievement. Instead, it looks as though we will have to rely on the idea of a shared identity in which we take some particular pride, and making sense of this identity will require us to speak of *race*. Of course, positive feelings drawn from shared identity are not automatically good, since the "achievements" may be undesirable or more properly seen as negative – many "white pride" movements, for example, are effectively neo-Nazi groups, and it is hard to see how any vindication for the concept of *race* is to be drawn from that. Nonetheless, the individual benefits to be had from identifying with one's racial group should be clear enough to make it obvious that the *eliminativist* case is not clear cut: there are reasons for thinking that racial labels can have positive impacts too.

Perhaps more important for the *preservationist* case, though, are what we can think of as a series of prudential reasons for wanting to hold on to *race*. In particular, the idea is that we might preserve *race*, not simply because it can have a positive impact on an individual's sense of self-esteem and so on, but because there is much work to be done in terms of social equality and political justice that we simply cannot do without the concept of *race* to hand. Consider, for example, the various statistics we gave about

---

14. John Arthur makes similar arguments, drawing upon and developing Rawls's account of self-respect (Arthur 2007: 141–4).

what it is like to be an Aboriginal Australian. The lowered life expectancy, the reduced educational opportunities, the greater health issues, the higher rates of unemployment – these are all due, in part, to *race* and the kinds of racial structures that exist in Australia. And while this might seem to be grist to the *eliminativist* mill, the problem, as far as the *preservationist* sees it is rather simple – when we eliminate *race*, we do not thereby correct these inequalities. If our language and thought is purged of *race* there will still be groups of people who suffer these social inequalities. However, if we retain the concept of *race* there is much we can do to redress these imbalances and correct some of the injustices that have occurred as a result of *race* thought and talk.

To take the point further, consider that the Australian government is investing money into what it calls "closing the gap". The idea is that money and targeted programmes will aim to reduce the discrepancy between the life expectancy, health, education and employment prospects of Indigenous and non-Indigenous Australians. However, without a concept of a *race*, it is hard to see how these programmes could be targeted and administered. If the Australian government sets aside A$90 million for the improvement of Aborigine antenatal healthcare, then without the appropriate racial classification there is no one to spend this money on.

Of course, we might maintain that there are categories other than *race* into which those most in need of social programmes and welfare fall, and that we can distribute and administer help via these classifications rather than *race*. While we have already noted that failing to acknowledge the role of *race* in social inequalities is to miss something very important – the lowered life expectancy of a Darug man, for example, is not due to his being Darug, but due to his being an Indigenous Australian – the suggestion here is more subtle than substituting *race* for ethnicity. It is more like the suggestion that we can dispense with *race* and still secure the redressing of racial inequalities by paying attention to such issues as class and culture. Nonetheless, it seems that any attempts to remove *race* and reduce racial inequalities to other social factors will miss something. As Lucius Outlaw notes:

> [D]uring the decades of the 1950s through the 1970s, the civil rights, Black Power, Chicano, and other movements assaulted and attempted the "great transformation" of this racial state; however, the assaults were partial, and thus not successful ...

because "all failed to grasp the comprehensive manner by which race is structured into the U.S. social fabric. All *reduced* race: to interest group, class faction, nationality, or cultural identity."

(Outlaw 1990)

The argument being made here is this: a failure to appreciate that the social inequality we must address is born of *race* will miss something crucial and ultimately prevent any redressing of such inequality. If I reduce the inequalities between Indigenous and non-Indigenous Australians to class, I have missed something about the social fabric of Australian society that has used a concept of *race* to allow such social problems to arise. Moreover, if I try to create programmes based on class to redress such problems I have again missed something – the inequality is not due to class, but to *race*. It may be true that many Indigenous Australians have lower socio-economic status, and by tackling problems associated with that we thereby help Indigenous Australians, but to ignore the fact that the lower socio-economic status of most Indigenous Australians is a result of their being racially classified as they are in Australian society makes this look wrong-headed. It is as though I am insisting on curing an endemic disease by treating the symptoms but refusing to remove the cause – I will treat the symptoms of your water-borne disease, but leave the infected water source untouched.

The *preservationist* arguments for defending the social impact of *race*, then, should be quite straightforward. First, the negatives of *race* are obvious, but this does not mean there are no positives to be had. The individual benefits of group identity for counteracting the negative images of *races*, and even as a source of self-esteem and pride, certainly give grounds for thinking that *race* could beneficially be preserved. In addition, there are simple prudential reasons for wanting to retain *race*. Many social *inequalities* and injustices exist as a result of *race* – this is central to the *eliminativist*'s reasons for wanting to purge us of *race* thought and talk. However, it seems clear that if we were to eliminate *race*, these long-developed injustices and inequalities would not somehow simply disappear too. We would have to work to redress the inequalities. However, how we could target the right people and the right problems, and make sure that our programmes are attending to the real causes of the injustice without a concept of *race* is hard to see.

Summary

We can summarize the *preservationist* position as we have outlined it here as follows.

The *eliminativist* argument is too quick. There are perfectly acceptable ways to show that *race* is real – albeit as a social kind. In particular, we can show that, contrary to the *eliminativists'* claims, we can take *race* to be socially constructed while taking the biological pretensions of our ordinary concept seriously. We can do this by telling a richer tale about the inter-action between our social practices and how this affects certain biological outcomes in terms of breeding populations. Or we can reconstrue the biological pretensions of our *race* concept in more modest terms as look-ing for reliance on some non-social facts such as macro-level appearances. Either way, we certainly need not accept the *eliminativist's* argument about the failure of *strong social constructionism* to capture our ordinary concept of *race*.

Additionally, there are good reasons for thinking that our concept of *race* should be preserved on grounds of both the beneficial effects to be had from adopting certain racial labels, and from the restorative and amel-iorative work that we need to do to redress past injustices inflicted through our concept of *race*.

RECONSTRUCTIONISM

It might seem that *eliminativism* and *preservationism* constitute the whole of the debate to be had here. Indeed, the strengths of one seem to trade on the weaknesses of the other, and an advance in one position seems to come at the expense of the other. For instance, the *eliminativist's* claim that we do and should alter our thought and talk to accommodate the discovery that some concept is empty seems to be a strength of the position. The *preser-vationist*, on the other hand, seems to be committed to the idea that we should maintain such thought and talk. This cannot be compelling unless the *preservationist* finds a way to undermine the *eliminativist* claim that our concept is empty. Similarly, the *preservationist's* claim that there are benefits to be had from identifying with our racial group, or that we should keep *race* as a tool for redressing social inequalities is more compelling than the *eliminativist* claim that *race* has no positive elements that can outweigh its negatives. And in this arena, the *eliminativist* must advance their position by showing that the benefits noted by the *preservationist* can be had through means other than *race*. However, despite what looks like a well mapped out argumentative landscape, there is a different series of approaches to the question we are concerned with here.

In the last ten or so years more philosophers of *race* are beginning to move away from the standard *eliminativist/preservationist* debate and towards what we are going to call *reconstructionism*.[15] *Reconstructionism* draws on the insights that we noted in Chapter 2 when we discussed how *reconstructionists* might view facts about the social aspects of *race*. You may recall that we noted that the key lesson the *reconstructionist* draws from the socio-historical facts about our *race* thought and talk was that the concept is malleable and is shaped by social factors. As interesting as the social, political and economic forces that have shaped our *race* concept are, it is more interesting that such forces can be pressed into service to bring about a reshaped notion of *race* in the future. For the *reconstructionist*, then, the answer to the question that we are asking ourselves in this chapter – "what should we do with *race*?" – is simple: we should reconstruct it. However, we cannot say just what that reconstruction should look like until we ask ourselves such additional questions as "what do we want our concept of *race* to be like?" and "what do we want a concept of *race* for?". What is more, when we have a better sense of what our reconstructed notion of *race* looks like, we can hopefully answer the question of what we should do with *race* in a way that gives us the strengths of both the *eliminativist* and the *preservationist* positions with none or few of their weaknesses.

There are various ways that we can go about reconstructing *race*. For instance, there are *reconstructionist* accounts that suggest reconstructing our *race* thought and talk with something like ethnicity as the central concept rather than *race* (see, for example, Corlett 2003). In this chapter we have already expressed worries about replacing *race* with *ethnicity* or some other concept such as *class*, so we won't pursue this any further. There are also *reconstructionist* accounts that suggest reconstructing our *race* concept into thought and talk about the process and practice of racialization (Blum 2002). Instead of describing someone as "black", we would describe them as "racialized as black in our society". However, in the remainder of

---

15. The notion of reconstruction for the concept of race is found in many places (e.g. Haslanger 2000) but the term as used here borrows most directly from Joshua Glasgow (Glasgow 2006, 2009a).

this chapter we shall look in more detail at two recent *reconstructionist* positions – Sally Haslanger's *ameliorative* definitional project and Joshua Glasgow's *substitutionist* account. As I have said, these are not the only kinds of *reconstructionism* that we could examine, but I take them to be most interesting because they are recent developments in the philosophy of *race*, and because they offer intriguing ways out of the *preservationist/eliminativist* debate.

Racial reconstruction I – developing *race* into an ameliorative concept

The first way of reconstructing *race* that we shall look at comes from work by Sally Haslanger (see Haslanger 2000, 2004, 2006). Haslanger points out that we can have a variety of definitional projects in mind when we talk about concepts such as *race* and *gender*. For instance, we can be concerned with something like giving a list of necessary and sufficient conditions for a concept, or we can be concerned with defining the concepts that seem to underpin our everyday practices. Haslanger calls these two kinds of definitional project *conceptual* and *descriptive*, respectively. We may well recognize the *descriptive* definitional project as similar to the kind of endeavour we engaged in during Chapter 1 – we tried to recover an account of *race* from our ordinary thought and talk. However, and most interesting for both Haslanger and us, is a third kind of definitional project which we shall call *ameliorative*.[16]

In an *ameliorative* definitional project, the whole point of providing a definition is to ask ourselves what we want these concepts to do for us, to what end we want to put them, and how can we best shape this definition as a tool that enables us to accomplish some particular desired end. As Haslanger puts it:

> [O]n an [ameliorative] approach, the question ... "What is race?" require[s] us to consider what work we want [this] concept to do for us; why do we need [it] at all? The responsibility is to define [it] for our purposes. In doing so, we will want to be responsive to some aspects of ordinary usage ... However, neither ordinary usage nor empirical investigation is overriding,

---

16. In Haslanger (2000), this kind of definitional project is called *analytic*, but this is altered in later papers to *ameliorative*. Given that this later term best captures the reconstructive intent of Haslanger's project we will use that term.

for there is a stipulative element to this project: *this* is the phenomenon we need to be thinking about. Let the term in question refer to it. On this approach, the world by itself cannot tell
us what ... race is; it is up to us to decide what in the world, if
anything, [it is].   (Haslanger 2000: 33–4)

Haslanger maintains that the main driver for reconstructing a concept of
race has to be social, and it has to be geared towards overcoming injustice.
To this end, we want our definition to capture just how inequalities occur,
what the injustices are, and against whom they are perpetrated. We are
interested in such a definition because crucial to redressing inequalities is
identifying their nature and whom they impact.

Now, notice that in one sense, this resonates strongly with the *preservationist* observation that we have much work to do if we are to overcome
the social injustices that have occurred in the name of *race*, and that key
to doing this is to have a concept of *race* to hand. The difference, however,
is that the concept of *race* which Haslanger thinks we need to make use of
need not simply be the old concept of *race* that got us into such a mire of
social inequity in the first place. Instead, it can be geared entirely towards
the aim of identifying where our ameliorative efforts are most needed and
best directed. It is in this sense that the ameliorative concept of *race* that
we find in Haslanger's account is *reconstructionism*.

The particular account of *race* that Haslanger identifies as serving our
needs, then, is this:

A group is racialised (in context C) iff its members are socially
positioned as subordinate or privileged along some dimension
(economic, political, legal, social, etc.) (in C) and the group is
"marked" as a target for this treatment by observed or imagined
bodily features presumed to be evidence of ancestral links to a
certain geographical region.   (Haslanger 2004: 7)

So, to be black in contemporary USA is to be economically, politically,
legally and socially subordinated or oppressed by virtue of being seen to
have physical traits such as black skin, which are presumed to be evidence
of ancestral links to Africa.

It is worth noting a couple of interesting things about this definition.
First, it draws on many of the commonplace assumptions about *race* that
we looked at in Chapter 1 – *race* is about somatic markers, ancestry and

geography. In that sense it contains some quite familiar elements. Second, and more importantly for the *reconstructionist* element of Haslanger's account, is that the notion of suppression and racial hierarchies is built directly into this definition. In our everyday thinking about *race*, we do not tend to think that to be black one must be oppressed, or that to be white one must be privileged. And of course it is this second element that is supposed to enable the reconstructed notion of *race* to do the ameliorative work that we require of it. If we need to identify and counteract racial injustices, then building the root cause of those injustices into our concept of *race* enables us to be clear about who we are working with, what we are working against, and what we are working towards.

This *reconstructionist* project is deeply interesting and we have only given the briefest of accounts of it here. It is obvious that concerning ourselves with some central questions about how we can redress the social injustices related to *race*, and pressing into service a concept of *race* that directs our efforts straight to those who suffer from the injustices is a useful tool. Nonetheless, it is worth pausing to raise one or two potential issues for such an account.

First, we might worry that such a definition seems to exclude non-suppressed black people and sets a negative criterion for inclusion within a *race*. It seems odd, at first blush, to say that you can only be black if you are the victim of oppression or that if you have been successful in life and show no signs of being oppressed you cannot count as black. However, for Haslanger, this is an acceptable part of the reconstructive project, as she says, "relative to the ... anti-racist values guiding our project – they [the excluded] are not the ones who matter" (Haslanger 2000: 46). And this response seems perfectly appropriate given that we are dealing with a reconstructed concept with particular aims of focusing on social injustice. However, should such exclusion undermine the ameliorative project, then such a concern may be more of an issue for Haslanger's account than it may initially appear. For instance, if it turns out that by excluding those who we might ordinarily count as black because they are not oppressed actually frustrates rather than furthers the redressing of social inequality then this concern has more bite. And, at least at a surface level, we can see how such a worry might go.

For example, when Barack Obama was inaugurated as the first black President of the USA, a common reaction among the black community was that this was a great positive because, among other reasons, it gave the message that no station in American society was closed to black people –

what about Donny?

every black child could aspire to the presidency and know that it was some-thing black people could attain. This kind of achievement looks as though it could contribute to the ameliorative project. However, if we stipulate that Barack Obama is not to count as black because he is not oppressed – and as an Ivy League-educated lawyer holding the highest office in the USA, it is hard to see how he can be oppressed – then it seems we have detracted from our ameliorative project.

A second issue, given that we'd hoped to bypass the *preservationist/ eliminativist* debate by having the positives of both positions with few of the negatives, is that this particular reconstruction may not deliver every-thing we want. To elaborate, Haslanger's account clearly meets many of the concerns that motivate the *preservationist*. We shape our concept of *race* to maximize its social utility, to redress social inequalities and injustices. Of course, if our concerns about excluding those who are not suppressed are correct then there are some limitations here but, for the most part, the positives of the *preservationist* position are retained. However, if we wanted to capture the *eliminativist* point that our thought and talk should reflect our discovery that there is no such thing as *race*, then this account seems to bypass such concerns.

In the first instance, the ameliorative definition is not explicitly con-cerned with providing an accurate definition of *race* as we currently use it. And whether we think *race* is a biological kind, or a social kind, or nei-ther, it's not clear that we mean *race* to include explicit reference to social position. Moreover, if the ordinary notion of *race* is deeply mistaken, then those mistakes need to find their way directly into the ameliorative defini-tion since it is via our beliefs about *race* that people are positioned into racial hierarchies. All of which makes no concession to any *eliminativist* inclination to have our thought and talk be sensitive to the facts about the reality of *race*. Of course, for Haslanger, the concern of her project is not to introduce a reconstructed notion of *race* in order to bring our *race* thought and talk into line with the ontological facts about *race*, but rather to bring about some redress for racial injustice and inequality, so this second worry may not be very deeply felt.

Racial reconstruction II – substituting *race* with *race**

The second *reconstructionist* project that we shall look at comes from Joshua Glasgow (2009a). As far as Glasgow is concerned, the *preservationist*'s concern to retain *race* is a good one, but the *eliminativist*'s call to have our thought and talk accord with the way the world is, is also a strong consideration. However, rather than adjust our thought and talk to reflect the emptiness of the *race* concept, Glasgow's project looks much more like an adjustment of our thought and talk so that the concept we refer to is a fully socially constructed *race*. In effect we drop the biological pretensions of our concept of *race*, adopt the *strong social constructionist* view, and consequently alter the world to reflect the apparent meaningfulness of our *race* thought and talk. This is a rather enigmatic way of putting it, but the idea is that we can introduce a new way of thinking and talking about race that embraces the socio-historical elements as wholly and solely reality conferring. This makes our *race* thought and talk line up with the way the world is.

Glasgow's idea is that we can reconstruct our *race* concept in three steps. First, we acknowledge that the way we currently speak of *race* is with biological intent, but recognize that there is a proximate concept of *race* which does not have any biological pretensions, and which recognizes that *race* is entirely socially constructed. We should, and can, use that concept too. Glasgow proposes that we retain the word "race" for both, for the time being, and perhaps trust to context to keep it clear which term we are using – the biologically loaded or wholly social term. To keep matters clear though, Glasgow proposes we use *race* to talk of our current, biologically loaded term and *race** to talk of our preferred *reconstructionist* social concept.

Second, we retain the broad racial groupings and *race* categorizations that we currently have and use *race* and *race** to refer to these. So the aim is that even when we intend to refer to entirely socially constructed *races*, we still aim to have our terms "black", "white", "Asian" and so on pick out roughly the same groups that our biologically loaded concept refers to. What this means is that in our reconstructed project our words and their references remain at least approximately the same, even though there is a conceptual difference between them.

Third, we aim for our *reconstructionist* project to lead to a point where, for reasons of not wanting to use empty concepts and to accord with the growing use of *race** to denote racial* groups, the concept of *race* is no longer used – instead we have the concept of *race** firmly ensconced in our thought and talk. At this point, the term "race" will be used as an entirely social kind without any pretension to having its objectivity conferred upon it by some non-social reality.

There are a couple of things to note about this view. First, the idea is that we introduce a replacement concept that we know accords with ontological reality and makes our use of the term "race" metaphysically and epistemically respectable. It will only be after repeated use that we begin to see our *race* thought and talk drop away to be replaced with *race** thought and talk. A second thing to note is that, because of the nature of social construction, there is currently no such thing as *race**. Let's assume that the *weak social constructionist* arguments are correct, and that although there is a possible concept for the *strong social constructionist* to pick out, it is not extant in our current use. However, by using the term and forming social practices and *racializing** conventions with this concept, *races** can be constructed and, in due course, we can have a thoroughly socially constructed concept.

Much of the argument for this particular *reconstructionist* project comes from seeing how and why such a reconstruction could work. But chief among its benefits are that it seems to enable us to run with the *preservationist* hare, and hunt with the *eliminativist* hounds – that is, we can get the benefit of both views. Consider that, the key strength of the *eliminativist* position is that it keeps us honest about our thought and talk. We really shouldn't persist in believing in and asserting empty concepts, and the emptiness of *race* certainly pushes us towards purging "race" from our thought and talk. If Glasgow is correct, we can reconstruct *race* into the much more honest *race**, and have our thought and talk made respectable as a result. If we mean to use a term which we know picks out an entirely socially constructed notion with no biological pretensions, then so long as that social kind exists, all is well.

Which brings us to the key strength of the *preservationist* position – its recognition of the utility of *race* for identity and for redressing racial inequality. The *reconstructionist* position that Glasgow advocates can give us this without asking of us that we fly in the face of *eliminativist* concerns. In constructing a racial* concept we try to latch on to the same groups picked out by our racial concepts (although we are clear that there is nothing biological binding these group members together). Accordingly, we institute practices and policies that allow for positive group identities, which embrace the shared experiences of the racial* groups, and which set about redressing some of the social ills created by *race* thought and talk. The very act of constructing *races** allows us to achieve the objectives that drive the *preservationist* desire to retain *race*. The very project of making our *race* thought and talk honest by introducing and constructing a nearby social kind of *race** involves addressing the concerns of the *preservationist* head on.

As with all of the views we have looked at in this chapter, there may be issues and worries of course. We might worry that while in many ways it is a good thing that Glasgow's account might offer a way to answer the *preservationist*'s need for *race*, the driving force is to make our thought and talk respectable. After all, the arguments for Glasgow's *reconstructionism* don't really suggest that *race** will serve our social purposes better than *race*, it is just that it will serve our epistemic purposes better without leaving us worse off in our projects to ameliorate racial inequality. Of course, this may be no bad result in the scheme of things, but for some the question of whether we should or should not retain *race* thought and talk should be judged first and foremost on questions of racial justice and equality.

We shall leave the discussion of *reconstructionism* here noting that as a reasonably recent research strain its strengths and weaknesses are yet to be fully explored. However, as a way out of the debate between *eliminativists* and *preservationists* it seems to offer a genuinely interesting way forward in questions about what we should do with our concept of *race*.

CONCLUSION

In this chapter we have tried to address the question of what we should do with *race*. We first examined the case for purging our thought and talk of *race*. This *eliminativist* position argued that there were important reasons for wanting our beliefs and assertions to closely reflect the way the world is, and since the concept of *race* is neither a biological nor a social kind, we must accept that it is not real and adjust our thought and talk accordingly. An additional element to the *eliminativist*'s argument is to suggest that the only time we might forgo the imperative to have our thought and talk accord with the world is if there are important moral or practical reasons for doing otherwise. Since *race* is largely seen as the root cause behind much inequality, injustice and personal suffering, it is hard to see under what circumstances we could want to retain *race*.

Next we looked at *preservationist* arguments which suggested that there may be reasons for thinking that the *eliminativist* is wrong – there are a variety of ways we can develop our *social constructionist* views so that it makes sense to see *race* as a social kind. In particular we looked at *social naturalism* and *pragmatic realism*. Further, we saw that the *preservationist* sees lots of good social reasons for retaining our *race* thought and talk, not least, that there are plenty of positive identity benefits. Moreover, *race* may turn out to be crucial for programmes that aim to redress previous racial injustices and inequalities.

The final position that we looked at was *reconstructionism*. This position suggested that our focus for *race* would not be on whether we keep or dispense with our present account of *race*, but whether we could use the social forces that we know play a key role in the nature of *race* to reconstruct the concept. In particular we saw two *reconstructionist* positions: one that focuses most strongly on the social needs for *race* thought and talk and defines *race* according to our social ameliorative needs; and another that focuses on pressing a concept of *race*, or rather, *race**, into service that marries up with a corresponding social kind and serves our social needs for such a concept.

CHAPTER FOUR

Racism

In the preceding three chapters of this book we have expended considerable effort in getting clear about what we think *race* is, what its social elements are and what we think its long-term prospects should be. In this chapter we turn our attention to the question of *racism*. *Racism* is clearly an important topic and, in many ways, it is a crucial reason for our concern with *race* – it is because so many injustices and inequalities occur in the name of *race* that we are concerned with what it is and whether we should reject it, retain it or rebuild it. But from a more philosophical point of view we face some similar dilemmas and concerns here as we did when we began looking at *race*. When we look around the world we feel quite confident that, for the most part, we can point to *racism* when we see it, and that we know when we've seen an instance of racial prejudice. We may not always be right, but we know what we're looking for. However, when we are asked to give a precise account of what *racism* is, we might well be stumped. And the reason is that in our day-to-day encounters we may have no more than a gut feeling that something is racist. To give a precise definition that captures that is going to be difficult for most of us. To see what we mean here consider the following three cases.

Case One: A local food store displays a large sign on the door that says "black people will not be served in this shop". Whenever a black person enters the store the proprietor becomes animated and orders the person from the store, frequently using racially pejorative language. In this instance I take it that most of us would be quite happy to say that this is an instance of *racism*.

Case Two: When looking for musicians for his college rock band, an aspiring singer says that he doesn't want to consider any black people.

Quizzed on why this is he says that he would happily form a band with black musicians if he were intending to form a funk or jazz band, but since black people aren't suited to rock music he doesn't want to include them. Having said that, if there aren't enough decent candidates he might compromise with a black drummer or bassist since the natural rhythm of black musicians could fit there. In this instance, I take it that most of us would want to say that this was an instance of *racism*, although some might say this singer is not as racist as he is terribly ill-informed.

Case Three: During a long-haul flight, passengers from standard class keep slipping behind the curtain into first class to use the toilet facilities there. This is partly because of the queues in standard class, and partly because the first class toilet is just nicer. The cabin crew seem to be ignoring this practice, but shortly after a family of black passengers begin to do the same thing, cabin crew begin to enforce the strict separation between standard and first class. Pressed on this, the cabin crew might quite genuinely state that they acted as and when they did because what had been an occasional breach of the rules was becoming too frequent. In this instance, I think some of us would say that this is an instance of *racism*, but we might be find it hard to say exactly why we thought so. Others, I guess, would want to say we were making a deal out of nothing.

If we want to give a more precise account of *racism*, and even give a workable definition of what it is, we will need to be able to say what these kinds of cases have in common, assuming they have any commonalities at all. We will have to get at where our gut feelings about Case Three come from, or why we have no doubts about Case One, or why we might excuse (or not) the singer in Case Two. And so on.

In this chapter, then, we are interested in trying to capture some broad and obvious facts about *racism* and use them as a guide for a more precise and philosophical definition of just what it is. A further interest that we shall pursue here is the near-universal opinion that *racism* is wrong – we all agree that *racism* is an invidious and negative thing that we should do without. We might even think that some kinds of *racism* are worse than others. And even those who declare that they are happy about *racism* and think there is something good in it – white supremacists for instance – are likely to be aware that they are being subversive and are embracing the wrongness of *racism* rather than making a case for its being right. From a philosophical point of view though, we are interested in capturing just what is it that makes it so undesirable, and wrong. Why do we think the three cases mentioned above are wrong? Why do we think that Case One is worse than Case Three (assuming we do)? Should we think that Case One is worse than Case Three (again assuming we do)?

In short, then, we are interested here in giving a philosophical definition of *racism* that enables us to make sense of the multiple instances of *racism* that we find in our day-to-day life, and which also allows us to make sense of why *racism* is wrong, and even why one kind of *racism* is more invidious than another. We will turn to these more philosophical issues and questions shortly but before we begin, we will spend a little time trying to map out the phenomenon of *racism* as we find it in the world. After all, it is the real world phenomenon of *racism* that we are looking to explain with our philosophical accounts, and more importantly, the three cases we have introduced above are not going to give us a full picture of the way *racism* occurs in our daily lives.

WHAT IS *RACISM* AND WHERE DO WE FIND IT?

In Chapter 1 we spent some time looking at a series of characteristics that, in our ordinary pre-theoretical thought and talk, we seem to connect to the notion of *race*. Although in this chapter we are also interested in what turns up in our pre-theoretical notions, fortunately we can draw on what is a vast body of sociological, anthropological and psychological work on the notion of *racism*. To begin with, then, let's look at a reasonably extensive characterization of *racism*:

1. *Racism* assumes there are human groups divided by the types of difference noted in Chapter 1 – somatic difference, heritage, geographical origin and so on.

However, this is not enough for obvious reasons. To think that there are people we can describe as "black" or "white" is not to be racist, and a commitment to *race* is not a commitment to *racism*.

2. *Racism* assumes one racial group is superior to another by virtue of the racial differences between them.

While this may be enough for *racism* in many instances, it may not yet capture what we think of as *racism* in many other cases. For example, we can easily imagine someone who thinks there are *races*, and who secretly thinks that the one *race*, R^1, is superior to another *race*, R^2, but says and does nothing that ever realizes or enforces this kind of thinking. For most of the cases of *racism* we think of, we would perhaps need something more.

3. *Racism* takes the superiority of one *race*, R^1, over another, R^2, to be grounds for R^1 dominating R^2, and exercising power and control over the lives and interests of the members of R^2.

Again, this seems to capture part of what we think of as *racism*. Using the assumptions that in the USA there are white people and black people, and that white people are superior to black people as grounds for controlling the lives and outcomes of black Americans looks racist. However, there may still be more to *racism* than this since we can imagine that members of R^1 assume themselves to be superior to members of R^2 and exercise power and control over R^2, dominating their lives, but that they do so in order to make life better for all. As unlikely as this is, we can still see how it might occur in a misguided but benevolent society. When we talk of *racism* we tend to mean something less benevolent than this.

4. *Racism* is the exercising of power and dominance by one racial group over another racial group, frequently and consistently resulting in the disadvantage of the dominated group at the expense of the dominating group. Further, this contributes to social, political, economic and personal inequalities created and enforced along racial lines.

This, finally, begins to look as though it gives a fairly full characterization of what we mean by *racism* in most instances – the assumption of *races* with relations of superiority and inferiority existing between them, such that the presumed superior group is able to dominate and exercise power over the dominated group to the detriment and disadvantage of members of that group *qua* members of that group.

This may already seem like a fairly extensive definition, but it is merely a starting point, especially since there is a range of other elements to *racism* that we will need to take into consideration. For instance, this definition may be a useful starting point, but consider the two following instances of what seem like racist behaviour.

Jack owns a car-tyre workshop and has a vacancy. However, he simply will not accept the idea of employing black people – they are lazy, dishonest, rude and disrespectful as far as Jack is concerned. It will be a desperate day before he fills his vacancy with a black candidate. When he fills the position, he selects a white candidate.

Karen also owns a car-tyre workshop, and also has a vacancy. She accepts applications from candidates regardless of *race*. Indeed, the majority of the applications she receives come from well-qualified black people. Unlike Jack, she does not believe that all black people are lazy, dishonest, rude or disrespectful. Indeed, if asked, she will state that she thinks *races* are equal and racial prejudice is abhorrent. However, when she fills the position none of the people who make her shortlist are black, and the white person she finally chooses looks under-qualified compared with some of the black candidates.

What gives in these two cases? Are they both instances of *racism*? In the case of Jack, it seems as though we do have a clear instance of *racism* – here is someone who thinks black people have a set of negative characteristics that their white counterparts do not share, and he uses this belief as grounds for denying black people the chance of gainful employment with his company. But what about Karen, who makes no apparently racist pronouncements? We can even take her at her word when she says she has no racist beliefs. Perhaps if we ask her why she took an under-qualified white candidate over the very many well-qualified black candidates she might say that she wanted to give the white candidate a chance, and that the other applicants would easily get another position. This doesn't look racist. But what if this keeps happening? What if Karen's company is expanding massively and positions become vacant all the time, yet the well-qualified black candidates are always passed over? What are we to make of that? We might well suspect *racism* there, but how can we make sense of it given the broad account that we have? One way is to note a difference between what is frequently called *overt racism* and *avert racism*.[1] We sometimes find terms such as *"explicit"* and *"implicit"* racism, or *"dominative"* and *"aversive"* racism, but we will retain "overt" and "avert". The idea behind the distinction is that there is a difference between our explicit unhidden and unabashed racist beliefs and actions, and those that are implicit, hidden and perhaps unavailable to us. In particular, we can have attitudes towards people of different *races* which are not entirely apparent to us, but which nonetheless direct our actions,

---

1. This distinction and the notion of aversive racism is due to Gaertner and Dovidio (1986).

rely on assumptions about negative racial characteristics, and lead to detrimental outcomes for members of that *race*.[2] In terms of our example above, it would come as no surprise if it turned out that Karen *did* harbour many implicit biases against black people, and though she does not show signs of overt *racism*, her actions are nonetheless based on avert *racism*.

Besides the broad notion of *racism* that we have here, there are other crucial distinctions that we need to take account of too. For example, closely related to the notion of *overt* and *avert racism* is a distinction between what we might call *direct* and *indirect racism*. Again, consider the following two examples.

In her local community, Clara organizes an after-school group for children, teaching them to sing choral music. However, Clara explicitly refuses to include black children in her programme arguing that as a people naturally endowed with the ability to sing, they would take up a place they did not need.

In his local community where there are a high number of low-income retirees, Tom manages a government-funded, free pet-companion service, which provides cats for company. However, since a high number of the local community are Romany Gypsies who consider cats to be *mochadi* (ritually unclean) many of those pensioners find they cannot really make use of the service.

The case of Clara seems to be a clear-cut case of *racism*. More importantly, its effects are quite direct – it impacts immediately and intentionally upon the black community, based on incorrect beliefs about *race*. The case of Tom, however, may feel a little less clear cut. First of all, there seems to be no malice intended. Indeed, the project is meant to provide a positive service for a needy group. Second, its negative effects seem to be accidental – why would Tom want his project to miss a proportion of its intended beneficiaries? But nonetheless a group is excluded and suffers negative outcomes for reasons related to *race*. And this is the point about indirectness – the negative outcome is had not as a direct intention of the action, but as a secondary or *indirect* effect of the action. And if you cannot see why this might count as *racism*, consider some other cases of indirect *racism*, such as before-school milk programmes for children that fail to take account of the fact that higher rates of lactose intolerance among black people mean

---

2. There are various sophisticated methods for uncovering our implicit biases. See, for example, the Implicit Association Test (Greenwald *et al.* 1998). Indeed, if you want to see just how these tests and implicit bias work, go try the tests at https://implicit.harvard.edu/implicit.

the black community is excluded. The important thing to note is that they come about through a failure to consider the important differences and needs of people that are due to their *race*. We can disempower and disadvantage people by actively using negative stereotypes to suppress them, and we can disempower and disadvantage people by ignoring them and their needs. The kinds of indirect *racism* we have noted here look as though they occur because of the latter.

One final thing we need to note here about *racism*, and along with it, a further distinction, is that we find it at various social levels. We'll note the three most obvious.

First, we find *racism* at the level of individual and personal interaction, and most of the cases we have talked about so far are instances of this *individual-level racism*. What we see at this level is the use of membership of a dominant group to exercise power and discrimination over members of a subordinated group. For instance, the usual kinds of racial name-calling, *race*-related violence, rejecting applications from people of a specific *race*, refusing service and so on. In many ways, this kind of individual level *racism*, when it is *overt* and *direct*, is the kind of the thing most of us have in mind when we think of *racism*.

Second, we find *racism* enacted through official channels and in the institutions through which we manage society. We shall call this level of *racism institutional racism*.[3] The idea is quite straightforward and captures the idea that the mechanisms through which we manage society are inherently oppressive and detrimental to the lives and prospects of people of particular *races*. For instance, if our educational system is funded by taking local taxes to fund local schools, then in black American communities, where the average income is less than in white American communities, the amount of money available to educate black children will be less than that available to educate white children. The knock-on effect of this will be that employment prospects and thus income will be reduced for black people. Similarly, if, as in the UK, our healthcare system requires that we register with the nearest doctor to where we live, and that our medical records are retained there, then travelling communities such as Romany Gypsies are *de facto* excluded from the normal healthcare system. These kinds of discrimination are part and parcel of social institutions. We can point to various others, such as the higher conviction rates for first time black offenders

---

3. The term is due to Stokely Carmichael and Charles Hamilton (1967) but it is very widely used.

in the USA and UK, or higher mortgage rates, or the greater difficulty in obtaining credit for black people in the USA (see Yinger 1995). Most of the clear instances of institutional *racism* that we might garner from history – Jim Crow-era USA, or apartheid South Africa for instance, are *overt* and *direct* forms of *institutional racism*, but much of what we might see today tends to be avert and/or indirect. It is all, nonetheless, institutional *racism*.[4]

The third and final level that we shall include in our discussions is what we shall call *cultural racism*. Discussion of cultural *racism* includes lots of terms such as *colour-blind racism, laissez-faire racism, new racism* and *unmarked racism*, and although these all pick out subtle differences in the phenomenon that we are interested in, we shall retain the notion of cultural *racism*. The concept of cultural *racism* is a recent and interesting one that might be usefully summed up, in the words of Eduardo Bonilla-Silva, as "racism without racists" (Bonilla-Silva 2003). The idea is that we frequently see racial prejudice treated as though it belongs to a past age, and current racial inequalities explained in terms of deep cultural differences. For instance, among immigrant families in Australia and the UK, speaking a language other than English at home is seen as a marker of socio-economic under-privilege and a marker for a lack of educational attainment. Yet among non-immigrant and white families, multi-lingualism is seen as a marker of culture and educational ability. This is due, of course, to the kinds of language spoken – speaking French and English is cultured and educated, speaking Urdu and English is not – and to the perceived degree of "integration". Similarly, assertiveness from white people is seen as directness, even honesty, but from black people it is seen as aggressiveness or "uppityness", and so on.

The real impact of cultural *racism* though is that it seeks to explain racial inequality in terms other than *racism*. The reason Aborigines in Australia have less educational and employment opportunities is not because the social structures are inherently suppressing this group of people, but because "they don't want to learn" or "they don't want to work – why would you when you can get everything you need handed out to you for free". And we can see how this assumption that cultural differences explain racial inequality becomes compounding. If a Romany Gypsy child shows a lack

---

4. Work on institutional racism is well established and beside the references already given, those interested would do well to look at Feagin (2006).

of interest in algebra, this is because "they aren't interested in school and learning", and both patience and educational opportunity are withdrawn. If a white child shows a lack of interest in algebra, this is because algebra is hard, or is not obvious to everyone, and no opportunities are likely to be withdrawn from the child by virtue of their *race*. If black people are presumed to be part of a culture that has no respect for the law, the law will be harsher upon them and so on. This general phenomenon is *cultural racism*.

SUMMARY

There are many elements and kinds of *racism* that we have not mentioned here – internalized *racism*, symbolic *racism*, and so on – but what we have mentioned certainly seems to capture a good proportion of the phenomenon of *racism* as it is identified by sociologists, psychologists and anthropologists. So what we have seen is that *racism* is, broadly speaking, the assumption of racial difference with relationships of superiority and inferiority existing between those *races*, and which grounds the exertion of power by a dominating group over a dominated group to the benefit of the former and to the detriment of the latter. Moreover, the exercise of this *racism* can be *overt* or *avert* – it can be known and acknowledged, or it can be unknown and result from implicit and hidden biases. Further, it can be *direct* or *indirect* – it can be unmediated and applied primarily to the detriment of a racial group, or it can result in poor outcomes for a racial group as a secondary and mediated effect. And finally, we find *racism* manifest at various levels of society – it can be enacted at a personal and *individual* level; it can be enacted via social organizations at an *institutional* level; and it can be enacted through widespread assumptions about the social practices and beliefs of *races* at a *cultural* level.

As we have already said, the topic of *racism* is a vast and complicated one, and disciplines other than philosophy have done considerable amounts of work to identify both what it is and what its effects are. Philosophers have some different concerns, which we shall look at in a moment, but the point of raising these ideas and notions about *racism* here is that they give us something to compare our philosophical accounts of *racism* with. While philosophers attempting to give interesting philosophical accounts of *racism* may feel that accounting for all of these notions is not important, or that failing to do so will not undermine their account, we will nonetheless want a philosophical account of *racism* to make clear connections with the kinds of considerations raised about *racism* here.

PHILOSOPHICAL ACCOUNTS OF *RACISM*

Given that we clearly know so much about *racism*, what it is, what it does, and so on, we might ask just why philosophers feel any need to give an account of it. There may well be philosophical questions and interests concerning *racism*, but given the wealth of sociological and psychological work already conducted on the topic, it's not clear why a philosophical explication of *racism* is of any use to philosophers or non-philosophers. However, philosophers have nonetheless spent considerable time and effort trying to give specifically philosophical definitions of *racism*. We shall look at three of these very shortly – a *belief/ideology model* of *racism* (the treatment of *racism* in terms of belief), a *behavioural model* of *racism* – (the treatment of *racism* in terms of actions) and an *affective model* of *racism* – (the treatment of *racism* in terms of feelings) – but first we shall say a little about just why a philosophical definition of *racism* might be of interest.

Why a philosophical account of *racism*?

For the most part philosophers believe that they have something to add to discussion of *racism* over and above the sociological and psychological contributions we have already noted. As Luc Faucher and Edouard Machery (2009) note:

> [T]he job of a philosopher consists of defining what race and racism are, and of understanding the moral issues these concepts raise. There is thus a division of labor between philosophers and psychologists: The former are interested in necessary truths and practice conceptual analysis; the latter are interested in contingent truths and use the empirical methods that are characteristic of science. Within this framework, a philosopher has nothing to expect from psychology.
>
> (Faucher and Machery 2009: 42)

We might still think, of course, that much of what we have already seen above provides the basis for a definition. However, one way to see the difference that philosophers might want to latch on to is that there has to be a distinction between what constitutes *racism*, and what is merely the effect or affordance of *racism*.[5]

To see why this matters, and why it seems to call for a specifically philosophical analysis of *racism*, consider that we characterized *racism* above as the assumption that there are *races* with relations of superiority and inferiority existing between them, which allows the exercising of power by one group over the other to the benefit of the former and to the detriment of the latter. We might, from a philosophical point of view, think that in this characterization we are running together questions of what *racism* is with what it allows and what the effects of that are. *Racism* might well just be the assumption of *races* with relations of superiority and inferiority existing between them. This assumption allows or affords the exercising of power relations, as empirical and historical analyses show. The effects of this action are racial inequality, as sociological and psychological analyses show. However, it is not immediately obvious that as philosophers we are deeply interested in anything but the constitutive questions. Moreover, it is not obvious, short of taking a philosophical pause and trying to extricate the various elements involved, that we can be entirely clear about which parts of the phenomenon are *racism*, and which bits are merely the effects of *racism*. Arguably, this will matter in our study of *racism*, and for the philosopher, the constitutive questions are philosophical questions *par excellence*.

This is not to say that the kinds of phenomenon we have mentioned above are not important – they are. If we produce deeply interesting accounts of the constitutive elements of *racism*, but these simply do not tie up with the various effects that we have noted, we know that they are inadequate for the task at hand. Philosophers may be correct in thinking that they can provide analyses that are, in some sense, prior to or detached from the empirical questions about *racism*, but this does not mean that these analyses of *racism* are not answerable to empirical considerations. With all this said then, let us now turn to philosophical analyses of *racism*.

---

5. This kind of notion is what drives J. L. A. Garcia's dissatisfaction with many non-philosophical accounts of racism (see, for example, Garcia 1999). For Garcia, we philosophers must concern ourselves first and foremost with the constitutive question and the provision of necessary and sufficient conditions.

The belief/ideology model of *racism*

The first account of *racism* that we shall look at treats belief and ideology as forming the core of a definition of *racism*. In its most extreme form the idea is that it is racist beliefs and racist ideology that form necessary and sufficient conditions for *racism*. So, for example, we might say that for something to be racist it must rely upon:

1. a belief in the reality of *races*
2. a belief in the superiority of one racial group over another.

Certain behaviours might follow from this that we would be inclined to call racist behaviours, but what makes them racist is that they emerge from these beliefs. Condition 1 is quite self-explanatory – it simply demands that we take the existence of *races* seriously. Condition 2 is also quite straight-forward, but we can see that this is the more *ideological* component of the account since it is in the detail of this condition that we see the account of superiority and inferiority drawn out. Ordinarily it involves the kind of ideas that we noted in Chapter 1 about the natural moral character of particular *races* and how these things enable us to form *races* into hier-archies. For instance, assumptions about the inferior mental capacities of black people, or the honesty of Asians and so on, mean we can rank *races* in such a way that white *races* are ordinarily seen as superior, more worthy, more suited to government and rule, and as having a greater right to access resources.

It should be obvious that while each of these conditions, considered on their own, is necessary on this account, considered on their own, they are not sufficient. If we do not believe in *races*, we cannot believe one to be superior to the other, and if we do not believe one *race* to be superior to the other, we are merely someone who believes in *races*. Taken together, though, we have jointly necessary and sufficient conditions for *racism* – that is, we have identified conditions which must hold for *racism* to exist and, once they are in place, nothing more is needed for *racism* to exist. So, something is racist if it relies on the belief that there are *races* and that one *race* is superior to another.

From this picture, which places belief front and centre in defining *racism*, we can easily see how the assumed wrongness of *racism* is explained. What makes *racism* wrong is that, as we have spent some time showing in this book, the beliefs are false. The notion that there are *races* – at least groupings that are something like those that our ordinary thought and talk demands – is erroneous. Consequently, the idea that one *race* is superior to another is also false. As we have noted before, it is incumbent upon us to make sure our beliefs accord with the way the world is. If we take false beliefs into the world and act upon them to the detriment of others, we are acting in a morally unacceptable way:

> [E]pistemically speaking, one has a duty to eschew error and pursue truth. And one also has a moral duty to be epistemically responsible (in the dutiful sense). To the extent that racist beliefs are false representations of self and/or others, one's failures to at least earnestly attempt to rid them from one's belief system constitutes a failure to live up to one's epistemic and moral duty. (Corlett 2003: 68)[6]

So what are to make of this account? We can judge this account along two, not entirely separable, strands. First, we can judge it by how well it meets the philosophical ambition of providing an account of the central constitutive elements of *racism* as a concept. And, second, we judge it by how well it captures and explains the kinds of sociological and psychological elements of *racism* that we noted at the beginning of this chapter.

In terms of the philosophical ambition, there may be some obvious worries. First of all, it is unclear that beliefs – either in *races* or in the superiority of one *race* over another – are necessary for *racism*. For example, we can quite easily imagine someone who does not believe in *races*, but who nonetheless manages to perform many apparently racist behaviours. Suppose that an extreme fear of black skin, without any accompanying notion that this a supposed *race* maker, leads someone to avoid any contact with black people, to attack them if they are in a confined space together, and to be repulsed by them in all quarters. We would probably want to say that this person was racist.

Similarly, it may be controversial that belief in *races* and a racial superiority/inferiority relation is sufficient for *racism*. We can imagine someone who holds these beliefs, but who is so removed from interaction with people of other *races* that they never get to reflect much on these ideas, nor

---

6. J. Angelo Corlett is not a simple *belief/ideology* theorist about racism, and we shall mention his account shortly. However, this is a very useful summary of the supposed wrongs of racism on the belief/ideology account.

enact any kind of behaviours by virtue of them. Perhaps they have never really met anyone from another *race* at all, are impressed by Enlightenment science, and believe in the testimony of people like Blumenbach who they read fifty years ago and have had little reason to think about since. If pushed, they would likely assent to the ideas of Enlightenment racial science – "sure, those Enlightenment scientists were serious and smart, I'm sure what they say is true". In such a case we might well feel as though we are hard-pushed to call this person a racist without some additional condition. They seem naïve and unworldly rather than racist.

There are also worries about the adequacy of the account to explain what is wrong with *racism*. As we have put it above, the wrongness of *racism* is to be explained in terms of irrationality. However, behaving responsibly with regard to our beliefs is not the same as behaving correctly with regards to moral action – what is epistemically right or wrong is not automatically what is morally right and wrong. For instance, as a soldier, my commanding officer might demand of me that I do something that is immoral, but it is in my self-interest to comply. It would be rational but immoral to perform the action, or maybe irrational but moral to abstain. These are murky waters and it is not obvious that the belief account of *racism* is sailing clearly through them.

With regard to capturing the kinds of sociological and psychological phenomenon that we mentioned earlier, we can perhaps start to see a little more clearly what the problems facing this account are. For instance, consider the various levels of *racism* that we identified. The belief account clearly does well in explaining the individual level of *racism* – beliefs are something that individuals have. However, when we begin to look at the institutional and cultural level, things begin to look more strained.

At an institutional level, the first question we can raise is quite obvious – how can institutions have beliefs? We might amend the view and say that institutions such as educational or healthcare ones and so on, have central tenets or guiding principles and we can identify the beliefs of the institution with these. But of course we will seldom find anything among these principles or tenets that looks anything like a statement that there are *races*, and that some *races* are superior to others. We might amend the view and say that if the beliefs of the practitioners who function within and manage the institution are racist then the social organization, by extension will be racist too. But again, this is not obviously so. We can easily imagine an institution that contains no racist members (by the belief account) but which we would want to count as racist all the same. Our library service might be full of kind and enlightened individuals, but because, for whatever reason, it excludes, alienates and works to the detriment of people from particular *races*, it looks like a racist institution.

At the cultural level, things look even more tricky since part and parcel of the cultural level of *racism* is that it can be and sometimes is explicitly assumed to rely on the idea that people believe they are living in an age without racial essentialism – *racism* without racists. If this form of *racism* makes clear space for the denial of certain kinds of *race* belief, how can a belief/ideology account make sense of this?

When it comes to the distinctions between overt and avert *racism*, and direct and indirect *racism*, this model, again, seems to have mixed fortunes. For example, overt and direct *racism* seem adequately explained on this model – I have clear beliefs about *races*, I act upon them. Avert and indirect *racism*, however, are less obviously explained on this model since my implicit biases are often a complete surprise to me and even when confronted with the results of an Implicit Association Test (IAT) showing my avert racist tendencies, I will still refuse to avow any of the beliefs needed to count as a racist. Further, the kinds of indirect *racism* that we mentioned above – badly thought-out milk programmes and pet-companion services – may come from a desire to make people's lives better, and certainly need not include beliefs that would count as racist on this model.

This all looks quite bad for the belief/ideology account, and I think as it stands, it doesn't give us the most robust account of *racism* that we can muster. This does not mean that the complaints we have made are the final word though. We can respond to these various points by either biting bullets or adding clauses to a belief/ideology account. We might respond to the differing fortunes in capturing the sociological and psychological elements of *racism* by saying that we cannot expect to capture elusive things such as *racism* that eschews racist belief – after all, cultural *racism* is not an entirely uncontroversial category. Or we might allow a broader account of belief to play a part here: perhaps we can include something more primitive or implicit among the kind of beliefs that count,[7] or perhaps we can allow that should the belief in *races* and racial superiority be a consequence of other more "front of mind" beliefs, then this counts as *racism*. This would certainly allow us to make better sense of avert and indirect *racism* on such a view.

---

7. For example, perhaps we can include a primitive and hidden doxastic category such as Tamar Gendler's notion of alief (see Gendler 2008).

Turning to complaints about the philosophical ambition of the view, we might say that the apparent breach of our necessary condition isn't an instance of *racism* at all – I might well have no ideas about what class and class division are, but fear people who have less money than me, and so by extension engage in what looks like very prejudicial practices against the working class. Does this mean I hold class prejudices? It is not clear, in the absence of some idea about what class is, that this can make sense. Of course, if we do make the kind of allowance for avert and indirect *racism* that we just mentioned, it would be hard to make this case, but since our necessary condition would be more accommodating anyway, all would still be well since the racist case would still fall within the model.

As for the apparent breach of the sufficient condition, perhaps we do need more clauses or conditions, but these need not stray away from the model of belief. Following on from the two conditions listed on page 124, for example, how about this condition:

3.   a resistance to recalcitrant evidence for those beliefs meeting conditions 1 and 2.

Clearly, this still a belief clause – it further qualifies the beliefs we formed about *races* and racial superiority. And in the kind of case envisaged above, if someone believed in *race* and racial superiority but they did not change their beliefs when presented with falsifying evidence, then they *would* be racist.

How adequate these answers are, I will leave to discussion. But we can at least see that the belief/ideology model has work to do, and that there are some avenues for exploration.

The behavioural model of *racism*

The next account of *racism* that we shall look at treats actions and behaviours as forming the core of our definition of *racism*. Again, in its simplest form the idea is that behaviours and actions that have detrimental outcomes are to be the focus of the necessary and sufficient conditions for something to be racist. So, we might say that for something to be racist it must:

1.   be aimed towards or enacted upon people or persons *qua* members of a *race*
2.   result in the disadvantage of those people or persons *qua* members of a *race*.

We can note a few things about this. First, there will obviously be beliefs and ideological elements involved here. For example, there seems to be a requirement that we identify *races* in these behaviours, which seems to rely on a belief in *races*. However, this is not really necessary since I might not believe in *races* but merely intend my actions to pick out those people that fall under what I take to be false categories. Actions and behaviours are meant to be central here. Again, condition 1 is reasonably self explanatory, but the idea is that for a behaviour to be racist it must be directed at someone because of their *race* – if someone who happens to be black is attacked because they are black this looks racist. If they are attacked because they are the next person the attacker meets after the decision to commit assault is made, this does not look racist. Condition 2 should also be reasonably clear. If I choose to act towards you because of your *race* this might seem as though it could lead to something racist, but it depends on the behaviour involved. If I steal all your worldly possessions and make sure you have no opportunities to make your life better, this looks racist. If I bestow worldly possessions upon you and open up opportunities to you, so long as I don't do this to the detriment of others by virtue of their *race*, I don't seem to have done anything racist.

Again, because of these types of consideration, it should be obvious that these two considerations are meant to be individually necessary and jointly sufficient. If I act towards you by virtue of your *race*, this isn't racist unless my actions cause you some harm, and if I aim to cause you harm by virtue of your *race* but don't perform any action towards you, the claim to *racism* begins to look to be impotent. I have to act and have that act disadvantage you *qua* member of your *race*.

On such a view of *racism*, it becomes quite straightforward how we account for the near-universal feeling that *racism* is wrong. The wrongness of *racism* on such a view comes from the immoral nature of the actions involved. It seems as though it is wrong to go out of our way to disadvantage someone because of racial membership – we might think that it is fine to disadvantage someone from performing some immoral action of their own, such as stealing or murdering, but being a member of a *race* is clearly not like that.[8] Being a member of a *race* seems morally neutral in

---

8. Some might think, of course, that *races* have a moral dimension and the characteristic of being black, say, involves certain kinds of immorality that need counteracting and disadvantaging. This is not the kind of case we have mind here and most of the time racist behaviour is not intended to be a moral crusade as much as it is meant to be the exercising of power.

that respect and to single someone out for negative treatment because of their *race* seems no more acceptable than to single someone out for negative treatment because they are female, or a science student, or six foot tall. In some respects, the wrongness of *racism* on a behavioural account is explained far more naturally than on a belief/ideology account. On the former view we can tap more or less directly into standard accounts of morality and questions of what makes an action right or wrong. On the latter view we have to rely on mapping epistemic right and wrong on to moral right and wrong, and as we noted, this is not so straightforward.

Again, trying to assess just how strong such an account is requires that we judge the view along two dimensions. First, how well does it meet the philosophical ambition of providing an account of the central, constitutive elements of *racism*? And second, how well does it capture the kinds of sociological and psychological phenomenon that we examined at the beginning of the chapter?

In terms of necessary and sufficient conditions, again, there seem to be some possible worries. The clearest worry is that conditions 1 and 2 may not really be necessary for *racism*. We can easily imagine someone who expresses the most contemptible and bile-ridden racist beliefs imaginable. And we can have no doubt that given half a chance to harm someone of a different *race*, this despicable individual would do it. However, we are able to find some relief from the fact that this person is so isolated from multiracial society that they never have, and are never likely to get a chance to enact any racist behaviour. Are they racist? You bet they are. Similarly, imagine someone who was white and who acted only towards members of their own *race*, but who did not intend to disadvantage these people, only to provide considerable advantage and opportunity. We might even imagine that for some reason or other this conferring of advantage upon members of the white *race* does not disadvantage members of other *races*. Is this person whose actions disadvantage no one a racist? I think many of us would believe they are.

In terms of the sufficiency of these conditions, there may also be problems. For example, suppose that we run a school for black students with an intensive and highly supportive educational programme. Our aim is to admit only children from that particular background and to counteract some of the poor educational opportunities that black children have. Our programme has been quite a success in helping our students into college and has drawn some ire from the media and even white supremacist groups. Suppose that as a publicity stunt a white supremacist family sends us an application form. We turn the white child away, exactly as the applicants intended, on the grounds that he is white and falls outside the intended recipients of our programme. Let us suppose that being turned away from this school does disadvantage the white student; he would have benefited from the education (and chance to go to college) and might even have had his view of the world significantly improved by being in an environment where he gets to meet smart and motivated black people. By the behavioural account we have acted towards someone in respect of their *race* and they have been disadvantaged as a result. Is this really racist? Some would argue that it is an instance of "reverse discrimination". Here though, I think we can perhaps concede that this is not a racist act. For us to say that this is racist, we would perhaps want there to be something else going on – such as, the *intent* of creating harm. But at that point, we are going beyond behaviours and looking at the mental states of the protagonists involved. More to the point though, we are going beyond the conditions we have in place, suggesting that this is not sufficient to account for *racism*.

What about capturing the sociological and psychological elements of *racism*? How well does the behavioural model do here? First of all, the behavioural model captures some levels of *racism* reasonably well in as much as we can see behavioural elements of *racism* there. For instance, individual behaviours and institutional behaviours can easily be directed at particular *races* with negative outcomes. An individual business owner may act to exclude people of particular *races* and deprive them of service and access; a university can set up exclusionary policies and deprive people of particular *races* of educational opportunities. However, we might sometimes feel as though this is not adequate to capture much individual and institutional *racism*. Individuals can behave in a manner as egalitarian as we might hope, but do so for fear of punishment and resent each non-racist behaviour they perform. They might quite obviously seethe with racist anger and belief. We still think they are racist. Similarly, an institution can have no overtly racist policies or outcomes, but be so filled with racist individuals that members of certain *races* simply don't feel as though they can flourish in that institution. We would want to say that such institutions have an issue with *race*, despite what look like non-racist behaviours.

At a cultural level, however, the behavioural model really does seem to struggle. Again, it seems as though it is possible to take up actions that count as cultural *racism* without targeting anyone at all by virtue of their *race*. I can easily assume that the reason black boys do less well in school is because contemporary self-image in black culture promotes machismo and anti-authoritarianism – black boys don't want to listen to anyone, let alone the predominantly white female teachers they find in primary schools. I don't even have to assume *races* to be anything over and above non fixed malleable cultures. I don't have to want this state of things to exist; however, I may also think that because it's a question of culture, it is up to black folks to fix it – I can't go around telling people how to change their cultures, that's paternalistic and imperial! This is typical cultural *racism*, but it is hard to make it fit the behavioural model neatly as we have stated it so far.

As for the distinctions between different types of *racism*, the behavioural model might give an intuitive explanation of overt and avert *racism*. The idea is that what makes us racist is as not a matter of what we believe, but of what we do. And whether I am explicitly negative in my actions towards black people, or whether some implicit bias guides my behaviour, the result is the same – I perform certain detrimental actions towards people *qua* members of a particular *race*. This seems to be a benefit of treating racism as a matter of behaviour. Of course, we might worry that this looks too simple – we do think there is a distinction there after all, and to make overt and avert *racism* look the same on a behavioural model seems to glide over the differences, and perhaps worse, makes it harder to get a sense of how the two might differ morally. What we mean here is this: overt *racism* is just that, overt and unabashed. Avert *racism* is hidden, something we are not always aware of and something which we seem to have no immediate control over. At first blush we might well want to say that the overt racist is more morally questionable than the avert racist. Treating both as though they are the same seems to rob of us the ability to say this.

In terms of the distinction between direct and indirect *racism*, the behavioural model does less well. Direct *racism*, for instance might well be explainable in behavioural terms – actions are taken directly towards someone with their *race* in mind. However, indirect *racism*, as the examples we mentioned show, does not have the racial status of those people who are excluded or who suffer negative effects in mind. It is by targeting actions on some other feature of a person – as an underprivileged child, or as a lonely pensioner – that we inadvertently affect them along a racial dimension. The behavioural account doesn't offer any obvious scope for explaining why this is racist.

Just as with the belief model, this might look damning, but the behavioural account might engage in various forms of bullet biting or the introduction of new clauses to deal with these worries. For instance, just as the belief/ideology theorist can state that we should not expect to capture everything with this account of the constitutive core of *racism*, and that some of the elements we mention – cultural *racism*, for example – are controversial, the behavioural theorist can do the same. Similarly with the worry about overt and avert *racism*: if the detrimental effects of these two kinds of *racism* are the same – and this is what the behavioural model captures – then perhaps we *should* treat them as equally morally questionable. It may well be that our sense that there is a difference is just misplaced. And with the question of direct and indirect *racism*, perhaps we need to make our account of what it means to act or behave more sophisticated so that we include a failure to act or behave – after all, it is by failing to take account of the racial dimensions of a person that indirect *racism* seems to occur.

With regard to the apparent failures of necessary and sufficient conditions, perhaps we might include not just actual acting, but the disposition to act, and not merely the disadvantaging of others, but also the promotion or compounding of inequality, and so on. There are various risks involved in this bending of necessary and sufficient conditions of course. For instance, if we do include a mere disposition to act, then given the finding of implicit bias tests such as the IAT, almost everyone is a racist. Indeed, given some of the results show that black people respond negatively to black faces even if they don't realize it and are thus predisposed to act on that fear – to be more cautious of black strangers than white strangers and so on – even black people are racists towards black people.[9] This looks as though it will need careful handling if it is not to make *racism* too ubiquitous to be plausible – there is probably more *racism* around than most people would like to think, but perhaps not as much as that.

There are plenty of other things we can consider about these possibilities and their effectiveness – the kind of avenues the behavioural model could pursue, and so on. However, we shall not pursue them further here. This much, though, is clear: there is much for any behavioural theorist to concern themselves with if they are to make this particular model workable and answerable to both our philosophical and empirical ambitions.

---

9. For example, Lieberman shows that even black people have a fear response to black faces and are likely to behave accordingly (Lieberman *et al.* 2005). Having this automatic response looks as though it will predispose everyone to act towards all black people as though they are a threat. This is clearly going to have detrimental effect on black people.

The affective model of *racism*

The final account of *racism* that we shall look at treats the feeling or motivation that lies behind a particular belief or action as forming the core of our definition of *racism*. In particular, the idea is that the presence of negative feeling or malevolent motivations gives us the basis of necessary and sufficient conditions for *racism*. So, for example, we can say that something is racist if, and only if:

1. it is motivated by malevolence, or a desire to see a negative outcome for people of a particular *race*
2. that malevolence or negativity is targeted towards people because of their *race*.

The obvious point here is that there may be certain behaviours and certain beliefs that we want to call racist, or which we think of as obvious instances of *racism*, but what makes them *racism* is that they stem from ill will directed towards *race*. Or in the words of J. L. A. Garcia, one of the main proponents of this type of account, *racism* is a matter of looking into the *heart* of the racist individual and finding "hatred and ill-will directed against a person or persons on account of their assigned race" (Garcia 1996: 7). And as before, we can see how these two conditions work together. I can harbour ill will or hatred towards someone of a particular *race*, and this can manifest itself in terms of beliefs and actions; that is, I can meet condition 1. However, if I harbour this ill will for reasons other than *race* – because this person has personal habits that I find repellent for instance – I cannot count as racist. If, however, I harbour such malevolent feelings and negative intent towards someone because of their *race* (that is, I meet condition 2), then I am a racist.

The immorality of *racism* on this model is explained by the immorality of the kind of negative and malevolent feelings that form the core of the racist ill will. In particular, feelings of hatred are immoral if they are harboured against others for non-moral reasons, because they are opposed to the kinds of good will feelings that we value.[10] Similarly, negative intent and the desire to see people of a particular *race* disadvantaged is immoral because it is opposed to such important moral principles as justice and

---

10. This is the view of J. L. A. Garcia (see, for example, Garcia 1996, 1997 and 1999), who sees racism as malevolence and its immorality coming from its opposition to benevolence.

equality.[11] Again, as with the behavioural model, this account of what makes *racism* moral or immoral looks more satisfying than the belief/ideology account in so far as it seems to tap directly into our accounts of ethics rather than requiring that we map epistemology onto morality. However, we can still see how the account of morality behind such a view seems subtly different to that behind the behavioural account. So, for example, the behavioural account looks as though it connects more directly to accounts which focus on what makes an action right or wrong, whereas the affective account seems to connect more directly to accounts which focus on the moral virtues and vices or moral agent. Not that this means these accounts necessarily require or presuppose particular accounts of morality, just that we can see how they connect more directly to our ethical theories.

As with the belief and behavioural models, trying to assess just how strong this account is requires that we judge the view by how well it meets the philosophical ambition of providing an account of the central, constitutive elements of *racism*. Further, we are interested in how well it captures the kind of empirical facts and distinctions that we drew from sociological and psychological views of *racism*.

Again, we can raise the same type of worries about this account giving necessary and sufficient conditions for *racism* as we have done for the others we have looked at. With regard to condition 1 for instance, is it really the case that we cannot have *racism* without malevolence? It seems quite intuitive that a person who harbours no ill will towards people of a particular *race* might nonetheless have racist beliefs, or perform racist actions, or be considered by others to be a racist. It is quite conceivable that one can be motivated by a desire to help people of a particular *race* whom one believes to be intellectually and morally deficient by virtue of their *race*, and for one's actions to turn out horribly disadvantageous to the people in question. The beliefs, the actions, and even the person appear to be racist.[12]

Similarly, we can imagine instances where ill will is felt towards people of a certain *race* by virtue of their *race*, but no clear racist belief or action occurs, and we would not feel inclined to call the person a racist. Suppose that I have a deep-seated fear and revulsion towards people of a particular

---

11. This view is most closely related to the views of W. Thomas Schmid (Schmid 1996), who sees racism as motivated by the desire to dominate through unequal consideration based on race.

12. There are many instances that we would most probably call racism that do not seem to involve negative intent or ill will. A preference for one's own race, indifference towards the race of others, and so on all seem to lead to racist beliefs and actions that lack the ill will that the affective model suggests.

race. This could be due to some indoctrination early in my life that I have long since forgotten. Nonetheless, if you were to perform tests for implicit bias, or scan my brain when I see pictures of people of this *race*, you would see revulsion and fear. However, I express nothing but genuine heart-felt admiration for people of this *race* when you engage me in conversation, and although I seldom get to direct behaviours towards people of this *race*, when I do my actions show nothing but benevolence. You might say I have a racist heart but a well-developed ability to keep it in check and to balance out its effects on my beliefs and actions. Am I a racist? If I am, it is not in a very simple or obvious way. Now it may turn out that the affective model doesn't necessarily count me as racist either, but we'll say more on this shortly.

How does this account fare with regard to the empirical considerations we introduced at the beginning of the chapter? To begin with, the account can perhaps capture some interesting elements of individual and institutional *racism*. For example, many of the worries that we had with regard to the belief and behavioural models was that we can envisage instances where people have no explicit beliefs or, given a lack of racial contact, no need to reflect upon them. Similarly, people may not get a chance to act negatively towards people of other *races* because of low contact or racial isolation. However, such circumstances make no difference on an affective account since the ill will that grounds such beliefs and actions is what is at issue rather the presence of the beliefs or actions themselves. If an individual hates a particular *race*, but has very few beliefs about *races*, and never gets to act, they are still racist.

Interestingly, there are similar explanatory benefits to the affective account when it comes to institutional level *racism* too. If an institution is grounded on a racially malevolent mission, then it results in institutional *racism*. Jim Crow laws and South African apartheid laws, for instance, stem from negative racial intent – to see one *race* deprived of the privileges afforded another *race*. However, we also have an interesting way of explaining why certain kinds of institution are not racist despite their focus on *race*. Recall, for example, the black school and educational programme that we imagined when talking of the behavioural model. We wanted to say there that such a school was not racist even though it denied access to white children and disadvantaged them as a result. On the affective account we can capture this intuition by noting that the school is founded on benevolent feelings and a desire to increase justice and equality, not on a hatred for white people and a desire to see negative results for them.

What is more, we can explain the assumption by some that the school is racist as a misunderstanding of the motivation behind such programmes – they see the motivation as a desire to promote the needs of black people by "doing down" white people; that is, as there being some negative racial intent involved. But of course, there isn't, so such institutions are not racist, and we can make sense of this on the affective model.

As for cultural *racism*, again there may be some improvement on the behavioural and belief models. The reason for this is that cultural *racism* is often characterized by a lack of commitment to *races* as part of the explanation of *racism* – cultural attitudes tend to be invoked instead. Further, there is often a refusal to think that any kind of action or behaviour is necessary – the assumption is that problems of racial inequality tend to arise because of problems with the cultural attitudes of particular *races*, so it is up to them to alter their cultural practices. For example, there is a widespread assumption that Indians, Pakistanis and Bangladeshis in the UK have lots of problems associated with ghettoism, but that part of the culture in such communities is to be isolationist – until *they* change this and integrate, the problems will persist.[13] Since the affective model of *racism* does not require explicit beliefs about *races* – indeed, there can be affective *racism* even with a steadfast commitment to the falsity of *races* (Garcia 1996: 7) – we can see how cultural *racism* might be explained on this model. There may still be some worries though.

Many people use cultural *racism* as a way to talk about *race* and even to justify racial inequality without taking on the mantle or label of racist. They do this because they quite clearly do not think this a desirable thing to be, nor do they want to be considered racist. A well-known marker of cultural *racism* is the phrase "I am not a racist, but ...". For example,

> Well, I'm gonna be, you understand, I'm not prejudice or racial or whatever. They're always given the smut jobs because they would do it. Then they stopped, they stopped doing [those jobs]. The welfare system got to be very, very easy. Why work if the government's gonna take care of you?
>
> (Sixty-year-old white American female quoted in Bonilla-Silva 2003)

---

13. Of course, matters are far more complex than this: there is refusal to acknowledge the problem of "white flight" on the one hand, and a refusal to see just how culturally mixed most Asian communities in the UK are on the other. For interesting work on this see Simpson (2004).

Here we see the view that black welfare dependence is widespread and due to black people's willingness to take handouts. This, I think, is racist. But the tentative prefix and disassociation with *racism* tells against viewing this as a piece of racial malevolence. And in this respect, cultural *racism* and affective accounts look to be at odds.

With regard to the various distinctions between different types of *racism* that we noted, we can again see that the affective account might explain overt and direct *racism* quite well – these kinds of *racism* do seem to come from a kind of racist ill will and a desire to dominate or keep in place particular kinds of *race*-related inequalities. However, the explanations of avert and indirect *racism* look more stretched. The kinds of implicit bias that lead to avert *racism* may well be characterized in terms of certain emotions – for instance, the increased amygdala activity when seeing black faces might well indicate fear or hatred – but this does not seem to be the kind of *felt* ill will or negative intent that is needed for *racism*. And in terms of indirect *racism*, we often do not have people's *race* in mind, let alone ill will towards it, when we devise programmes or perform actions that lead to this kind of indirect *racism*.

Again, the affective theorist can counteract some of these worries by biting bullets or amending the necessary and sufficient conditions accordingly. For example, the affective theorist might maintain that their account gives us the chance to recognize further subtleties within concepts such as indirect *racism* – we might think that some of the instances of indirect *racism* are not really racist because the negative impacts on *races* simply could not be foreseen, whereas others are racist because a little regard for the needs of another *race* could easily have forestalled the inequity. If we can characterize this difference in terms of will – in the former no amount of good will could have made a difference, in the latter a blatant disregard for racial difference might well count as ill will – then we have acquired an explanatory subtlety through the affective account that we did not have previously. Similarly, with cultural *racism*, much will depend on just how we define malevolence or ill will or negative intent. If we treat the situation with *racism* to be such that a lack of positive intent is enough to count as having negative intent, then we can explain much cultural *racism* as what we might call racial indifference. However, seeing whatever is not part of the solution as part of the problem may well characterize many more actions, beliefs and people as racist than we would otherwise want.

As for the worries about necessary and sufficient conditions, we might maintain that for an individual or institution to be racist this racial ill will or negative intent has to be effective. After all, the case that we mentioned earlier against the sufficiency of the two conditions of an affective account simply had the racist heart making no impact on belief or behaviour. It seems that we are on safe ground if we maintain that a difference that makes no difference is really no difference at all – the racial ill will must have an effect somewhere if there is to be *racism*. But this may well lead us to question just where our intuitions about when there is and is not *racism* come from – after all, in this case we seem to have to introduce beliefs and behaviours to define *racism*, and at the same time we frequently seem to think that *racism* can exist without ill will.

We have presented a fairly simple form of the affective account here, and just as with the belief/ideology and behavioural models, there are more or less sophisticated versions of it. What these various considerations show is not that this account is deeply flawed, but that there are plenty of issues to negotiate and pre-theoretical intuitions to navigate, and much empirical work to accommodate. Whatever emendations or arguments are made, the affective theorist is unlikely to satisfy all the considerations, but the task confronting this account is to find ways to set aside some issues and embrace or resolve others.

WHERE NOW?

Looking at these three accounts of *racism* we can see that there are problems. In the broad terms in which we have examined them, all fail to meet the philosophical ambitions behind giving a philosophical account of *racism* in some way. The belief account seems inadequate for capturing instances of *racism* where belief is absent yet clearly racist behaviour is present. Similarly, the behavioural account seems inadequate for capturing instances of *racism* where belief and intent are present yet action is absent. And the affective account seems inadequate for capturing cases where benevolent but racist beliefs and behaviours are present. What's more, all fail to adequately explain the empirical facts that we were interested in – all can capture some dimension of overt and direct *racism*, and individual and institutional *racism*, but avert and indirect *racism* look problematic, especially for the belief and affective accounts. And cultural *racism*, which is increasingly identified as the most prevalent form of *racism*, troubles all accounts. What, then, as philosophers of *race*, are we to do here?

With regard to the empirical data we could simply abandon any concern to capture or accord with what the psychologists and sociologists are saying. Indeed, there are some complaints that too many philosophers of *race* have already done this, and that therein lie many of the problems we face in giving philosophical accounts.[14] But it is not clear that is a good strategy:

> [P]sychology can fuel new arguments relevant to the debates about the nature and moral significance of racism. … When some philosophical arguments rely on claims about the racist mind, psychology can keep our unreliable folk understanding of the mind in check. It can also reveal new, non-obvious features of the racist mind that are relevant for these arguments. … [L]imiting oneself to a mundane understanding of the racist mind in effect means depriving oneself of original insights and arguments about the nature and moral significance of racism.
> (Faucher and Machery 2009: 60)

Another option is to rethink, or be clearer about, just what our philosophical ambitions are in giving an account of *racism*. So far we have suggested that we want to give an account that gives necessary and sufficient conditions, but why? Do we intend these conditions to be wholly descriptive of either our pre-theoretical intuitions or empirical accounts of what *racism* is? In which case, our theories live and die by how well they capture these facts. If, however, we intend our accounts to have some prescriptive intent too, then we have room for manoeuvre regarding fit with intuitions and empirical accounts.

Similarly, we might question whether we are being too ambitious in wanting to give a unified account of *racism* at all. Perhaps the problem that besets us with these accounts is that they are trying to explain a complex, changing and multifaceted phenomenon – it should be of no surprise, then, that these accounts fail to capture all aspects of such a chimeric beast as *racism*. While this means we might stop trying to provide a unified account and partition our accounts to explain different elements of *racism*, I think it is worth noting that the three accounts we have looked at are not the only philosophical theories of *racism* that we could develop. Indeed there are

---

14. For example, Faucher and Machery (2009: 41) note that "with very few exceptions … philosophers have not expressed much interest in what psychology reveals about the way we think about race or about the phenomenon of racism".

other extant philosophical theories of *racism* that do not fit neatly into the categories we have examined here, but which can be pressed into giving us a unified account of *racism*. To close out this chapter, then, we shall gesture at two broad strategies for giving a different account of *racism*.

The first strategy is to note that while none of the belief, behavioural or affective models of *racism* do everything we might hope for, between them they seem to get most things right. Perhaps, then, we should try to develop "hybrid" accounts. And this seems as though it could be a useful strategy. However, it is worth sounding a word of caution about how such a strategy might play out.

Consider, for example, the *cognitive-behavioural* account of J. Angelo Corlett. Corlett maintains that we should combine some cognitive element, such as a belief in *races* and racial hierarchy, with a behavioural element such as an act, an omission or an attempt based on one's racial belief. He calls these two elements *ethnic prejudice* and *ethnic discrimination* respectively, and thinks the two are necessary and sufficient for *racism* (Corlett 2003: 65–6). There are obviously further details, but an obvious worry we might have about such an account is that it seems to be restricting and makes *racism* rarer than it might seem to be – if something has to involve a belief *and* a behaviour to be racist, then fewer things will count as racist than if it merely required a belief, or if it merely required a behaviour.[15] And of course, the more elements we add, the more restrictive the definition becomes. Moreover, some elements of *racism* were not satisfactorily captured by any of the three accounts – cultural *racism* and avert *racism* – and it is hard to see that combining the elements into a hybrid account would automatically help here.

A second strategy is to look deeper and see if there is something more basic that both unifies the various accounts we have mentioned and captures more of the phenomenon of *racism* than we have previously been able to. The kinds of accounts that we see here are Paul Taylor's view of *racism as disregard* (Taylor 2004a), and Joshua Glasgow's account of *racism as disrespect* (Glasgow 2009b). The important thing about these views is that disrespect or disregard are not judged in terms of the felt attitude, but

---

15. Intriguingly, it turns out that Corlett sees *ethnic prejudice* in such a way that racism turns out to be so ubiquitous as to be inescapable. *Ethnic prejudice* so invades our lives and thinking that all ordinary thinkers at some point engage with it. Given the ubiquity of *ethnic prejudice*, we cannot but engage in *ethnic discrimination*. While Corlett might not worry about this, it seems to be a counterintuitive result. For greater discussion on this, see Mills (2005).

can instead be applied to behaviours, beliefs or attitudes.[16] The key definitional point of such accounts is that we can treat something as being racist if, and only if, it is disrespectful towards or disregarding of people of a certain *race qua* members of that racial group. We won't go into the many finer details of these views, but we can see how a belief, a behaviour, some attitude or intent, a person, an institution, a cultural stance, and so on can be disregarding and/or disrespecting. Or how an instance of disregard or disrespect can be direct or indirect, or overt or avert. Take the examples of indirect *racism* and cultural *racism*. A social welfare programme that fails to take account the racial elements of its intended recipients seems to be a clear case of disregard or disrespect – I simply have not taken the needs of certain people *qua* racial group into account. Similarly with cultural *racism*, an explanation of racial inequality in terms of cultural attitudes might rest on thin racial beliefs (or an outright denial of the reality of *race*), show no explicitly racialized behaviours, and manifest no overtly negative or hateful attitudes. Nonetheless, cultural *racism* is premised on an outright disregard for the impact of *race* thought and talk and can easily be seen as disrespectful towards members of a racial group considered as members of that racial group – it grossly underestimates the impact of *race* on ordinary lives.

Again, there may be problems capturing some elements or nuances of the phenomena but we are less interested in those here than we are in the fact that such accounts point the way towards giving a unified account of *racism* without positing beliefs, behaviours or attitudes as the basis of *racism*.

CONCLUSION

In this chapter, then, we have looked at a range of interesting empirical facts about *racism* as we find it in contemporary society. In particular we drew on work by sociologists and psychologists and drew out distinctions between direct and indirect *racism* and overt and avert *racism*, and identified three social levels at which one might find *racism* – the individual, the institutional and the cultural. We then examined three distinctly

16. See Glasgow (2009b: 82–3) for the important details of what he calls *deattitudinalized* notions of disrespect and disregard.

philosophical accounts of *racism*, all of which attempt to give necessary and sufficient conditions for *racism* in terms of belief, behaviour, or affective states such as malevolence or negative intent. We saw that none of those accounts seemed to meet either its philosophical ambition of providing necessary and sufficient conditions, or our wish to capture the empirical facts. Finally, we looked briefly at some alternatives to these approaches including the possibility of pursuing accounts of *racism* in terms of *disregard* and *disrespect*.

In our next chapter we shall look at some social issues and programmes that, in a variety of ways, draw on our concerns about the injustices and inequalities that arise from *racism*. In particular, we will examine areas where it seems we might have a practical reason for using *race*, but where concerns of *racism* seem to tell against this.

CHAPTER FIVE

The everyday impact of
race and *racism*

Throughout this book we have been concerned with lots of what we might call "definitional questions" about *race* and *racism*. That is, we've tried to get clear about just what *race* and *racism* are. Something else that we have frequently mentioned, right from the beginning of the book, is that the notion of *race* and the practice of *racism* have a remarkable impact on our day-to-day lives. In this chapter, we shall spend some time looking at philosophical contributions to a debate that takes place along the fault line between these two areas – that is, we will now turn our attention to the interaction of questions of *race* and *racism* with questions of social policy. In particular, we are interested in seeing just what it is that philosophy can bring to such concerns.

Intriguingly, there are very many areas where the interaction of our ideas about *race* and *racism* on the one hand, and their impact on our daily lives on the other can lead to deep and interesting philosophical inquiry. Consider, for instance, the following examples.

We have quite strong feelings of moral censure against certain racist words and terms. In the UK, it is acceptable for you to call me a "Romany Gypsy", or "traveller", and in some instances, "gypsy". However, it is morally unacceptable for you to call me a "pikey" or "gypo". In the USA it is acceptable, for the most part, to call black people "black" or "African-Americans", but there are very many unacceptable racial terms and slurs. But what is it that makes these unacceptable terms wrong? Is it simply because they are racist? We can easily imagine uses of "traveller" and "black" that are racist, but this doesn't seem to make those terms wrong in and of themselves.

And do our accounts of *racism* enable us to make sense of this? Perhaps it is because there is some semantic peculiarity about the pejorative term. Yet both pejorative and non-pejorative terms refer, putatively at least, to the same things. Perhaps it is because of power relations – what really makes a difference here has less to do with word meanings, and more to do with the power imbalances that some uses of these words illustrate. And we can ask many more such questions (see, for example, Himma 2002, and Anderson and Lepore in press).

In a similar vein, we have lots of beliefs about what we might call *procreative and parental liberty* when dealing with reproduction and parenthood – we think that, in principle, parents have choices about when to have their children and how to raise them. I might want to have children before I'm thirty-five or to have two children with a specific interval between them, or I might want to raise them as vegans or Christians, and so on. In some respects, we extend some of this choice to medically assisted conception too. Nonetheless, we are often unsure why or how *race* and *racism* should impact upon these kinds of decision. For example, an infertile black woman in Italy in the early 1990s was given medical assistance to conceive and give birth to a white child. Around the same time, a clinic in the UK turned down requests from a Pakistani family to have a blonde-haired, blue-eyed daughter with fair skin.[1] Both families' requests were based on ideas about the likely future experiences of their children given their *races* – whiter and lighter would make for easier and better lives. These parents' intentions are to act to protect their children from *racism*, and they are acknowledging the racial and racist facts of the world in which they live. But they also seem, in turn, to be compounding that *racism*. Exactly what should medical professionals do in these circumstances? And how should they reach their decisions? The ethical and legal implications of being able to select the *race* of our offspring are deeply interesting, and made even more so when we introduce factors about the reality of *race*.[2]

Very close to questions about the interaction of *race* and the ethics of reproductive science and medically assisted conception are questions such as organ donation. Put simply, what should medical practitioners do if offered organ donations but with what seem to be racist provisos?

---

1. See Willan and Hawkes (1993) for a report on both of these cases.
2. For discussion on this, see, for instance, Berkowitz and Snyder (1998).

Suppose I assert that you may harvest my organs for donation upon my death, but only so long as they are not used for people of a particular *race*. How should a medical professional respond to that offer? Intriguingly, such cases do occur.[3] But the concern is this: if these cases are instances of *racism* – and it is interesting how our accounts of *racism* might fare in explaining them – there seems to be a good ethical reason for refusing the offer. But there is a corresponding medical duty to save lives, which seems to mean there are considerations for accepting the offer. *Racism* is odious and immoral, but how does our moral stance towards it interact with other moral and ethical positions we have to take in our daily lives?[4]

Finally, consider the question of affirmative action. Although we will not consider the question of affirmative action in detail in this chapter, it is an area where philosophy, *race, racism* and questions of social policy have interacted for a long time. This has led to vast amounts of work and sometimes sprawling debates, and philosophers have been fruitful contributors for some time. Affirmative action requires certain actions from employers or government agencies to make opportunities for underrepresented groups, including racial groups. Of course, much of the detail depends on where in the world we look at such policies and programmes, but lots of philosophical questions arise on the back of such practices. Exactly what should we aim to provide for under-represented groups: equality of opportunity or equality of outcome? Are both of these philosophically interesting? Is affirmative action trying to compensate for past ills, tackle current inequalities, pave the way to a more equal future, or what? The answers will affect the strength of the arguments for and against affirmative action. And there are many other arguments that arise here too.[5]

There are very many more areas where *race*, daily life and social policy interact in philosophically interesting ways, but in the rest of this chapter we shall concern ourselves with an extended examination of just one: racial profiling, and particularly criminal racial profiling. There are a couple of reasons for tackling this topic.

---

3. A British Department of Health investigation into conditional organ donation in 2000 reports on just such a case from the late 1990s.
4. For more on the moral questions around racist organ donation see, for example, Wilkinson (2007).
5. I mention instructive literature on affirmative action in the further reading section for this chapter, although it is worth noting that the philosophical work on affirmative action and positive discrimination is really very large.

One consideration is that racial profiling is, as the name suggests, crucially focused on issues of *race* and *racism*. Questions of racial language can be seen as a special case of broader pejorative language; questions of *race* and reproductive science or organ donation can be seen as special cases within broader bio-medical ethics; even affirmative action for *races* is entangled in broader questions of affirmative action for underrepresented groups. We are interested in seeing how philosophers can contribute to these debates, but we are *especially* interested in seeing what a philosopher armed with some of the insights we have drawn during the course of this book might contribute. As such, the more we can keep our topic exclusively about *race*, the better.

Another consideration is that, quite understandably, racial profiling raises very strong opinions among philosophers and non-philosophers alike. If I am of a particular *race*, then being subjected to certain treatments in view of that can have many effects on my day-to-day life, and the strength of my opinions about the practice will reflect this. Similarly, some see a refusal to use racial profiling to reduce crime, for example, as weak-willed and stemming from a fear of being labelled racist. Since there are such strong opinions and intuitive reactions to the question of racial profiling, bringing philosophical insight to bear can hopefully show just how much philosophy has to contribute.

Finally, a practical consideration: there are some areas where a little reflection tells us that philosophy and philosophers have much to contribute. Racial profiling is one, and affirmative action is another. However, given our concerns in this chapter – to illustrate just what philosophers with a well worked out understanding of *race* and *racism* can bring to such debates – we would do well to keep to a manageable topic. Affirmative action is too big a topic for our needs here, and in many ways it has run its philosophical course in terms of making tangible contributions to policy-makers. Racial profiling on the other hand is different.

As J. Angelo Corlett notes, "Philosophers have devoted relatively little attention to the ethics of what has become known as 'racial profiling' in criminal justice contexts" (Corlett 2011: 21). What this means is that the topic is both manageable enough to allow us to meet the aims of our chapter, and the debate is at a stage where philosophers can still make contributions that are clear enough to be heard above the political din. As philosophers, it seems that we can still bring something important to the table on matters that have a deep impact and are hugely important for how people live their lives.

RACIAL PROFILING

The notion of profiling is actually a rather simple one. We use information about groups and put it to particular ends. For instance, in contemporary Western society, advertisers know that men are more likely to watch TV programmes with particular kinds of content. Armed with this information, the advertiser can place information about products they want to market to men around particular programmes. Government agencies and policy-makers can use similar profiling strategies. For example, airport, customs and border control officials can use particular facts about passengers, including their nationality, the clothes they wear, how their ticket was purchased, what kind of group (if any) they travel with, how much luggage they carry, their travel history and their itinerary, to build profiles of likely terrorists, drug traffickers, illegal immigrants and so on. There are also similar profiling systems in place for taxation and internal revenue agencies looking for tax fraud – the features of the profile are such factors as large charitable donations or self-employment. Similarly, social welfare systems checking whether reported cases are likely to be instances of abuse use factors such as income of the family, number of siblings, and so on.

While profiling in this respect is clearly useful and may not raise too much irritation among those of us who find ourselves audited for tax or subject to some additional questions and searching at airport customs, when it comes to racial profiling matters seem to be different. Racial profiling is like the kinds of profiling we have already mentioned except that that chief marker or fact used is a person's *race*. However, *race* is often seen as a key marker or indicator of criminality, and even of the likely perpetrator of particular types of crime. So, at its most simple, when we are looking at profiling particular categories of people, most frequently criminals, welfare dependants, and threats to our safety, we can and often do use *race*.

Racial profiling begins to get philosophically interesting when we note two things about our reaction to it.

First, many of us think that profiling people by using *race* is straightforwardly and obviously wrong. The reason for this is quite simply that many of the instances that first spring to mind when we talk of racial profiling are obviously bad. For instance, it is often done unofficially by shopkeepers who monitor customers of a particular *race* to the point of harassment, or by teachers who see pupils of a certain *race* as destined for a life where education is of no use and wasted. And even when it is done within the auspices of official institutions and policy, such as criminal profiling by police officers, we worry that is misapplied and over-zealous. All of this smacks of *racism*, both individual and institutional, overt and avert, and we are all agreed, I hope, that *racism* is not something we should accept.

Second, many of us can see the utility of profiling, and are often impressed by it. The apparent insight that serial killers are most likely to be white males with particular backgrounds and family histories is deeply interesting and, we assume, a useful tool in identifying the perpetrator of particular crimes. We also don't necessarily mind the idea that our government can save lots of money by targeting its resources in the right places, whether this is for crime, healthcare, education, defence or border control. If profiling is an appropriate tool for this, then it seems wrong of us to undermine the greater social good that this brings.

From these two facts, important philosophical questions begin to emerge. It is obvious that the kinds of racial profiling we worry about are wrong, and cannot be justified – these are instances of *racism* and we simply do not want to see a continuation of racial injustice and inequality in modern society. However, given the kinds of social benefit that profiling can arguably lead to, it seems we must also ask whether there is any kind of racial profiling that is acceptable. If we were able to frame a system of racial profiling that was not obviously bad in the ways that we might currently worry about, would this be justifiable? Or is racial profiling simply wrong by virtue of using *race* as a marker?

When we put the problem like this, the shape of the philosophical enterprise here is quite clear. First, we need to identify what a philosophically interesting instance of racial profiling would look like – what would a viable and not obviously bad instance of racial profiling be like? And second, we need to assess whether this kind of racial profiling is justifiable or not. Let us begin with the first task.

Philosophically interesting racial profiling

By suggesting that we need a philosophically interesting account of racial profiling, what we mean is that the obviously bad cases of racial profiling – cases where we can quite clearly see *racism* at play – do little to capture our attention here. They are clearly wrong and no attempt to justify them will get past our intuitive objections to them. However, should there be cases that lack the features that make these instances obviously bad, then we might be able to set aside our worries about the racial aspects of the practice and reap some of the social benefits that profiling seems to offer. But what would an interesting case of racial profiling look like?

We can begin to see what an interesting instance of racial profiling would look like by noting just what it is about the obviously bad cases that make us so uneasy. While we will be able to point to many things that leave us troubled by such cases, there are three features that loom large, which we shall focus on here.

The first feature of bad cases that makes them troubling is that the tool used to connect a particular characteristic with a particular profile often seems to be suspect or inappropriate in some way. What we mean here is that in any practice of profiling, a particular tool is used to connect some characteristic with some profile. For example, statistical analyses and the experience of forensic accountants connect the characteristic of making large charitable donations with tax evasion. However, in instances of racial profiling we are often concerned that the tools used are wrong or mislead-ing. Take, for instance, the case of a shopkeeper who follows black custom-ers around his store, treating them with suspicion and making them feel uncomfortable. Here the shopkeeper is using a kind of unofficial racial pro-filing based on some stereotype that black people are thieves and criminals. Here our worry (among many things that might concern us) is that stereo-types are a terrible basis upon which to generalize from the characteristic of being black to the characteristic of being a criminal. We use stereotypes all the time, of course, but we know they are deeply unreliable and probably shouldn't ground such divisive and invasive practices.

We can take this insight further and apply it to those official cases that concern us too. For example, in the late 1960s through the 1980s and beyond in Britain, a weak correlation was noted between mugging crimes and young black men, especially in London. What was not clear was how much this was due to unofficial targeting of black men by the police, or to media reporting, and so on. However, official crime statistics showed that there was no major *race*-specific crime wave to be concerned about, and Britain should be no more concerned with the nature of this correlation than with the correlation between white males and bank fraud. Nonetheless, British governments enacted a series of policies that focused enforcement on black people and on black communities, all of which was done with the putative aim of reducing crime and making dangerous areas safe.[6]

---

6. For a detailed breakdown of this state of affairs and its various racial and racist implications, see Hall *et al.* (1978).

This kind of case, and this period in modern British police practices more than any other, is rife with the kinds of racial profiling that make many so uneasy about the practice. And our concern here is that while the policy looks official – it is enacted through the auspices of government rather than randomly by individuals – it still uses the wrong tool, or perhaps uses the right tool badly, in order to connect a characteristic such as *race* to a particular profile such as being a criminal. In short, we are happier to see official use of a tool in racial profiling, and we may even be happy to see something like statistics and proper analysis, rather than a reliance on crass stereotypes functioning as the tool that connects *race* with, say, criminality. However, what we are keen to see is that the tool is used appropriately. The first feature of the bad cases that seems to drive our intuition that they are obviously wrong, then, is that either the wrong tool is used or the right tool is used badly to connect a particular characteristic such as *race* to a particular profile such as violent crime.

The second feature of the bad cases of racial profiling is perhaps much easier to state than our first concern, and is that we worry about the possibility of abuse. For example, imagine that statistics and respectable analysis might show that a particular racial group, R, is far more likely to drive without proper documentation. We decide, for some well-considered reason, that greater social utility is served by not having unlicensed drivers on our roads and we set up a policing practice which allows stop-and-check, targeting R in particular. If police merely stopped drivers and asked to see documentation, we might feel that the many law-abiding members of R faced an extra burden by being inconvenienced, but otherwise, all was well. If, however, the police used these stop-and-check searches to carry out lots of other unrelated inquiries – frisk searches, drug tests, DNA swabs, aggressive questioning about who owns the car, where the driver is going, where they have been, where they obtained any possessions or cash they might be carrying, and so on, we begin to feel uneasy. And the reason for this is simple; we feel that the police are now abusing the policy and by extension abusing members of R. We might tolerate the burden of a minor time inconvenience on account of our *race* if a greater social good is secured. But if this turns into unnecessarily invasive questioning and searching, people being treated as though they are criminals unless they can prove their innocence, then we think this to be an abuse of racial profiling and an abuse of people by virtue of their *race*. We simply do not want to allow for that possibility.

The further worry that we often have with racial profiling, and especially in the kinds of bad case that spring to mind for many of us when we
think of such practices, is that it is precisely this kind of abuse that occurs.
For example, Czech airport authorities and employment agencies have
previously identified which passengers and which applicants are Romany
Gypsies. The reason for doing this, officially, is standard border control and
to monitor equal employment opportunities. However, the profiling has
been used to stem and reduce migration from this group (see, for example,
Mirga 2000). This seems to go beyond the putative reasons for profiling
and looks like an abuse.

The third and final feature of bad cases of racial profiling is when it is
disproportionate, or used on a scale that it out of line with its supposed
social benefit. We can think of disproportionality in a couple of ways here,
both of which will lead us to think that racial profiling is problematic:

First of all, simple disproportional use of racial profiling which borders
on abuse is clearly problematic. Suppose that I am of a particular *race*, R,
which is profiled as driving unlicensed. On a short journey to work I am
stopped by the police, who want to check my documents. All is well and
I am allowed to go on my way. However, a few minutes later I am stopped
again by another patrol who want to see my licence. All is well and I am
allowed to go on my way. However, ... and so on. It turns out that the
majority of police attention is spent on policing this problem. Perhaps the
statistical analysis that shows the connection between being of *race* R and
committing the offence in question is very clear and police feel confident
that they can have many successes in directing their attentions in this way.
However, we can see clearly how this is an application of the policy out of
proportion with its social benefit and that as a member of R, I am being
asked to bear a burden which looks unacceptable.

Second, we can imagine that statistics show that 65 per cent of those
who perpetrate a particular crime are of *race* R^1, 25 per cent are of *race* R^2,
8 per cent are of *race* R^3 and 2 per cent of *race* R^4. However, when policing
to counteract or prevent the crime in question, the only people who are
subjected to police attention are members of R^1. Again, it looks as though
members of R^1 are being subjected to police attention in a way that is out of
proportion with what is socially beneficial, and out of proportion with the
suggested profile.

Whenever we see these kinds of disproportional treatment, we will tend
to think of racial profiling as being bad. And as it happens frequently, this is
exactly what happens where racial profiling is used. The crime prevention

policies directed at black youth in Britain from the 1970s to the 1990s, for instance, were objectionable for this very reason, among many others. Police attention was directed disproportionately towards black areas and towards abating a moral panic far out of proportion with the scale of the problem. Moreover, the targeting of black males for police attention and the negative feeling caused by heavy-handed police presence in black communities was so great that it contributed to *race*-related rioting in some of Britain's major cities during the 1980s. It is this kind of disproportionate use of racial profiling that many find troubling.

What these three features of the bad cases of racial profiling tell us then is, quite simply, that a philosophically interesting case of racial profiling will lack any or all of these three features. So, the kinds of racial profiling that we might not automatically rule out as obviously bad, and upon which we focus when we ask whether racial profiling can be justified, are of the following kind:

1. the tool used to connect *race* to a particular profile is accurate, appropriate, and used correctly
2. the use of racial profiling does not result in or include any abuse which, separate from the question of whether racial profiling is acceptable, is itself morally unjustifiable
3. the use of racial profiling is applied in proportion to broader concerns of fairness, other social benefits, and the scope of the tool we have based our profile upon.

These conditions are fairly self-explanatory, and in many ways are clearly interrelated. However, it's worth briefly emphasizing how we might see them working. For instance, condition 1 rules out tools such as stereotypes, hearsay, suspicions or "gut-feelings" and statistics and analyses that are misapplied. It does allow such things as good statistical evidence where we can clearly separate correlation and cause and where the conclusions are not allowed to out run the findings. For instance, if our statistics suggest that 75 per cent of heroin dealers are Asian, we cannot form our profile with the claim that all heroin dealers are Asian or all Asians are heroin dealers. Condition 2, again, is straightforward and we can see how it is supposed to ensure that our profiling practices are used for what they are supposed to be used for – if we are profiling for heroin traffickers we must not subject people to tests and checks for things such as tax evasion, we must not victimize and alienate those whom our policy affects beyond some appropriate initial screening or check. And condition 3 means that we must ensure that our practices do not take up more of our attention or resources or focus on particular groups in a way that outstrips the obvious social benefit. For instance, if we have a reliable tool to determine that members of R^1 make up 75 per cent of perpetrators of crime C^1 and we also know that, in terms of seriousness, C^1 detracts from the broader social good by many magnitudes less than crime C^2, then we need to make sure that our policing practices reflect that. If we pursue C^1 with greater vigour than C^2 (because we have a useful profiling tool, say), and in pursuing C^1 we focus exclusively on R^1, we are using racial profiling disproportionately.

Now that we have some sense of what a philosophically interesting case of racial profiling would look like – it uses a good tool to connect *race* to a profile, it involves no abuse and it is applied proportionately – we can ask, given the apparent social benefits of racial profiling (of this "good" kind), is it acceptable or justifiable?

The case for racial profiling

Let us suppose that we can have practices of racial profiling which meet the three conditions outlined above. Of course, we have no reason to think that this would be easy to obtain; after all we live in a racist society with many forms of *racism*. All the same, the philosophically interesting question is one where we assume that we *can* counteract these problems and purge racial profiling of any obvious *racism*. In that case, would racial profiling be acceptable?

To answer this question positively – to say that yes, this kind of racial profiling would be acceptable – we would need to establish that such a practice causes no *unacceptable* harms. What we mean here is this, if racial profiling causes harms then it should not be tolerated. This is why we think that the kinds of profiling that fail to meet the three conditions we mentioned are unacceptable – they cause harm. However, we don't think causing any harm whatsoever is enough to rule something out. For example, it is often the case that when we give children vaccinations we cause them some distress when we push the needle into their arm or leg. And there is a clear sense in which we harm them – we damage their flesh. However, we also think that the discomfort of a needle is such a minor and trifling harm when compared with the harm caused by the infectious disease that the vaccination is designed to prevent that we can set this aside. When we can set aside harms in this manner, we tend to think that the practice does not cause an *unacceptable harm.*

There are other ways in which we might try to set harms aside, and we shall look at one of them in what follows, but the point here is obvious – we can defend racial profiling if we can show that it either causes no harms, or that whatever harms its does cause can be set aside as acceptable. So how might such an argument go?

First of all, we can identify the potential harms of racial profiling as stemming from two sources: the invocation of *race* and racial identity as the basic indicating characteristic in our profile, and the burden of having special attention called to a particular group *qua* racial group as part of the application of our profiling practice. If there are no harms or only acceptable harms arising from these sources, then we look to have grounds for thinking that racial profiling is acceptable.

With regard to the first potential source of harms – those that stem from the racial element of racial profiling – we can see that some damages are likely to arise here. For instance, if I am of a particular racial group, then in the kind of society where we tend to find practices of racial profiling, we will also find *racism* and lots of differential treatment based on *race*. For example, the notion of Romany Gypsy criminality is very widespread in Britain and Europe, despite poor and questionable evidence for this. The result is that Romany Gypsies are often subjected to negative treatment by virtue of their *race* and the stereotypical views about them. However, suppose that an acceptable form of racial profiling shows that Romany Gypsies do perpetrate a particular kind of offence more frequently than those of other *races* – driving unlicensed say. Although the police might use the statistics correctly, without abuse, and in proportion, the backdrop of being singled out for racist treatment in so many dimensions of day-to-day existence means that this treatment will have a negative effect, lead to resentment, and compound the *racism* experienced by this group. In short, it will be a reminder of the many racist and negative experiences that members of this group have in their daily lives.

We can see that this kind of result may well constitute a considerable harm too. For instance, when we see how these kinds of harm might work in many other settings, we can see why such harms might be taken as unacceptable in the context of racial profiling. Consider that it is common practice for television and radio stations to alter their schedules or playlists to accommodate recent events and minimize any potential offence. A clear example is that the Warner Brothers channel in the USA rescheduled an episode of *Buffy The Vampire Slayer*, called "Earshot", in which a student was depicted loading a gun in a bell-tower. It had originally been due to air only one week after the Columbine High School shootings. Similarly, after the 11 September 2001 terror attacks, Clear Channel radio issued a list of songs which it recommended its stations did not play, given heightened public sensitivity to certain topics and terms (see, for example, Graybow 2001). It is obvious that these songs, or television episodes might cause some harm by inadvertently stimulating raw emotions and feelings. The concern here, then, might be that, just as we think it right and proper to reschedule programs whose topics may cause distress to a sensitive public, we might also minimize harm by not adopting racial profiling. Though the profiling itself need not be racist, it aggravates sensitivities and distress due to broader *racism* within society and for that reason perhaps constitutes an unacceptable harm.

There may, however, be an argument here that in a case such as racial profiling this kind of harm is acceptable. The thought is that we must distinguish between the presence of the harm and what causes it. For example, we can see that the harm caused in the kinds of cases we have mentioned are not directly due to either the songs, programmes or to the practice of racial profiling itself, but to something else. The harm caused by playing an episode of *Buffy the Vampire Slayer* one week after the Columbine High School shootings is not due to the TV show, but to the crime committed in Columbine. Similarly, the harms that we identified as arising from directing our racial profiling toward a particular *race* are not caused by the profiling practice itself, but by the underlying *racism* in society. In this way we can see that racial profiling does not *cause* any special harms of its own by virtue of its racial element, but merely *directs attention* to pre-existing harms. The question, then, is whether or not we should resist racial profiling because it might draw attention to pre-existing harms, or whether there are good reasons for accepting this feature of the practice.

Initially, it might seem that when some practice is harmful in so far as it draws attention to pre-existing harms, we do quite often withdraw from that action. Warner Brothers didn't air *Buffy The Vampire Slayer*; Clear Channel avoided playing certain songs. By extension, we might think it is obvious that we should withdraw from racial profiling since it draws the attention of members of a particular *race* to the harms they experience by virtue of being the *race* they are. But of course, in rescheduling programmes or adapting our radio playlists, we are sacrificing very small benefits for a much greater good. In the case of racial profiling, however, the cost of forgoing the practice might be much greater. The kind of racial profiling we are interested in is well founded upon statistics and practised without abuse. Further, the broader social benefit of removing a particular crime or practice is well noted. This seems to give a strong reason for tolerating some harm.

An additional consideration is that while racial profiling does not add to the harms felt – as we have noted, the harms of racial profiling we are considering here arise simply from directing attention to pre-existing harms – stopping racial profiling would do nothing to remove or diminish those harms. If we stopped our racial profiling to reduce a particular crime, the harms of *racism* to which racial profiling draws unwelcome attention would still be there, would still be felt, and would still impact negatively upon the lives of those that our policies would have targeted. Put like this, it seems that the harms had here are probably acceptable. Withdrawing from profiling would do nothing to diminish the harms felt and would also mean that we have sacrificed a considerable social benefit. Retaining profiling would mean that we draw unwanted attention to the racist treatment suffered by the group that our policies target, but we would also see considerable benefit in the reduction of crime.

When we turn to the kinds of harm that might arise from the profiling element of racial profiling we can see that, again, damages are likely to arise. For example, when we profile a particular group, for whatever reason, they are subject to special attention that is likely to inconvenience them, certain actions and events are made more prone to intervention from police or authorities, and the kinds of irritation or resentment that anyone might feel by virtue of such practices is likely to be increased. It seems obvious that no matter how well practised racial profiling is, those who carry the burden of its focus will feel that they are scrutinized more than others and are more likely to feel as though they are subject to undue suspicion or intrusion. Feeling constantly scrutinized, growing resentful towards police and facing the threat of having mundane activities interrupted by police are clearly harms. Even if we are not subject to racial profiling, we can all appreciate how such intervention and threats of intervention can be harming. After all, why should I have to add an extra thirty minutes on to every journey I make after dark simply because of my *race*?

Once again, though, these harms are only a problem if they are unacceptable, and they are only unacceptable if they outweigh the greater social benefit of whatever profiling practices we engage in. And, given that we are dealing with racial profiling practices that are not abusive or disproportionate, we can assume that a racial group is inconvenienced and targeted only so far as the profile suggests and only to the extent of the social utility that the profiling practice can fulfil. What this means is that the harms here should hopefully be like the distress and discomfort of having an injection, considered against the broader benefits of immunity. A good practice with racial profiling will not pursue the policies beyond the social benefit and so the impact should be felt accordingly. As such, the kinds of harm inherent in any profiling practice will be no more intolerable or unfair on a racial group than the balancing of motor insurance payments against risk according to the age of the driver – irritating for some, but understandable and bearable.

What this means then is that we may well have grounds for thinking that racial profiling, if enacted in accord with the three conditions we have mentioned, could be justifiable or acceptable. There may be harms associated with its racial element, but these are due to the broader *racism* of society to which racial profiling would draw a targeted group's attention. Refusing to use racial profiling on these grounds would be at the cost of the social benefits to be had from reducing certain kinds of crime, and would do nothing to reduce the harms of *racism* either. As such, these harms are acceptable. Similarly, there may be harms associated with the profiling element, but these are mostly issues of inconvenience, resentment and the feeling of being unfairly under suspicion. And while these can be treated as genuinely harmful, they are outweighed by the social benefits to be had by responsible and well practiced racial profiling. These harms are arguably acceptable too.

The case against racial profiling

Despite the various arguments that any potential harms arising from racial profiling are acceptable, we may have some reason to worry. Of course, we can raise lots of concerns that by virtue of living in a racist society we can never be sure that racial profiling, however much it seems to meet the three conditions we have set, is free of problematic assumptions. Our statistics, the kinds of tool we might use to connect *race* to a profile and so on, have to be drawn from somewhere, and it is hard to see how we can be certain that we have extricated ourselves from the effects of *racism*, however subtle. Just looking at crime, for example, we have to base our statistics on something and the racial identity of those convicted seems like a sensible place to start. However, when we consider such issues as the higher first time conviction rates for black Americans over their white counterparts, we have some grounds for concern that the source of our statistics may be biased and problematic.[7] Similarly, we have to ask ourselves what role *racism* might play in our decisions to pursue racial profiling policies rather than some other social policy. It is not obvious that reducing certain kinds of crime, for instance, can only be achieved through racial profiling, even if the statistical tool is robust and free of *racism*.

Whilst these concerns and arguments are worthwhile and interesting, we shall not pursue them here. We shall continue to keep hold of the assumption that meeting our three conditions makes a case of racial profiling good, and that the question in hand is whether that kind of racial profiling can be justified. So far, we have seen some arguments that it can, since the harms that it may give rise to are tolerable. Here, we shall challenge the possibility of justifying racial profiling by looking at how we might challenge those arguments. So, first, we shall look at the claim that the harms of racial profiling related to its use of *race* are not deep and are due instead to underlying *racism*. We shall then examine the claim that the harms of racial profiling due to the very nature of profiling are tolerable because they are outweighed by greater social benefit.

The first thing we might note is that just because a harm is somehow parasitic on pre-existing and separate harms that need not somehow diminish it. As we pointed out before, a television programme's depiction of shooting is harmful only in so far as reminds us of a pre-existing and separately harmful event, such as the Columbine High School shootings, but we are still prepared to withdraw from showing the programme. Forgoing scheduled televisionprogramming is not a great loss when compared to the benefits of showing sensitivity to public feeling. Forgoing racial profiling is arguably a greater loss. However, we also have to consider the other element in this claim – it might be that racial profiling has greater social benefits than having a reliable schedule for our television programmes, but it might also be that not showing sensitivity to the unwelcome reminder of *racism* that racial profiling poses is a markedly greater harm than not showing sensitivity to public feelings about high-school shootings.

Whilst insensitivity to the general public's feeling of horror or distress about a particular event can easily be overridden by a practice with real

---

7. For the huge disparities in the treatment of black and white Americans in the criminal justice system of the USA see, for example, Crocker (2003) or Austin and Allen (2000).

social benefits, when these practices begin to impact on directly affected individuals things are much less clear. For example, we might decide that a public awareness programme directed at raising awareness of date rape is enough of a social benefit that our general discomfort with talk about such things can be overridden. However, if our policy inadvertently involves compelling date-rape victims to relive their experiences in a deeply traumatic and public way, we would think that the policy needs rethinking. General discomfort or sensitivity is one thing, but direct provocation of victims' feelings is another, far more serious matter. And the worry, of course, is that racial profiling is more like this latter provocation of feelings than the former.

A further consideration against the claim that a harm that merely draws attention to pre-existing harms can be easily tolerated when the social benefit is high is that in the case of *racial* profiling, this may itself be racist. To see how we might make this argument, think back to our last chapter on *racism*. In that chapter we looked at various ways of accounting for *racism* and amongst our final considerations were ways of treating *racism* as disregard or disrespect. On such accounts, we can treat something as racist if and only if it is disrespectful towards or disregarding of people of a certain *race qua* members of that racial group. The kind of considerations that speak in favour of adopting racial profiling despite the fact that it acts as a reminder to members of a particular racial group that they are subject to *racism* seem to call upon us to actively disregard the feelings of a particular racial group. If this is a viable account of *racism*, then the kind of harm that merely draws attention to pre-existing harms may not be a deep harm in its own right, but setting it aside in considerations of racial profiling is – it is an act of *racism*, and I take it that we all take *racism* to be a harm.

There are other considerations that might hold against the putative harms of racial profiling that, whilst due to its invocation of *race*, are not simply parasitic upon the pre-existing harms of *racism*. The presence of such separate and self-standing harms would add further weight to the suggestion that we should not accept the practice of racial profiling. And in particular, it looks as though there *are* a series of harms that could actively contribute to the underlying *racism* that members of a racially profiled group encounter. Here we shall mention three broad instances of this kind of harm:

First, if a member of a particular racial group is viewed negatively by society at large, then being racially profiled for such things as crime prevention is likely to remind members of that group how they are viewed.

Put like this, of course, this is merely a non-contributing harm – it seems to be harmful only in so far as it draws upon the pre-existing harms caused by the racist views held within broader society. However, if we think back to the various discussions in Chapter 3 about what we should do with *race* thought and talk, we noted that an undesirable feature of *race* and racial labelling is that some groups actively live under and embrace *negative* labels and identities. We mentioned in particular Romany Gypsies and illiteracy, but this phenomenon, widely known as *internalized racialism* and *internalized racism* is recognized as occurring in many racial groups. And the harms of such a phenomenon are wide ranging: there are the obvious feelings of negativity and irritation at being seen in this way; there are the various way in which such ideas can be self-limiting and prevent flourishing in certain areas; and internal racialism/racism is even known to lead to very serious mental health issues including self-harm and body dismorphia (see, for example, Cokley 2002 for more on internalized racism). These are clear harms that result quite directly from a person being constantly reminded of the negative way in which society sees them as someone of a particular *race*.

Second, racial profiling, even if it meets the three conditions we have suggested, seems to draw an official and explicit connection between people of a particular *race* and particular social problems such as crime. These connections are worrying in so far as they endorse many views about *race* and the characteristics of particular *races* that arguably lead to *racism*. Of course, the unfounded connection of such characteristics as criminality, immorality, laziness and so on as somehow being inherent among particular *races* is harmful – it is wrong and arguably it grounds certain kinds of *racism* – and in one sense racial profiling merely draws attention to that. However, there is a sense in which racial profiling makes it harder for us to undermine these ideas about *race* and racial characteristic because it relies upon drawing an *official* connection between the two things, and so ossifies and endorses the idea in ordinary concepts of *race*. If we cite statistics (using them properly, without abuse and in proportion etc.) that show that members of some *race* are more likely to perpetrate welfare fraud crimes, and the broader societal view is that members of that *race* have a natural inclination towards theft and are work-shy, lazy non-contributors, then we seem to have provided official endorsement of the view. After all, if members of some profiled *race* are not the ingrained thieves and freeloaders we all take them to be, then why does the government use racial profiling to stop them stealing and freeloading? While the prejudices that already exist in society may well be a pre-existing harm, inadvertently confirming and compounding those prejudices seems to be a separate harm that racial profiling brings to the table.

Third, racial profiling, even if it accords with our strictures on abuse and proportion, is likely to *exacerbate racism* and certain racial inequalities by virtue of the fact that it takes place against the backdrop of a racist and *race*-conscious society. We can see how this exacerbation might function in two ways. To begin with, it will exacerbate *racism* and racial inequality when combined with the kind of *endorsement* that racial profiling gives to certain views about *race*. For example, suppose that racial profiling inadvertently endorses the view that black people are prone to criminality. Further, suppose that this leads employers to show some reluctance in employing black people, especially for positions of responsibility where trustworthiness is deemed paramount. As it happens, black people already hold fewer of these positions of responsibility with the accompanying higher pay and social status. Here we see an inequality exacerbated by virtue of the endorsement that racial profiling might give to a particular view about racial characteristics. This, of course, is a simplistic example, but we can see how it might exacerbate well-known racial inequalities relating to employment, education, and even housing – if the criminality of black people is clearly endorsed by official government policies, why would anyone want to employ black people in positions of trust, teach in schools where they are present or live in the same neighbourhood?

Another way in which racial profiling might exacerbate current racial inequalities is through what we might think of as *self-policing*. Racial profiling, no matter how well managed, is likely to remind those members of a profiled *race* that they are subject to particular inequalities. It is also likely to lead to certain inconveniences – stop and search, extra scrutiny and so on. And while the inconveniences might be proportional, and the *racism* that members of a particular group are reminded of a pre-existing harm, it is nonetheless likely to lead to changes in behaviour. If I am black and commute to a mainly white area to work but frequently face "stop and search" during this commute, or frequently have it noted that I am one of the few black people in this mainly white area, I will perhaps police my own behaviour so that I work closer to where I live, so I don't have to commute after dark, and so on. If well-paid jobs are focused in these white areas, I am more likely to simply forgo a well-paid job. Similarly, if living in a mainly white area means being subjected to "stop and search" more frequently in my own neighbourhood and in full view of my neighbours, I am less likely to live there. If driving a new car means drawing police attention to myself, I will drive an old car. The worry is obvious: with so many racial inequalities arising from where we live, where we work, what we own and aspire to own, which opportunities we see open to us and so on, anything which makes us self-police to the detriment of greater racial equality is a harm. Racial profiling looks as though it can do this.

If these three worries make sense, then the claim that the *race* element of racial profiling may contribute no harm in its own right above directing our attention to the pre-existing harms of *racism* and racial inequality cannot be maintained. We might have reasons for thinking that invoking *race* here can compound many issues of negative identity related to *race*, can give the appearance of official endorsement to racist views or inaccurate ideas about *race*, and can exacerbate racial inequality by grounding the actions that lead to racial injustices through either endorsement of racist and inaccurate views or through self-policing. These harms are all related to drawing attention to the pre-existing harms of *racism*, but they are nonetheless harms separate and additional to those pre-existing harms.

When we turn to claims that the harms of racial profiling arise by virtue of the inconveniences of profiling we might also have some reason for thinking that even these harms are not acceptable. Recall that one claim made in favour of racial profiling being justifiable is that harms such as being inconvenienced or feeling resentment and so on are weighed against the greater social good that racial profiling brings. In particular, if we are ensuring that our racial profiling practices are proportional we will ensure that we never target groups disproportionately or focus on this profiled crime to the exclusion of other social issues and so on. What this means is that the harms of profiling are minor enough to be set aside when considered against the greater social benefits of reducing crimes, protecting borders, ensuring tax revenues are collected properly, and so on. However, it may be the case that when we introduce *race*, these harms are not so minor as all that. And again, this may be because we are neglecting the inherent *racism* and racialization in society at large.

In terms of the effects of racialization we can see how it may well magnify the extent and degree of inconvenience. Consider, for example, that small delays at airports, some additional questions or bag searches might be tolerable given that most of us travel by air far less frequently than we use other means of transport. Similarly, for most of us, we make one tax return per year and will be subjected to increased scrutiny by revenue services at most once per year by virtue of displaying certain characteristics in the profile. Put like this, we can see why such inconveniences and feelings of resentment and irritation can be tolerable. I am a traveller with a ticket paid for with cash only on infrequent occasions. I am a taxpayer with large charitable donations on my tax return just once a year. I may resent knowing that this will always mean I am subject to special scrutiny by border security and audit by tax officials, but I trigger the profile only rarely. Being of a particular *race* is not like this.

If my *race* is the characteristic triggering some profile targeted by official policy, then the fact that we live in a racialized society where we are all of us raced means that I display the characteristic that places me in the targeted profile every living moment of my life. If being black defines a profiled *race*, and I am black, then I am open to the inconveniences of profiling every day, not simply when I fly or return taxes. We can see how this might count as considerably more than the minor inconvenience posed by other instances of profiling, and that the irritation and resentment generated would be many magnitudes greater. The harms of this may not be so minor. Moreover, when we observe that those harms are visited across a whole group and sector of society – one with a greater cohesion and social presence than cash-only light travellers or taxable citizens with large donations to charity – we can see how the harms might have quite considerable weight after all. Of course, even this may not outweigh the social benefits of racial profiling but we can at least question the notion that the harms of profiling remain minor when a characteristic such as *race* is part of the profile, especially given that we live in a racialized society.

A second more serious set of considerations comes from observing that the minor harms of profiling have to be set against the fact that our society is not only racialized, but also racist. And particularly important here are not the kinds of *direct* and *overt racism* that we frequently have in mind. We can rule *direct* and *overt racism* out of racial profiling by *fiat* if we like. And in many ways this was what our three conditions were meant to do. We already know that racial profiling that targets *races* for racist reasons is wrong and cannot be justified. However, avert *racism* may pose an interesting problem here. We must be clear though that the worry is not that racial profiling itself may be avertly racist – after all, we wanted our statistics and tools for connecting characteristics to a profile to be scientifically robust and we might even demand that factors such as implicit bias be built into the forming of statistical analyses and gathering of evidence. The worry is that the avert *racism* and implicit biases which evidence suggests is so widespread, even among those who explicitly find *racism* to be appalling and abhorrent, will be found among those who must enact these policies. To see the worry, let us consider an example.

Suppose we use a robust, well-controlled statistical analysis that draws a connection between black youths and street crime. Further, we have a policing programme that involves training in the proper treatment of the people who are targeted, and which ensures that the programme is enacted without abuse and in proportion to both the statistics and the potential social benefits. We can also imagine that police officers are carefully vetted so that they are anti-racist and progressive, and that we even have a genuinely representative proportion of black police officers helping to carry out this programme. However, after some time of enacting this programme two young innocent black men are shot dead during a stop-and-search, and there are multiple complaints of police being too rough and intimidating in their treatment. How could this be, given how careful we have been with the racial profiling we have instantiated? After investigation to discover if our officers are racist, or if the programme is ignoring our strictures on abuse and proportion, we discover that all is enacted as we intended and our officers are not racists. Indeed, the two shootings involved black officers who are deeply distraught and affected by the events they were involved in. It turns out that the answer to why our programme has lead to these undesirable outcomes may be down to implicit bias. But let us elaborate.

There is a lot of research that shows that many of our subconscious responses to people of particular *races* might be negative and potentially harmful. Two pieces of research are particular important to us here.

The first shows that when Americans encounter a black face they respond to it fearfully. Research by Matthew Lieberman and his colleagues show that when completing various matching tests with black and white faces, subjects, when they saw a black face, showed heightened activity in the amygdala area of the brain, an area that responds to fear and threat (Lieberman *et al.* 2005). What is more, the fMRI scans used to chart amygdala response showed that it made no difference whether those tested were black or white; people of both *races* responded to black faces as though there was a threat. As Lieberman noted in an interview with *New Scientist*:

"I think the results are very specific to being raised in this society where the portrayal of African Americans is not very positive, on average," says Matthew Lieberman at the University of

California, Los Angeles, US, who led the study. "It suggests that those cultural messages are not harmless." (Gosline 2005)

The second is research into what is frequently called "weapon bias". Work by B. Keith Payne, for instance, shows that when asked to make split-second decisions about whether or not a presented object is a gun or something harmless, subjects misidentify harmless objects as firearms more frequently when they are shown black faces beforehand (see Payne 2005, 2006). What is more, this weapon bias is found just as frequently among those who express no explicit racial biases or racist views.

This now allows us to make sense of how the apparently well-managed and *race*-sensitive racial profiling practices that we envisaged might still lead to complaints of police intimidation, rough behaviour and even shooting deaths. Police are stopping and searching young black males who are statistically profiled as being potential perpetrators of crimes. The police are, as Lieberman's research shows, likely to be fearful and think they are responding to threat simply by virtue of dealing with a black face. As is well known, we often respond to fear and threat in ways that are themselves fear-inducing and threatening. This would help to explain the complaints of intimidation and rough behaviour. The police are also more likely to misperceive non-threatening objects as firearms, again, simply by virtue of dealing with black people. This might well explain why there have been shootings of innocent black men during the enactment of the profiling policy that we envisaged. And we can imagine that all of this takes place without any explicit *racism* or racist attitudes coming from the police officers, and we might even allow that black police officers have received complaints to the same degree as white officers.

The upshot of this scenario should be clear. The harms of racial profiling that arise from the nature of profiling itself may actually be markedly more damaging than simple inconvenience when it comes to the inclusion of *race*. There are very many cases of police shootings that mirror the examples we have in mind here – Amadou Diallo, a young black man who was shot in New York in 1999 by police who mistakenly thought he had a gun; Tyisha Miller, a young black female, who was shot in her car by police in Riverside California in 1998; Robert Russ and Latanya Haggerty, young black adults shot in Chicago in 1999 by black police officers; Oscar Grant, who was shot by a transport officer in Oakland in 2009 who thought he was reaching for a gun; Travis McNeal, a black man shot by Hispanic police officers in Miami in 2011. And there are thousands more cases besides. Of course, in these cases we cannot rule out explicit *racism* in the stipulative way we did for our example. Nonetheless, we can see by simply extending the damage caused by real cases – harms inflicted upon individuals, their families, broader communities, and even police officers – just how much serious damage racial profiling could create.

If these various arguments are right, then, we may have serious reason to think that even with conditions in place, racial profiling cannot be justified. Even if we concede that the main harm of racial profiling is to remind those targeted of a series of pre-existing harms it is not straightforwardly obvious that this is tolerable. Reminding of harms can be a serious harm in its own right. Moreover, it is not clear that, by drawing attention to those pre-existing harms, racial profiling does not thereby generate any harms of its own – it may be that issues of negative identity and self-image are compounded, incorrect or racist notions are endorsed, and racial inequalities exacerbated. Similarly, the harms inherent in profiling – inconvenience for members of targeted groups, resentment, ill feeling and so on – may not be as minor as they ordinarily seem to be once *race* becomes a factor. Living in a racialized society where one's *race* is a constant feature of one's life means that being the target of a particular profiling practice is a constant feature of one's life too. This is markedly more inconveniencing, alienating and worthy of deep resentment than being targeted in other profiling practices. And finally, living in a society where implicit bias and avert *racism* exist so widely, the effect on those who must enforce racial profiling policy may lead to seriously damaging outcomes, such as police shootings and heavy-handed policing. Even with a well-managed, well-intentioned racial profiling policy, the effects of these kinds of bias and *racism* may be pervasive enough to mean that there are deeply serious harms to take account of – harms which are serious enough to be intolerable.

So far we have argued against racial profiling by attempting to counteract the claims made in the case given for racial profiling. In particular, we have tried to show that the harms arising from the racial element of the practice may be more serious than simply drawing attention to pre-existing harms, and we have tried to show that the harms arising from the profiling element of the practice may be made more serious by virtue of the broader background of racialization and *racism*. However, there are other arguments we could give against racial profiling – even the very restricted notion we have in mind. We shall, however, finish here by mentioning just one: the claim that racial profiling could quite easily create feedback loops which make it, in a sense, self-fulfilling.

To see the complaint, consider the following example.[8] Suppose that there is a widespread belief among taxi drivers that males hailing taxis after dark are more likely to be robbers or fare dodgers. As a result, there is a growing reluctance among taxi drivers to take male passengers after dark. This reluctance is so widespread that it becomes increasingly difficult for males to catch a taxi at night-time. A natural response to this is that males who would ordinarily travel at night either simply do not bother and rearrange their affairs so there is no longer any need, or they make alternative travel arrangements. A further upshot of this is that of those males trying to hail a taxi after dark a greater proportion are now likely to be robbers and fare dodgers. The honest travellers who need reliable transport have gone to other sources; those who see taxis as an easy target remain.

This, of course, is an instance of unofficial and unfair profiling based on stereotypes, and is obviously wrong. However, we can see how such self-fulfilment might go when we look at racial profiling, even of the philosophically interesting kind. If statistics show members of a particular *race* are more likely to commit street crimes after dark, then innocent members of those *races* are likely to withdraw from behaviours that see them subject to police attention – we have already mentioned this likelihood when we talked about self-policing. What this means is that those members of a profiled racial group who the police do come into contact with will perhaps become increasingly likely to have committed the crime that the police are checking for. Of course, there are many provisos that come with this kind of complaint – perpetrators of a crime are as likely to change behaviours to avoid police attention (although for different reasons); it may be impossible for innocent people to change their behaviours substantially in some cases (driving may be the only realistic option despite the increased police attention). Regardless, it should be quite clear what the worry here is: the connection between *race* and crime that the profiling relies on may actually be further strengthened by the practice. If this is so then this seems to make some of the harms we mentioned above seem even more problematic – if an official connection between *race* and crime leads to negative self-identity issues, endorsement of problematic ideas about *races* and exacerbation of inequalities, then inadvertently strengthening that connection might presumably lead to a strengthening of those harms. All of this looks bad for racial profiling.

---

8. This kind example is given by John Arthur (2007: 48) in his discussion of racial profiling and is, I think, a particularly instructive example of how the worry might go.

Summary

We have looked at cases for and against what we have called a philosophically interesting account of racial profiling. In particular we saw that when we have a well-refined case of racial profiling, one that actively puts in place conditions on proper use and attempts to rule out *racism*, we can construct a case for adopting such practices. That case, as we saw, relied upon showing that whatever harms still arose were tolerable. In particular the claim was that such harms were tolerable because the chief harm was pre-existing *racism* in society and racial profiling did not add to that. Moreover, abstaining from such practices would not reduce those damages. Similarly, harms that come from any profiling practices – inconvenience, resentment and so on – are minor when measured against the social benefits to be had through racial profiling.

We also constructed a case against racial profiling by tackling the claims made for thinking that racial profiling could be justifiable. In particular we noted that racial profiling might contribute to the pre-existing harms above and beyond merely directing attention to them. We also noted that against the backdrop of a racialized and racist society, the minor harms of profiling become much more serious when *race* is the characteristic that the profile draws upon. These arguments seem to raise considerable problems for racial profiling – even with careful constraints on how we generate racial profiling,when we apply it and so on, there are still lots of worrying outcomes circling around the practice. However, it is worth noting that, as ever, the arguments are not conclusive and the debate is not closed.

It is possible for us to return to the arguments that suggest the harms of racial profiling to be intolerable and raise concerns about those. However, I take it that this would most likely involve showing that the benefits of racial profiling are such that even these harms are tolerable. An alternative, and I suspect more promising, strategy is to return to the question of what makes for a good case of racial profiling – perhaps we have not yet formulated what the best practice should look like. For example, we might think that finding very public and very official ways to acknowledge and show gratitude for the extra burden that particular racial groups experience when we practise racial profiling would be a useful addition. This might have a few clear advantages over the simple conditions we suggested: it would perhaps help to diminish the negative feelings that come from being reminded about being subject to *racism* since clear gratitude and acknowledgement of the service to the broader social good is included here; it would diminish the endorsement of unfounded racist and racial views since it would clearly acknowledge that the targeted racial group is not a problem to society, but a public servant; and it would hopefully prevent the exacerbation of racial inequalities as a result. We might also want to include other provisions in an account of a fully appropriate, acceptable and thereby philosophically interesting case of racial profiling. Special selection and special training for those who are to enforce such policies, especially in techniques designed to counteract avert *racism* and implicit bias, might prove to make such practices more justifiable too. This is not something we shall pursue further here.

CONCLUSION

In this chapter, then, we have brought our philosophical understanding of *race* and *racism* to philosophical debates where these matters have direct impact on our lives. In particular we have focused on the question of racial profiling. We spent some time trying to get clear about what a philosophically interesting account of racial profiling would look like – after all, the kinds of racist, clearly prejudicial and damaging uses of racial profiling that often come to light are clearly wrong and pose no philosophical or ethical challenge. They are wrong and we should not engage with them. However, with a suitably refined notion of racial profiling we saw that there may be reasons for thinking such an account could be justified, and might thereby be tolerated if used for some social benefit in our society. We also saw that there are various ways to challenge the justifiability and tolerability of even this refined notion of racial profiling.

In many ways, this way of turning our understanding of *race* and *racism* to questions of policy and areas where *race* and *racism* seem to have the strongest impact on our lives is a desirable end for philosophers of *race*. It is good to see that *race* is largely constructed and has none of the metaphysical weight we might have thought it to have. And it is good to ask ourselves if, why, and in what form we should keep *race* concepts. Similarly, understanding what *racism* is and why it is wrong is important and philosophically motivating in its own right. However, seeing just how these kinds of questions, insights, and concerns come to bear in matters of policy and broader social life is an important achievement. Questions of positive and negative racial identity play a part in our considerations of what to do with *race* concepts – they are deeply important in such considerations.

Knowing this means that we are perhaps less likely to set issues of negative racial identity aside when we look at social policy. Similarly, knowing just how multifaceted *racism* is, and knowing that our most fruitful way of handling that topic may be to look at approaches that rely on disrespect and disregard, has impact on how we view social policy questions too. The ubiquity of *racism*, especially avert *racism* and implicit bias, has to make us think long and hard about just how harmful a policy such as racial profiling might be. And we can also see the potential for addressing other "applied" questions too. Most important, though, is that we see that the deeper philosophical understanding of *race* and *racism* that we have tried to develop in this book is of inestimable value, not just in its own rights, but also in applying ourselves to everyday issues and social concerns.

Further reading

In this section we shall look at some of the themes and topics introduced in the five chapters of this book, and mention useful papers and research for those who want to pursue such matters in greater depth. The aim is not to be exhaustive, but rather to point towards good recent work that is informative or which will be suggestive of fruitful avenues for further study and research.

CHAPTER 1: IS *RACE* REAL?

In this chapter we talked about the assumed defining characteristics of *race*. We tried to justify identifying those characteristics in terms of the practices and assumptions of ordinary language users. This practice of relying on ordinary language users is shared and defended most prominently by Joshua Glasgow. In particular see chapters 2 and 3 of Glasgow, *A Theory of Race* (2009a).

Other techniques we could use in trying to recover a basic concept of *race* might include empirical work from the social sciences. Although there is not a wealth of such work, there is some. For instance, Morning, "Toward a Sociology of Racial Conceptualisation for the 21st Century" (2009) reflects and supports much of our pre-theoretical list of characteristics.

However, within philosophy, the most frequently-used approach for identifying our everyday concept of *race* relies on identifying expert opinion on *race* and racial characteristics. Particularly useful sources on this view are Appiah, "Race, Culture, Identity: Misunderstood Connections" (1996) and Taylor, "Appiah's Uncompleted Argument: W. E. B. Du Bois and the Reality of Race" (2000).

A related question is just which elements of the cluster of characteristics that form our ordinary concept of *race* we think should form the working core of our more philosophical concept. Some tend to use the broader cluster of characteristics – for example, Zack in "Life After Race" (1997a) and "The Philosophic Meaning of Race" (1997b), or Smedley and Smedley in "Race as Biology is Fiction, Racism as a Social Problem is Real" (2005). Others identify or argue for a refined core – Hardimon in "The Ordinary Concept of Race" (2003) suggests the three characteristics that we identified in this book; Glasgow thinks the core of our philosophical concept of *race* should include a refined notion of our first characteristic only - see *A Theory of Race* (2009a). There is some debate between Glasgow and Hardimon about just how thin our philosophical core should be, and this is also of interest – see Glasgow, "In Defence of a Four-Part Theory: Replies to Hardimon, Haslanger, Mallon and Zack" (2009c) and Hardimon, "Wallace Simpson was Wrong: Remarks on Joshua Glasgow's *A Theory of Race*" (2009).

In the latter half of the chapter we talked about how well our concept was supported by science and biology. A good and thorough examination of how far short of scientific credibility our ordinary concept falls is Zack, *Philosophy of Science and Race* (2002).

CHAPTER 2: IS *RACE* SOCIAL?

In this chapter we examined the social and historical aspects of *race*, and examined three views about how we might interpret those social historical facts. The view of the social elements that we introduced drew strong connections between slavery in the age of empire building, and scientific endorsement in the Age of Enlightenment. A useful, and in many ways comparable account is given in Fredrickson, *Racism: A Short History* (2002). There are studies that emphasize different aspects of the social and historical elements of *race* and *racism*, but especially interesting are those that note the connection between capitalism and *race* – the best of these are perhaps Williams, *Capitalism and Slavery* (1944) and Brodkin, "Global Capitalism: What's Race Got to Do with It?" (2000).

For those who wish to examine the details of racial formations in the USA in greater detail, Omi and Winant's *Racial Formation in the United States* (1986) is indispensable. For those who wish to examine the details of racial formations in Brazil in greater detail, Telles's *Race in Another America: The Significance of Skin Color in Brazil* (2004) is an excellent source.

Chapter 2 also saw the discussion of social constructionism. We did not discuss the broader philosophical issues that surround the notion social construction and for the most part took for granted the idea that something could be real yet socially constructed. For a good general sense of what social construction is and what the broader philosophical issues are, the interested reader would do well to consult Mallon, "A Field Guide to Social Construction" (2007), Searle, *The Construction of Social Reality* (1995) and Hacking, *The Social Construction of What?* (1999).

The best representative examples of philosophical work that is committed to the idea that *race* is a social construct can be found in chapter 3 of Mills, *Blackness Visible: Essays on Philosophy and Race* (1998) and Sundstrom, "Race as a Human Kind" (2002). For the weaker view that the social elements of race give us racial identities but not social reality, see Appiah, "Race, Culture, Identity: Misunderstood Connections" (1996), the primary source of this view. For the best *reconstructionist* views see Haslanger, "Gender and Race: What Are They? What Do We Want Them To Be?" (2000) and "Future Genders? Future Races?" (2004) and Glasgow, "A Third Way in the Race Debate" (2006) and chapter 7 of *A Theory of Race* (2009a).

An additional area of interest that we discussed in the chapter was the problem posed for social constructionists by the phenomenon of passing and travelling. Those interested in this debate should see Michaels, "The No-Drop Rule" (1994), Piper, "Passing for White, Passing for Black" (1992), Mallon, "Passing, Travelling and Reality: Social Constructionism and the Metaphysics of Race" (2004) and Glasgow, "Three Things Realist Constructionism About Race – Or Anything Else – Can Do" (2007) for the best and most central work in this area.

CHAPTER 3: WHAT SHOULD WE DO WITH *RACE*?

In this chapter we examined three philosophical views on what we should aim to do with our concept of *race* given the scientific and social facts discussed in Chapters 1 and 2. In particular we discussed *eliminativism*, *preservationism* and *reconstructionism*.

Important *race eliminativist* work can be found in Appiah, "The Uncompleted Argument: Du Bois and the Illusion of Race" (1995) and "Race, Culture, Identity: Misunderstood Connections" (1996), Blum, *"I Am Not a Racist But ....: The Moral Quandary of Race* (2002), Corlett, *Race, Racism and Reparations* (2003), Zack, "The Philosophic Meaning of Race" (1997b) and *Philosophy of Science and Race* (2002). Important *preservationist* work can be found in Outlaw, "Toward A Critical Theory of Race" (1990), "On W. E. B. Du Bois's 'The Conservation of Races'" (1995), "'Conserve' Races? In Defense of W. E. B. Du Bois" (1996a) and *On Race and Philosophy* (1996b), Mills, *Blackness Visible: Essays on Philosophy and Race* (1998), Sundstrom, "Race as a Human Kind" (2002), Taylor, "Appiah's Uncompleted Argument: W. E. B. Du Bois and the Reality of Race" (2000), *Race: A Philosophical Introduction* (2004a) and "Pragmatism and Race" (2004b). Important *reconstructionist* work is found in Haslanger, "Gender and Race: What Are They? What Do We Want Them To Be?" (2000) and "Future Genders? Future Races?" (2004), Glasgow, "A Third Way in the Race Debate" (2006) and *A Theory of Race* (2009a). In addition we can find *reconstructionist* elements in some *eliminativists'* work: Blum in *"I Am Not a Racist But ...": The Moral Quandary of Race* (2002) thinks that while *race* should be eliminated it can be replaced or reconstructed into *racialization*; and Corlett in *Race, Racism and Reparations* (2003) thinks that *race* can be replaced or reconstructed in terms of ethnicity.

Research that is strongly connected to the question of what we should do about *race*, but which we did not discuss in this chapter, is the idea that *race* might reconstructed in terms of its biological element rather than its social element. Work on reconstructed biological notions of *race* includes Andreason, "A New Perspective on the Race Debate" (1998), "The Cladistic Race Concept: A Defense" (2004) and "The Meaning of 'Race': Folk Conceptions and the New Biology of Race" (2005), and Kitcher, "Race, Ethnicity, Biology, Culture" (1999). Glasgow, "On the New Biology of Race" (2003) is a useful commentary on Andreason's work and Spencer, "What 'Biological Racial Realism' Should Mean" (in press) is an interesting discussion on the notion of *biological kind* required for this kind of *reconstructionism*.

CHAPTER 4: *RACISM*

In this chapter we looked at various philosophical accounts of *racism*. In particular we examined three accounts of *racism*: the belief model, the behavioural model and the affective model. We also concluded by looking at some potential hybrid views, and accounts that took *racism* to be grounded on disregard or disrespect.

The clearest and most important belief accounts can be found in Appiah, "Racisms" (1990) and "Racism: History of Hatred: A Review of George Frederickson's *Racism: A Short History*" (2002), although there are also elements of a belief account in Shelby, "Is Racism in the Heart?" (2002b) and Lengbeyer, "Racism and Impure Hearts" (2004). Good examples of the behavioural model of *racism* can be found in Philips, "Racist Acts and Racist Humor" (1984) and Frederickson, *Racism: A Short History* (2002). The affective model is most closely associated with J. L. A. Garcia and can be found in Garcia, "The Heart of Racism" (1996), "Current Conceptions of Racism" (1997) and "Philosophical Analysis and the Moral Concept of Racism" (1999). There is also interesting criticism of Garcia's view to be found in Mills, "Heart's Attack: A Critique of Jorge Garcia's Volitional Conception of Racism" (2003) and Shelby, "Is Racism in the Heart?" (2002b) and Faucher and Machery, "Racism: Against Jorge Garcia's Moral and Psychological Monism" (2009). Variations on the affective view can be found in Schmid's, "The Definition of Racism" (1996), where he takes what he calls a *motivational view*, and in Arthur, *Race Equality and the Burdens of History* (2007), who takes an *indifference view*.

Among the most interesting hybrid views – those that combine elements of these three basic positions – are *Race, Racism and Reparations* (2003), where Corlett combines behaviour and belief, and "The Nature of Racism" (2004) where Dummett combines behaviour and an affective type of view. The most important accounts of *racism* as disregard and disrespect are found in Taylor, *Race: A Philosophical Introduction* (2004a) and Glasgow, "Racism as Disrespect" (2009b).

Among the assumptions that we made in this chapter about *race* are that we can give a single unified account of *racism* and most of the research we have mentioned here shares this assumption. There is, however, important work that suggests a philosophical analysis of *racism* will need to be more pluralistic and accept that we may not be able to account for all instances of *racism* with a single view. The most interesting of this is found in Blum,

"I Am Not a Racist But ...": *The Moral Quandary of Race* (2002) and Headley, "Philosophical Analysis and The Problem of Defining Racism" (2006).

A further assumption was that a philosophical account of *racism* must make sense of why *racism* is wrong. Although this is a widely shared assumption, again, it is not universal and some philosophers think it is a mistake to load an account of *racism* with this additional burden. The most important of this work is Mills, "Heart's Attack: A Critique of Jorge Garcia's Volitional Conception of Racism" (2003) and Shelby, "Is Racism in the Heart?" (2002b).

CHAPTER 5: THE EVERYDAY IMPACT OF *RACE* AND *RACISM*

In this chapter we examined the impact of *race* and *racism* on our everyday life. In particular we looked at the notion of racial profiling and brought our philosophical understanding of *race* and *racism* to bear on the debate. We also mentioned other such areas where philosophers and philosophy has some bearing and potential to affect the discussion.

In terms of racial profiling we outlined a positive case that drew heavily on Risse and Zeckhauser, "Racial Profiling" (2004). Further support is given in Risse, "Racial Profiling: A Reply to Two Critics" (2007). Other arguments in broad support of racial profiling are given by Arthur, *Race Equality and the Burdens of History* (2007). Particularly useful for the negative case is Lever, "Why Racial Profiling Is Hard to Justify: A Response to Risse and Zeckhauser" (2005) and "What's Wrong with Racial Profiling? Another Look at the Problem" (2007). Other useful discussion is found in Lippert-Rasmussen, "Racial Profiling Versus Community" (2006), Corlett, "Profiling Color" (2011), and Thomsen, "The Art of the Unseen: Three Challenges for Racial Profiling" (2011).

A broader and useful discussion of the idea that racial profiling must take place against a background of pre-existing harms and that this must be accounted for if the practice is to be justified is given by Bou-Habib, "Racial Profiling and Background Injustice" (2011).

A useful discussion of racial profiling as it is used in medicine and healthcare is given in Wasserman, "Is Racial Profiling More Benign in Medicine than in Law Enforcement?" (2011) and provides an interesting case where our intuitions about profiling maybe less clear than in the case of criminal profiling.

Aside from racial profiling we mentioned other areas where *race* and *racism* have a more everyday impact. In particular we mentioned affirmative action. This is a very broad area, but anyone looking for a useful overview of the arguments would do well to consult Mosley, "A Defense of Affirmative Action" (2005) and Wolf-Devine, "Preferential Policies Have Become Toxic" (2005). Kranz, *Affirmative Action* (2002) provides a useful overview of the background to affirmative action in the USA along with summaries of the most important landmark legal cases. Sowell, *Affirmative Action around the World: An Empirical Study* (2004) provides details of affirmative action policies from different countries, which is useful given that so much of the discussion tends to focus on how such a policy is managed in the USA. Arthur, *Race Equality and the Burdens of History* (2007) gives an interesting and extended case against affirmative action, with an especially useful discussion of merit. And for a further discussion of the notion of merit as it is used in affirmative action see Davis, "Race as Merit" (1983).

Bibliography

Anderson, Luvell & Ernie Lepore. In press. "Slurring Words". *Noûs*.

Andreason, Robin O. 1998. "A New Perspective on the Race Debate". *The British Journal of the Philosophy of Science* **49**(2): 199–225.

Andreason, Robin O. 2004. "The Cladistic Race Concept: A Defense". *Biology and Philosophy* **19**: 425–42.

Andreason, Robin O. 2005. "The Meaning of 'Race': Folk Conceptions and the New Biology of Race". *The Journal of Philosophy* **102**: 94–106.

Antony, Louise. M. 2002. "Embodiment and Epistemology". In *Oxford Handbook of Epistemology*, Paul K. Moser (ed.), 463–78. Oxford: Oxford University Press.

Appiah, Kwame A. 1990. "Racisms". In *Anatomy of Racism*, D. T. Goldberg (ed.), 3–17. Minneapolis, MN: University of Minnesota Press.

Appiah, Kwame A. 1992. *In My Father's House: Africa in the Philosophy of Culture*. New York: Oxford University Press.

Appiah, Kwame A. 1995. "The Uncompleted Argument: Du Bois and the Illusion of Race". In *Overcoming Racism and Sexism*, L. Bell & D. Blumenfeld (eds), 59–78. Lanham, MD: Rowman and Littlefield.

Appiah, Kwame A. 1996. "Race, Culture, Identity: Misunderstood Connections". In *Color Conscious: The Political Morality of Race*. K. A. Appiah & A. Guttmann (eds), 30–105. Princeton, NJ: Princeton University Press.

Appiah, Kwame A. 2002. "Racism: History of Hatred". *New York Times* (August 4), www.nytimes.com/2002/08/04/books/review/O4APPIAT.html?pagewanted=all (accessed May 2012).

Arthur, John 2007. *Race Equality and the Burdens of History*. Cambridge: Cambridge University Press.

Austin, R. & M. Allen 2000. "Racial Disparity in Arrest Rates as an Explanation of Racial Disparity in Commitment to Pennsylvania's Prisons". *Journal of Research in Crime and Delinquency* **37**(2): 200–20.

Australian Bureau of Statistics 2008. *The Health and Welfare of Australia's Aboriginal and Torres Strait Islander Peoples*, Brian Pink and Penny Allbon (compilers/authors). Canberra: Australian Bureau of Statistics.

Bascara, Victor. 2006. *Model-Minority Imperialism*. Minneapolis, MN: University of Minnesota Press.

Berkowitz, Jonathan & Jack Snyder 1998 "Racism and Sexism in Medically Assisted Conception". *Bioethics* **12**(1): 25–44.

Block, Ned 1995. "How Heritability Misleads about Race". *Cognition* **56**: 99–128.

Blum, Lawrence 2002. *"I Am Not a Racist But ...": The Moral Quandary of Race*. Ithaca, NY: Cornell University Press.

Blumenbach, Johann Friederich [1795] 1997. "On the Degeneration of Species". In *Race and the Enlightenment*, Emmanuel Chukwudi Eze (ed.), 79–90. Cambridge: Blackwell.

Bond, Selina & Cash, Thomas 1992. "Black Beauty: Skin Color and Body Images Among African American College Women". *Journal of Applied Social Psychology* **22**: 874–88.

Bonilla-Silva, Eduardo 2003. *Racism Without Racists: Color-Blind Racism and the Persistence of Racial Inequality in the United States*. Lanham, MD: Rowan & Littlefield.

Bou-Habib, Paul 2011. "Racial Profiling and Background Injustice". *Journal of Ethics* **15**: 33–46.

Boxill, Bernard 2001. "Introduction". In *Race and Racism*, Bernard Boxill (ed.), 1–42. Oxford: Oxford University Press.

Brace, C. Loring 2005. *"Race" is a Four-Letter Word: The Genesis of the Concept*. New York: Oxford University Press.

Brika, Ben, Lemaine Gérard & James S. Jackson 1997. *Racism and Xenophobia in Europe*. Brussels: European Commission.

Brodkin, Karen 2000. "Global Capitalism: What's Race Got to Do with It?" *American Ethnologist* **27**(2): 237–56.

Carmichael, Stokely & Charles Hamilton 1967. *Black Power: The Politics of Liberation in America*. New York: Random House.

Cavalli-Sforza, L. L., P. Menozzi & A. Piazza 1994. *History and Geography of Human Genes*. Princeton, NJ: Princeton University Press.

Chaucer, Geoffrey 1974. "The Nun's Priest's Tale". In *The Complete Works of Geoffrey Chaucer*, F. N. Robinson (ed.), 237–46. Oxford: Oxford University Press.

Cholbi, Michael 2006. "Race, Capital Punishment, and the Cost of Murder". *Philosophical Studies* **127**: 255–82.

Cokley, Kevin 2002. "Testing Cross's Revised Racial Identity Model: An Examination of the Relationship between Racial Identity and Internalized Racialism". *The Journal of Counselling Psychology* **49**(1): 476–83.

Corlett, J. Angelo 2003. *Race, Racism and Reparations*. Ithaca, NY: Cornell University Press.

Corlett. J. Angelo. 2011. "Profiling Color". *Journal of Ethics* **15**: 21–32.

Crocker, D. 2003 "Addressing the Real World of Racial Injustice in the Criminal Justice System". *The Journal of Criminal Law and Criminology* **93**(4): 827–79.

Davis, Michael 1983. "Race as Merit". *Mind* **92**: 347–67.

Dummett, Michael 2004. "The Nature of Racism". In *Racism in Mind*, Michael. P. Levine & Tamas Pataki (eds), 27–34. Ithaca, NY: Cornell University Press.

Dunn, Kevin 2003. "Racism in Australia: Findings of a Survey on Racist Attitudes and Experiences of Racism". *National Europe Centre Paper No. 77*. University of Sydney.

Dunn, Kevin, James Forrest, Ian Burnley, & Amy McDonald. 2004. "Constructing Racism in Australia". *Australian Journal of Social Issues* **39**(4): 409–30.

Duster, Troy 2002. "Would 'Race' Disappear if the United States Officially Stopped Collecting Data on it?". *ASA News* (19 August), www2.asanet.org/media/race.html (accessed May 2012).

Eldridge, Kathryn Roe 2002. "Racial Disparities in the Capital System: Invidious or Accidental?". *Washington and Lee School of Law Capital Defense Journal* (Spring): 305–25.

Entine, Jon 2000. *Taboo: Why Blacks Dominate Sports and We're Afraid to Talk About It*. New York: Public Affairs.

Faucher, Luc & Edouard Machery 2009. "Racism: Against Jorge Garcia's Moral and Psychological Monism". *Philosophy of the Social Sciences* **39**(1): 41–62.

Fausto-Sterling, Anne 1995. "Gender, Race, and Nation: The Comparative Anatomy of 'Hottentot' Women in Europe, 1814–1817". In *Deviant Bodies*, Jennifer Terry & Jacqueline Urla (eds), 19–48. Bloomington, IN: Indiana University Press.

Feagin, Joe R. 2006. *Systemic Racism: A Theory of Oppression*. New York: Routledge.

Fischer, Claude S., Michael Hout, Martín Sánchez Jankowski, Samuel R. Lucas, Ann Swidler & Kim Voss. 1996. *Inequality by Design: Cracking the Bell Curve Myth*. Princeton, NJ: Princeton University Press.

Fredrickson, George 2002. *Racism: A Short History*. Princeton, NJ: Princeton University Press.

Gaertner, Samuel L. & John F. Dovidio 1986. "The Aversive Form of Racism". In *Prejudice, Discrimination, and Racism*, John F. Dovidio & Samuel L. Gaertner (eds), 61–89. Orlando, FL: Academic Press.

Garcia, J. L. A. 1996. "The Heart of Racism". *Journal of Social Philosophy* **27**: 5–45.

Garcia, J. L. A. 1997. "Current Conceptions of Racism: A Critical Examination of Some Recent Social Philosophy". *Journal of Social Philosophy* **28**: 5–42.

Garcia, J. L. A. 1999. "Philosophical Analysis and the Moral Concept of Racism". *Philosophy and Social Criticism* **25**(5): 1–32.

Garvin, J. L. & F. H. Hooper (eds) 1956. *Encyclopaedia Britannica* 14th Edition. Chicago, IL: Chicago University Press.

Gendler, Szabo Tamar 2008 "Alief and Belief". *Journal of Philosophy* **105**(10): 634–63.

Glasgow, Joshua 2003. "On the New Biology of Race". *Journal of Philosophy* **100**(9): 456–74.

Glasgow, Joshua 2006. "A Third Way in the Race Debate". *The Journal of Political Philosophy* **14**: 163–85.

Glasgow, Joshua 2007. "Three Things Realist Constructionism About Race – Or Anything Else – Can Do". *Journal of Social Philosophy* **38**: 554–68.

Glasgow, Joshua 2009a. *A Theory of Race*. New York: Routledge.

Glasgow, Joshua 2009b. "Racism as Disrespect". *Ethics* **120**: 64–93.

Glasgow, Joshua 2009c. "In Defence of a Four-Part Theory: Replies to Hardimon, Haslanger, Mallon and Zack". In *Symposia on Gender Race and Philosophy* **5**(2), http://web.mit.edu/sgrp/2009/no2/Glasgow1009.pdf (accessed May 2012).

Gosline, Anna 2005. "Brain Scans Reveal Racial Biases". *New Scientist* (8 May), www.newscientist.com/article/dn7355-brain-scans-reveal-racial-biases.html (accessed May 2012).

Gould, Stephen Jay 1982. "The Hottentot Venus". *Natural History* **91**(1): 20–27.

Graybow, Steve 2001. "Ban Rumours Dispelled, Songs Don't Suffer". *Billboard Magazine* (13 October).

Greenwald, A., D. McGhee & J. Schwartz 1998. "Measuring Individual Differences in Implicit Cognition: The Implicit Association Test". *Journal of Personality and Social Psychology* **74**(6): 1464–80.

Hacking, Ian 1999. *The Social Construction of What?* Cambridge, MA: Harvard University Press.

Halberstram, D. 1987. "The Stuff Dreams Are Made Of". *Sports Illustrated* (29 June).

Hall, Stuart, Chas Critcher, Tony Jefferson, John N. Clarke & Brian Roberts. 1978. *Policing the Crisis: Mugging, the State, and Law and Order*. New York: Holmes & Meier.

Hardimon, Michael O. 2003. "The Ordinary Concept of Race". *Journal of Philosophy* **100**(9): 437–55.

Hardimon, Michael O. 2009. "Wallace Simpson was Wrong: Remarks on Joshua Glasgow's *A Theory of Race*". *Symposia on Gender Race and Philosophy* **5**(2): 1–10.

Haslanger, Sally 2000. "Gender and Race: What Are They? What Do We Want Them To Be?" *Noûs* **34**: 31–55.

Haslanger, Sally 2004. "Future Genders? Future Races?". *Philosophic Exchange* **34**: 4–27.

Haslanger, Sally 2006. "Philosophical Analysis and Social Kinds: What Good are our Intuitions?". *Proceedings of the Aristotelian Society* **80**(suppl.): 89–118.

Headley, Clevis 2006. "Philosophical Analysis and The Problem of Defining Racism". *Philosophia Africana* **9**(1): 1–16.

Herrnstein, Richard J. & Charles Murray 1994. *The Bell Curve: Intelligence and Class Structure in American Life*. New York: Free Press.

Himma, Kenneth Einar 2002. "Definition of Unconscionable Slurs". *The Journal of Social Philosophy* **33**(3): 512–22.

Huxley, Julian 1938. "Clines: An Auxiliary Taxonomic Principle". *Nature* **142**: 219–20.

Isaac, Benjamin 2004. *The Invention of Racism in Classical Antiquity*. Princeton, NJ: Princeton University Press.

Jablonski, Nina, G. 2004. "The Evolution of Human Skin and Skin Color". *Annual Review of Anthropology* **33**: 585–623.

Jones, Nicholas, A. & Amy Symens Smith 2001. "The Two or More Races Population: 2000". In *Census 2000 Brief*, www.census.gov (accessed February 2012).

Kaessmann, H., V. Wiebe & S. Paabo 1999. "Extensive Nuclear DNA Sequence Diversity among Chimpanzees". *Science* **286**(5442): 1159–62.

Kelly, D. & Roedder, E. 2008. "Racial Cognition and the Ethics of Implicit Bias". *Philosophy Compass* **3**(3): 522–40.

Kitano, T., C. Schwarz, B. Nickel, & S. Paabo 2003. "Gene Diversity Patterns at 10 X-Chromosomal Loci in Humans and Chimpanzees". *Molecular Biology and Evolution* **20**(8): 1281–9.

Kitcher, Phillip 1999. "Race, Ethnicity, Biology, Culture". In *Racism*, L. Harris (ed.), 87–120. Amherst NY: Humanity Press.

Kranz, Rachel 2002. *Affirmative Action*. New York: Facts on File.

Labelle, Micheline 1978. *Idéologie de Coleur et Classes Sociales en Häiti*. Montréal: Presses de l'Université de Montréal.

Lengbeyer, L. A. 2004. "Racism and Impure Hearts". In *Racism in Mind*, M. P. Levine & T. Pataki (eds), 158–78. Ithaca, NY: Cornell University Press.

Lever, Annabelle 2005. "Why Racial Profiling Is Hard to Justify: A Response to Risse and Zeckhauser". *Philosophy & Public Affairs* **33**(1): 94–110.

Lever, Annabelle 2007. "What's Wrong with Racial Profiling? Another Look at the Problem". *Criminal Justice Ethics* **26**(1): 20–28.

Lewontin, Richard D. 1972. "The Apportionment of Human Diversity". *Evolutionary Biology* **6**: 381–98.

Lieberman, Matthew D., Ahmed Hariri, Johanna M. Jarco, Naomi I. Eisenberger & Susan Bookheimer 2005. "An fMRI Investigation of Race-Related Amygdala Activity in African-American and Caucasian-American Individuals". *Nature and Neuroscience* **8**: 720–22.

Linnaeus, Carl [1758] 1997. "The God-Given Order of Nature". In *Race and the Enlightenment*, Emmanuel Chukwudi Eze (ed.), 10–14. Malden, MA: Blackwell.

Lippert-Rasmussen, Kasper 2006. "Racial Profiling Versus Community". *Journal of Applied Philosophy* **23**(2): 191–205.

Livingstone, Frank B. 1962. "On the Non-Existence of Human Races". *Current Anthropology* **3**(3): 279.

Mallon, Ron 2004. "Passing, Travelling and Reality: Social Constructionism and the Metaphysics of Race". *Noûs* **38**(4): 644–73.

Mallon, Ron 2007. "A Field Guide to Social Construction". *Philosophy Compass* **2**(1): 93–108.

Manne, Robert 2001. "In Denial: The Stolen Generations and the Right". *Australian Quarterly Essay* **1**: 1–113.

Michaels, Walter Benn 1994. "The No-Drop Rule". *Critical Inquiry* **20**: 758–69.

Mills, Charles 1998. *Blackness Visible: Essays on Philosophy and Race*. Ithaca, NY: Cornell University Press.

Mills, Charles 2003. "Heart's Attack: A Critique of Jorge Garcia's Volitional Conception of Racism". *The Journal of Ethics* **7**: 29–62.

Mills, Charles 2005 "Reconceptualising Race and Racism? A Critique of J. Angelo Corlett". *Journal of Social Philosophy* **36**(4): 546–58.

Mirga, Andrzej 2000. *Roma and the Law: Demythologizing the Gypsy Criminality Stereotype*. Princeton, NJ: Project on Ethnic Relations.

Morning, Ann 2009. "Toward a Sociology of Racial Conceptualisation for the 21st Century". *Social Forces* **87**(3): 1167–92.

Mosley, Albert 2005. "A Defense of Affirmative Action". In *Contemporary Debates in Applied Ethics,* Andrew Cohen & Christopher Wellman (eds), 43–58. Oxford: Blackwell.

Newport, Frank, Jack Ludwig& Sheila Kearney 2001. "Gallup Poll Social Audit: Black–White Relations in the United States – 2001 Update" www.gallup.com/poll/file/125972/sr010711.pdf (accessed February 2012).

Okely, Judith 1983. *The Traveller-Gypsies*. Cambridge: Cambridge University Press.

Omi, Michael & Howard Winant 1986. *Racial Formation in the United States*. New York: Routledge.

Ostriker, Jeremiah P., Paul W. Holland, Charlotte V. Kuh & James A. Voytuk 2009. *A Guide to the Methodology of the National Research Council Assessment of Doctorate Programs*. Washington, DC: National Research Council.

Outlaw, Lucius T. 1990. "Toward A Critical Theory of Race". In *Race and Racism,* Bernard Boxill (ed.), 58–82. 2001. Oxford: Oxford University Press.

Outlaw, Lucius 1995. "On W. E. B. Du Bois's 'The Conservation of Races'". In *Overcoming Racism and Sexism,* L. A. Bell & D. Blumenfeld (eds), 79–102. Lanham, MD: University Press of America.

Outlaw, Lucius 1996a. "'Conserve' Races? In Defense of W. E. B. Du Bois". In *W. E. B. Du Bois on Race and Culture,* Bernard Bell, Emily Grosholz & James Stewart (eds), 15–38. New York: Routledge.

Outlaw, Lucius T. 1996b. *On Race and Philosophy*. New York: Routledge.

Pager, Devah 2003. "The Mark of a Criminal Record". *American Journal of Sociology* **108**(5): 937–75.

Payne, B. K. 2005. "Conceptualizing Control in Social Cognition: The Role of Automatic and Controlled Processes in Misperceiving a Weapon". *Journal of Personality Social Psychology* **81**: 181–92.

Payne, B. K. 2006 "Weapon Bias: Split-Second Decisions and Unintended Stereo-typing". *Current Directions in Psychological Science.* **15**: 287–91.

Peffley, Mark, Jon Hurwitz & Paul M. Sniderman 1997. "Racial Stereotypes and Whites' Political Views of Blacks in the Context of Welfare and Crime". *American Journal of Political Science* **41**(1): 30–6.

Piper, Adrian 1992. "Passing for White, Passing for Black". *Transition* **58**: 4–32.

Philips, Michael 1984. "Racist Acts and Racist Humor". *Canadian Journal of Philosophy* **14**: 75–96.

Post, Richard H. 1962. "Population Differences in Vision Acuity: A Review, with Speculative Notes on Selection Relaxation". *Eugenics Quarterly* **9**(4): 189–212.

Risse, Mathias 2007 "Racial Profiling: A Reply to Two Critics". *Criminal Justice Ethics* **26**(1): 4–19.

Risse, Mathias & Zeckhauser, Richard 2004. "Racial Profiling". *Philosophy & Public Affairs* **32**(2): 131–70.

Rockquemore. Kerry Anne 2002. "Negotiating the Colour Line: The Gendered Process of Racial Identity Construction among Black/White Biracial Women". *Gender and Society* **16**(4): 485–503.

Rockquemore, Kerry Ann & David L. Brunsma 2002. *Beyond Black: Biracial Identity in America.* Thousand Oaks, CA: Sage.

Root, Michael 2000. "How We Divide the World". *Philosophy of Science* 67(suppl.): 628–39.

Rosenfeld, Michael J. 2008. "Racial, Educational and Religious Endogamy in the United States: A Comparative Historical Perspective". *Social Forces* **87**(1): 1–33.

Roth, Philip 2000. *The Human Stain.* New York: Vintage.

Saul, Jennifer M. 2003. *Feminism: Issues and Arguments.* Oxford: Oxford University Press.

Saul, Jennifer 2006. "Philosophical Analysis and Social Kinds: Gender and Race." *Proceedings of the Aristotelian Society* **80**(suppl.): 119–43.

Schmid, W. Thomas 1996. "The Definition of Racism". *Journal of Applied Philosophy* **13**(1): 31–40.

Searle, John 1995. *The Construction of Social Reality.* New York: Free Press.

Shelby, Tommie 2002a. "Foundations of Black Solidarity: Collective Identity or Common Oppression". *Ethics* **112**: 231–66.

Shelby, Tommie 2002b. "Is Racism in the Heart?". *Journal of Social Philosophy* **33**: 411–20.

Shelby, Tommie 2003. "Two Conceptions of Black Nationalism: Martin Delany on the Meaning of Black Political Solidarity". *Political Theory* **31**(5): 664–92.

Shelby, Tommie 2005. *We Who are Dark: The Philosophical Foundations of Black Solidarity.* Cambridge, MA: Harvard University Press.

Shriver, Mark D., Esteban J Parra, Sonia Dios, Carolina Bonilla, Heather Norton, Celina Jovel, Carrie Pfaff, Cecily Jones, Aisha Massac, Neil Cameron, Archie Baron, Tabitha Jackson, George Argyropoulos, Li Jin, Clive J Hoggart, Paul

M McKeigue & Rick A Kittles. 2003. "Skin Pigmentation, Bio-Geographical Ancestry and Admixture Mapping". *Human Genetics* **112**: 387–99.

Simpson, Ludi 2004. "Statistics of Racial Segregation: Measures, Evidence and Policy". *Urban Studies* **41**(3): 661–81.

Skidmore, Thomas 2003. "Racial Mixture and Affirmative Action: The Cases of Brazil and the United States". *American Historical Review* **108** (5): 1391–96.

Smedley, Audrey & Brian Smedley 2005. "Race as Biology is Fiction, Racism as a Social Problem is Real: Anthropological and Historical Perspectives on the Social Construction of Race". *American Psychologist* **60**: 16–26.

Snowden, Frank M. Jr. 1983. *Before Color Prejudice: The Ancient View of Blacks*. Cambridge, MA: Harvard University Press.

Sowell, Thomas 2004. *Affirmative Action around the World: An Empirical Study*. New Haven, CT: Yale University Press.

Spencer, Quayshawn. In press. "What 'Biological Racial Realism' Should Mean". *Philosophical Studies*.

Steele, Claude M. & Joshua Aronson 1998. "Stereotype Threat and the Test Performance of Academically Successful African Americans". In *The Black-White Test Score Gap*, Christopher Jencks & Meredith Phillips (eds), 401–27. Washington DC: Brookings Institution Press.

Stone, A. C., R. C. Griffiths, S. L. Zegura & M. F. Hammer 2002. "High Levels of Y-Chromosome Nucleotide Diversity in the Genus". *Proceedings of the National Academy of Sciences of the United States of America* **99**(1): 438.

Stone, Jeff, Zachary Perry & John Darley 1997. "'White Men Can't Jump': Evidence for the Perceptual Confirmation of Racial Stereotypes Following a Basketball Game". *Basic and Applied Social Psychology* **19**(3): 291–306.

Sundstrom, Ronald 2002. "Race as a Human Kind". *Philosophy and Social Criticism* **28**(1): 91–115.

Survey Research Center 1991. *National Race and Politics Survey*. Berkeley, CA: University of California at Berkeley.

Survey Research Center 2004. *National Race and Politics Survey*. Berkeley, CA: University of California at Berkeley.

Taylor, Hugh R. 1981. "Racial Variations in Vision". *American Journal of Epidemiology* **113**(1): 62–80.

Taylor, Paul C. 2000. "Appiah's Uncompleted Argument: W. E. B. Du Bois and the Reality of Race". *Social Theory and Practice* **26**: 103–28.

Taylor, Paul C. 2004a. *Race: A Philosophical Introduction*. Cambridge: Polity Press.

Taylor, Paul C. 2004b. "Pragmatism and Race". In *Pragmatism and the Problem of Race*, Bill E. Lawson & Donald F. Koch (eds), 162–76. Bloomington, IN: Indiana University Press.

Taylor, Paul C. 2005. "Three Questions About Race, Racism and Reparations". *Journal of Social Philosophy* **36**(4): 559–67.

Telles, Edward E. 2004. *Race in Another America: The Significance of Skin Color in Brazil*. Princeton, NJ: Princeton University Press.

Thomsen, Frej Klem 2011. "The Art of the Unseen: Three Challenges for Racial Profiling". *Journal of Ethics* **15**: 89–117.

Todorov, T. 2000. "Race and Racism". In *Theories of Race and Racism*, L. Back & J. Solomos (eds), 64–70. London: Routledge.

Twain, Mark. [1894] 1976. *The Tragedy of Pudd'nhead Wilson*. Vol. 1. Langston Hughes (ed.). New York: Bantam.

Wasserman, David 2011. "Is Racial Profiling More Benign in Medicine than in Law Enforcement?". *Journal of Ethics* **15**: 119–129.

Webster, Yehudi 2003. "Racial Classification: A Wrong Turn". *Footnotes: Newsletter of the American Sociological Association* **31**:(1). Public Forum.

Wilkinson, T. M. 2007. "Racist Organ Donors and Saving Lives". *Bioethics* **21**(2): 63–74.

Willan, P, & N. Hawkes, 1993. "White Baby Born To Black Mother", *The Times*, (31 December): 1.

Williams, Eric 1944. *Capitalism and Slavery*. Chapel Hill, NC: University of North Carolina Press.

Winnant, Michael 2001. *The World Is a Ghetto: Race and Democracy Since World War II*. New York: Basic Books.

Wolf-Devine, Celia 2005. "Preferential Policies Have Become Toxic". In *Contemporary Debates in Applied Ethics*, Andrew Cohen & Christopher Wellman (eds), 59–74. Oxford: Blackwell.

Yinger, John 1995. *Closed Doors, Opportunities Lost: The Continuing Costs of Housing Discrimination*. New York: Russell Sage Foundation.

Zack, Naomi 1997a. "Life After Race". In *American Mixed Race: The Culture of Microdiversity*, N. Zack (ed.), 297–308. Lanham, MD: Rowman & Littlefield.

Zack, Naomi 1997b. "Race and Philosophic Meaning". In *Race/Sex: Their Sameness, Difference, and Interplay*, N. Zack (ed.), 29–44. New York: Routledge.

Zack, Naomi 2002. *Philosophy of Science and Race*. New York: Routledge.

Index

n following a page number denotes footnote; *t* denotes table